FOUNDING

ST. LOUIS

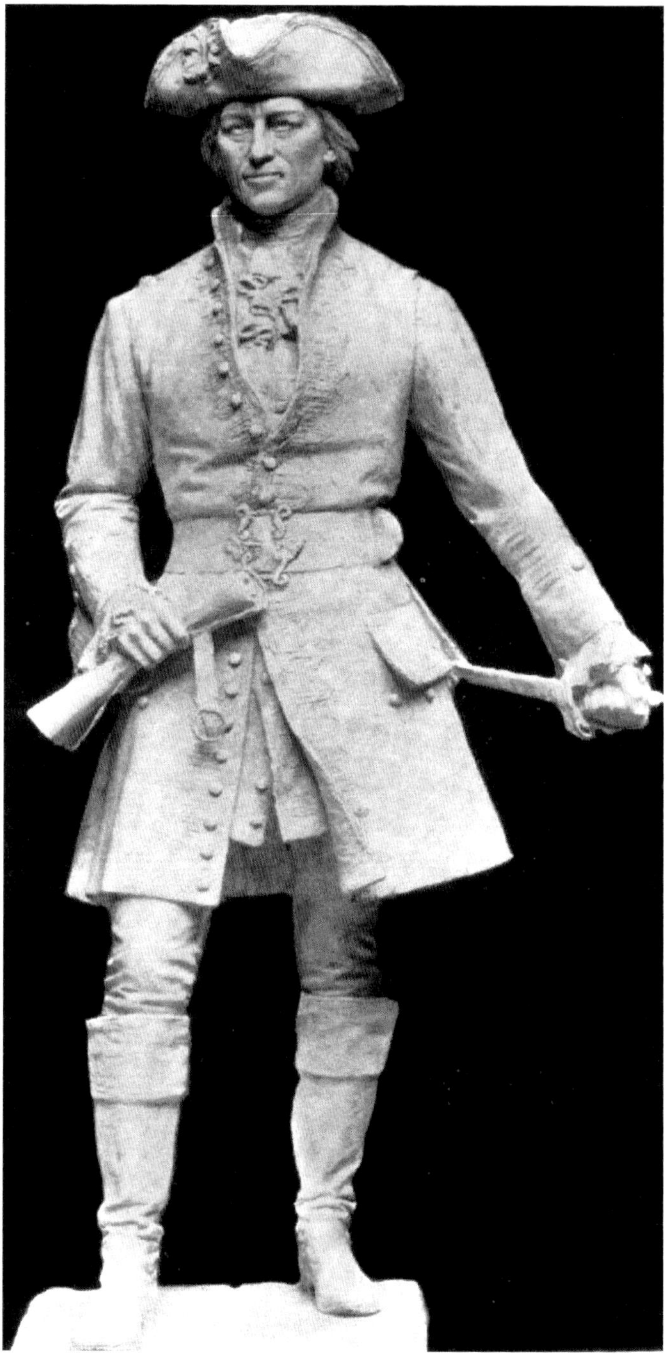

Statue of Laclède by Jonathan Scott Hartley, with facial features of grandson Pierre Chouteau Jr. *From* Grandeurs of the Universal Exposition at St. Louis *(1904)*.

FOUNDING ST. LOUIS

FIRST CITY *of the* NEW WEST

J. Frederick Fausz

THE History PRESS

Published by The History Press
Charleston, SC 29403
www.historypress.net

Cover image: *Laclede Landing at Present Site of St. Louis* (detail) by Oscar Edward Berninghaus (circa 1914). *Courtesy Saint Louis Art Museum. Gift of August A. Busch Jr.*

First published 2011
Second printing 2012
Third printing 2013

Manufactured in the United States

ISBN 978.1.60949.016.4

Library of Congress Cataloging-in-Publication Data

Fausz, J. Frederick.
Founding St. Louis : first city of the new West / J. Frederick Fausz.
p. cm.
Includes bibliographical references.
ISBN 978-1-60949-016-4
1. Saint Louis (Mo.)--History. 2. Saint Louis (Mo.)--History--Pictorial works. 3. Laclède-Liguest, Pierre de, 1724-1778. 4. Chouteau, Auguste, 1750-1829. 5. French Americans--Missouri--Saint Louis--History. 6. Frontier and pioneer life--Missouri--Saint Louis. 7. City planning--Missouri--Saint Louis--History. 8. Osage Indians--Missouri--Saint Louis--History. 9. Saint Louis (Mo.)--Ethnic relations. 10. Saint Louis (Mo.)--Commerce--History. I. Title. II. Title: Founding Saint Louis.
F474.S257F38 2010
977.8'66--dc22
2010043552

To Jeanette and John,
who joined me on a journey from the Chesapeake
to a West that was new to us and has never grown old.

Contents

Acknowledgements

Historians are like voyageurs, traveling upstream and downstream between the then and now along endless rivers of time. As adventurers in the foreign territory of distant ages, they struggle with new currents (of thought), lost cargo (missing records) and treacherous snags (errors that continually resurface) in seeking the portages (thematic links) that connect the past with the present, ensuring that there will be new voyages of discovery in the future. Fortunately, historians rarely travel alone and need many helpful hands to advance their craft (buoyant research).

In 1991, I was a history professor at St. Mary's College of Maryland, living in a watery world of crabbers and oystermen only a few miles from where the Potomac River flows into the Chesapeake Bay. My research focused on Indian relations with English colonists along the seventeenth-century Atlantic Coast, and all of my past publications had dealt with that era and area. But my "big book" on Jamestown was put on hold when I became the first dean of the new Pierre Laclede Honors College at the University of Missouri–St. Louis (UMSL). I had never heard of the man and knew little about the early history of the city.

Being an ignorant but curious outsider was an advantage, since each new discovery was exciting. I immersed myself in the region's fascinating history as a public speaker for the Missouri Humanities Council and the Missouri History Museum. The first books I purchased to support that research were *The First Chouteaus: River Barons of Early St. Louis* by William E. Foley and C. David Rice and James Neal Primm's *Lion of the Valley: St. Louis, Missouri, 1764–1980.* I will be forever grateful to Bill and Neal for generously sharing their vast knowledge with me. In 1999, I was fortunate to spend an entire semester as a research fellow at the library and archives of the Missouri History Museum, and I extend my appreciation to President Bob Archibald for that transformative experience. His excellent staff members deserve my thanks, especially Ellen Thomasson, for providing wonderful illustrations in record time; Barnes M. "Barney" Bradshaw, for hosting my public presentations; and three editors of *Gateway Magazine*, who nurtured my interest in using illustrations to make history come alive for the general public—a commitment shared by The History Press.

I also thank Dr. Bob Moore of the National Park Service at the Gateway Arch for his friendship, wisdom and permission to use his excellent illustration of St. Louis in 1804. He put me in touch with Jennifer R. Clark, archivist at the Jefferson National Expansion Museum, who was most helpful in providing other illustrations. I am grateful to Dr. Kathleen Nigro, whose suberb administration of an NEH (National Endowment of the Humanities) grant during the Lewis and Clark bicentennial funded the thirteen thousand miles I drove to take my "Museum on Wheels" to many rural communities in four states. Her continued encouragement, along with Jerry Garrett and other friends in the St. Louis chapter of the Lewis and Clark Trail Heritage Foundation, is most appreciated. I also acknowledge the assistance of friends in the Osage Nation; Tim O'Neil of the *St. Louis Post-Dispatch*; Bill Swagerty, a buddy since our travels with the incomparable Francis "Fritz" Jennings; and Steve Smith of the Royale Food & Spirits, whose intellectual patrons like a dash of history with their cocktails. I am most grateful to my department chairperson, Andrew Hurley, for his sustained support and to colleagues Peter Acsay and Steve Rowan for many stimulating conversations about the history of Missouri.

Particularly helpful in the production of this book were: Dr. Jon Kukla, a dear friend since our Chesapeake days; former UMSL students Sharon Person, Steven Stuckey and Doc Luecke; Darrell Duensing and his staff at the Fort de Chartres State Historic Site; Lesley Barker, director of the Bolduc House Museum in Ste. Genevieve; Susan Newton at Winterthur Museum; Jason Gray, Ella Rothgangel and Cathryn Gowan of the Saint Louis Art Museum; Marshall McClure of MarshallArts in Norfolk, Virginia; and Helen Valle Crist, Emily Horton and Cece Boyer Myers of the Center for French Colonial Studies. I am forever indebted to Ian Stokes of the United Kingdom and Jean Caillabet of New Zealand, who granted permission to use their beautiful photographs of Béarn, as well as the Saint Louis Mercantile Library at the University of Missouri–St. Louis for providing access to Auguste Chouteau's original "Narrative of the Settlement of St. Louis," which launched my research into the many unanswered—and even unasked—questions about the founding of St. Louis. This book would be very deficient without Shannon Lee Dawdy's excellent study of the merchant rogues of New Orleans, Kathleen DuVal's keen insights about the Native Ground between the Missouri and Arkansas Rivers and M.J. Morgan's path-breaking environmental history of colonial Illinois. Finally, I thank the talented staff of The History Press for their confidence and patience, including Laura All, who provided the contract; publications director Adam Ferrell, who oversaw every aspect of the project with astonishing good humor; and senior editor Jaime Muehl, whose talents in copyediting are exceeded only by her cheerfulness.

My citations recognize the many intellectual debts I owe to other historians, and my dedication acknowledges how privileged I am to have a wonderful wife and supportive son who love history as much as I do.

A Note on Terminology

Throughout this book, "French" will refer to natives of France, as well as Canadians (*Canadiens*), Creoles and Caribbean islanders of French descent who were born in the Western Hemisphere, spoke various forms of the French language *and* adhered to Roman Catholic and/or secular traditions associated with the cultural homeland of France. The recent preference for using "Francophone" or "French-speaking" is awkward and inaccurate, since being of French descent implied much more than language alone.

The geography of French America in the mid-1700s resembled the fleur-de-lis, with the prominent center portion representing the long Mississippi River that connected Canada in the far north with Louisiana (*Louisiane*) in the Deep South. The large, curving upper petals of that lily symbol extended across both sides of that dominant waterway to encompass France's claims to the trans-Appalachian region (eastern Louisiana) and the trans-Mississippi territory (western Louisiana). The line across the lower, smaller petals corresponds to the Arkansas River boundary between "Lower" and "Upper" Louisiana. Present-day Missouri was included in the latter, but St. Louis and Ste. Genevieve were also considered part of *Le Pays des Illinois* (the Illinois Country), which encompassed both sides of the Mississippi River in that region. Treaties at the end of the French and Indian War made that river an international boundary line, with France's former territories now governed by Great Britain in the East and Spain in the West. *San Luis de Ylinueses* (St. Louis of the Illinois) was a regional capital of Spanish *Luisiana* administered from New Orleans for the remainder of the eighteenth century.

A Note on Terminology

In 1800, Spain retroceded New Orleans and western Louisiana to France, which then sold that region to the United States in the Louisiana Purchase of 1803. The term "Missouri" only became an official territorial designation under the United States, nine years after that transaction. Throughout this book, "Louisiana" will refer to New Orleans and the trans-Mississippi West, irrespective of French, Spanish or U.S. governance and different spellings in each language.

Introduction

A French Heritage Lost and Found

Honors rendered to the dead, we know, cannot affect them…but it serves to excite the living to emulate their virtues and their worth.
—Pierre Chouteau Sr.

On Tuesday, February 24, 1829, the *Missouri Republican* reported that "the venerable" Auguste Chouteau, "Patriarch of St. Louis," had died that morning. Thus "closed a life of singular usefulness" stretching over eight decades, during which that masterful merchant had earned "the esteem of his fellow citizens" by "his philanthropy, his unpretending benevolence, and the amenity of his manners." Chouteau died in his magnificent mansion just a few steps from the imposing Mississippi riverfront that had shaped his success. The thriving port of an inland empire that surrounded Chouteau's grave and outlived his passing was a fitting monument to its "First Citizen." Almost exactly sixty-five years before his death, he had landed at that site as a precocious boy of fourteen and began building a new and novel French town that was destined for greatness in the American West.[1]

From a boy who paddled log canoes during the reigns of Bourbon kings to an aging "river baron" who profited from far-flung fleets of trading vessels under American presidents, Chouteau succeeded in translating childhood dreams into adult realities until St. Louis fulfilled the prediction to become "one of the finest cities of America." The elevated landscape of St. Louis resembled a natural amphitheater, and upon that "stage," Chouteau played leading roles in countless dramas over many eventful decades. Some of his "scripts" were written across the Atlantic by

European diplomats, who negotiated three Paris treaties in tidy twenty-year cycles. The treaty that ended France's New World empire in 1763 created a unique opportunity for its abandoned colonists to preserve their culture and expand their commerce by moving west of the Mississippi. That led Chouteau and his stepfather, Pierre Laclède, to found the first permanent town near the confluence of the continent's two longest rivers. Chouteau supervised the construction of buildings and went on to dominate the St. Louis real estate market for six decades. The Paris pact of 1783 that concluded the American Revolution made U.S. expansion a growing concern for then-thriving St. Louisans, but Chouteau increased his fortune and developed his diplomatic skills over the next twenty years to prepare for future challenges. Although the Louisiana Purchase Treaty of 1803 forever transformed French St. Louis and its long alliance with the Osage Indians, Chouteau worked with U.S. officials to make his prosperous city the first administrative capital of the American West, achieving more wealth and new fame for his influential family dynasty for almost a century after Laclède's death.[2]

Combining the attributes of a daring entrepreneur and a cautious accountant, Chouteau adapted to the shifting currents of both rivers and politics—proving that at least one French-American was not a mere pawn in the fickle diplomacy of European nations. His birth into a French family of New Orleans made him a Creole; his turbulent childhood in that port city of international trade molded his future as an adventurous merchant; and his long career as an Indian diplomat developed his enlightened appreciation of humanity in all its variety. No one personified a broader range of the French heritage in mid-America than Chouteau, who lived in Louisiana, Illinois and Missouri and linked the Great Lakes with the Gulf of Mexico through his expansive business enterprises, finally fulfilling the goals of earlier Frenchmen who wanted to connect Canada, Illinois and Louisiana by commerce and culture.

Not even death could stop Chouteau from promoting his city. Almost thirty years after his passing, and more than fifty years after he wrote it, Chouteau's "Narrative of the Settlement of St. Louis" first came to public attention just before the Civil War. That rare document is arguably his most precious legacy, for few U.S. cities are fortunate to have a personal account of their origins by someone who was present at the creation. Chouteau's "Narrative" captures the special moment when St. Louis was born on a vacant prairie, making time stand still as an immutable benchmark of beginnings for an ever-changing metropolis in pursuit of modernity.

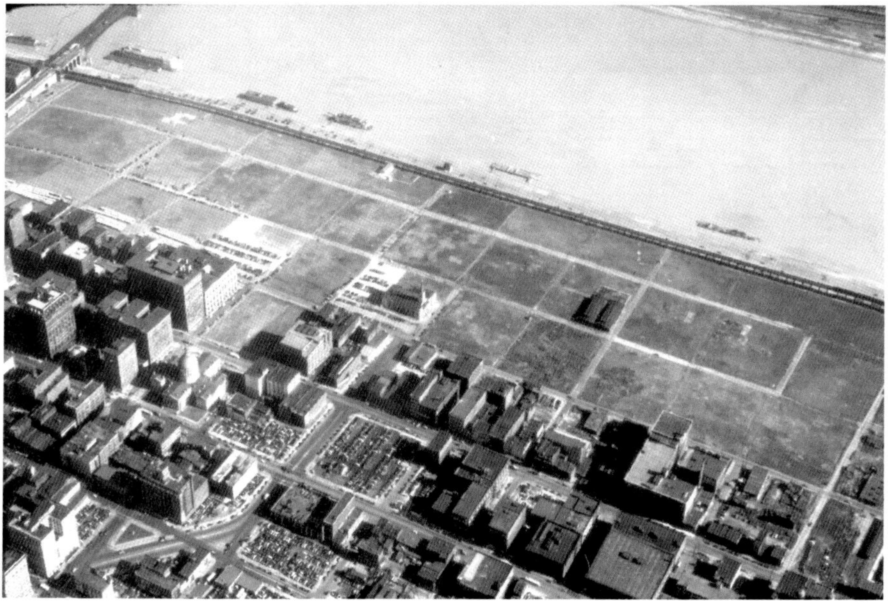

Site of French St. Louis, showing outlines of original town grid after demolition ended in 1942. *Courtesy National Park Service, Jefferson National Expansion Memorial, VREF-17954.*

Chouteau's observations inspired this book, because words are all we have to remind us of St. Louis's French colonial era. Every physical feature of the frontier town that Laclède and Chouteau knew and nurtured disappeared long ago, despite the enviable "French contribution to architecture and town planning" that enriched the continental landscape. "No professional archaeological investigations have ever been performed on a French Colonial site within Missouri's St. Louis metropolitan area," and "St. Louis achieved the unique, if dubious, status in North America of entirely obliterating its original urban core in one fell swoop." The construction of the Gateway Arch erased the last rare remnants of French St. Louis that had survived into the twentieth century, by bulldozing the city's oldest forty blocks along the riverfront and then burying even the outlines of the eighteenth-century town under tons of dirt needed to support that massive monument. Once all of the tangible remains of that French colonial world had literally disappeared, it became much easier to forget that the earlier "L&C team" of Laclède and Chouteau founded St. Louis as the orginal gateway to the *Osage* West before Meriwether Lewis and William Clark were even born. And St. Louis would not even exist if those indispensable and *not-so-*"savage" Indian hunters had not provided the fur wealth from a very *useful* "wilderness" to make St. Louis a progressive, prosperous and peaceful community of urbane consumers engaged in international commerce.[3]

Despite the prominent fleur-de-lis on the city's flag, most St. Louisans know little, and seem to care less, about the French heritage of St. Louis. That amnesia is reflected in the hoopla about remodeling the grounds of the Gateway Arch in time to celebrate the 50th anniversary of its completion. St. Louis mayor Francis Slay stated recently that "come October 28, 2015, we'll have something really big to celebrate." But where is the public enthusiasm and official interest in commemorating the 250th anniversary of the *founding of St. Louis* that will occur *even earlier*—on February 15, 2014? That is a far more significant milestone in the history of any U.S. city and deserves the biggest celebration in the metropolitan area and throughout Missouri, since our state had its origins here as well.[4]

The Gateway Arch is the tail wagging the dog, because it only honors *Jefferson* national expansion—the belated "discovery" of a long-flourishing French capital in the West by Anglo-Americans from Virginia, who then ousted the very Indians who helped make St. Louis such a unique and successful multicultural city. Why do we give all the credit and attention to the later "pioneers" who *passed through* St. Louis on their way to settle on stolen Indian homelands in a West *made* "wild" by aggressive U.S. policies? The Louisiana Purchase was a traumatic event for many outnumbered and intimidated French St. Louisans, and they bent over backward to demonstrate their loyalty and helpfulness to the United States. They were already "Americans" in terms of geography but sought inclusion as citizens in the American nation as well—at almost any cost. Historian Robert J. Moore Jr. contends that replacing the French identity and legacy was "a deliberate campaign by the early American administrators and residents, after the Louisiana Purchase, to…erase…the French colonial culture, and by later historians to marginalize and trivialize it." Descendants of the French founders demonstrated their patriotic allegiance by embracing President Jefferson more than any people outside of Virginia—naming the state capital for him, acquiring his original tombstone to display on the state university campus and erecting the first public building (the Missouri History Museum) to honor him, forty years before the Jefferson Memorial was built in Washington, D.C.[5]

Yale historian Jay Gitlin observed that "the French have remained invisible, in part because their story demands that we accept a frontier past that transcends our old dichotomies of heroes and villains, settlers and Indians." The process of "Americanization" required an acceptance of pervasive anglocentric prejudices that excluded French and Indian ancestors from our country's historical narrative. Military conquest became the truest measure of national greatness after France lost its American empire in 1763 and the British lost theirs in 1783. Both were replaced by Jefferson's "Empire of Liberty," a forerunner of nineteenth-century Manifest Destiny, which credited divinely approved continental expansion to the "superiority" of the English language, Protestant religion and a government determined to eradicate "heathen savages" and "howling wilderness" as obstacles to U.S. dominance.[6]

A century after the Louisiana Purchase, historians were still glorifying the cultural conquest of the French and Indians. Despite a career of translating French colonial documents, Clarence W. Alvord observed in 1920 that "the most important event in the history of the United States and one of the most momentous in the history of humanity [was] the occupation of the great Mississippi valley by men of *English* speech." He asserted that the "few Gallic families" living there became "mere castaways in the conquest of the west," which was preordained in order to expand American democracy: "It may be that Fate demanded from them [the French], as it did from the Indians, a sacrifice for the greater good." As late as 2007, a respected scholar supported the myth of that erroneous "disappearance" by asserting that "the French left North America in 1763"—confusing the king who pulled out with 100,000 French speakers who continued to live in what another author called France's "Ghost Empire."[7]

No historian more clearly allowed the Jeffersonian ideology of Anglo-American superiority to cloud his judgments than Richard C. Wade. His 1959 book, *The Urban Frontier: The Rise of Western Cities, 1790–1830*, successfully challenged Frederick Jackson Turner's dated assertions about frontier development, finding that "towns were the spearheads of the frontier" rather than small, crude hunting camps. Even though Wade acknowledged St. Louis as "the oldest of the western cities," his bias was obvious when he claimed that it "grew very slowly" due to a "gay and relaxed" French population. He noted that its "ruling group was refined [but] contained few dynamic leaders." St. Louis, he wrote, was "long regarded as a savage place" with a "stigma" for "wildness" and an "Indian problem." His claim that "by 1815, the outlines of St. Louis's economy had been established," with commerce being "the fundamental activity," gave all credit to U.S. citizens after the Louisiana Purchase, while ignoring the profitable French-Osage alliance in the global fur trade for fifty previous years.[8]

This book challenges those old prejudices that have distorted the past for too long. It is an ethnohistorical "biography" of French *and Indian* St.

Louis from conception to adolescence, beginning before the city's founding in 1764 and concluding shortly after the Louisiana Purchase. I contend that St. Louis, as the first city in the "New West" of the Missouri River Valley, was the notable climax of France's legacy in North America because it integrated previous components of that cultural heritage to create a unique and laudable experiment in *alternative* frontier living at the end of the colonial era. Planned in the South by France's last two royal governors of Louisiana, perpetuating the traditions of Canadian fur trading in the North and populated by French Illinois colonists from the East, St. Louis preserved and enhanced that composite inheritance in the West long after New Orleans was Hispanicized, Canada became Anglicized and Illinois was Americanized. As the last officially authorized French settlement within the present boundaries of the United States, St. Louis attracted émigrés from every part of France and its North American empire, while the Osage Indians welcomed them with a fur trade that promised instant success. It was appropriate that Laclède "opened" that gateway to the western wealth of Indian hunters because his surname means "gate" in the Béarnais language of his birth province.

St. Louis was created solely for commerce, without military or missionary motives, and the early residents commited themselves to something new—an admirable, alternative western frontier based on multicultural cooperation, generating profits without profiting from genocide. The young settlement was so imaginatively conceived, innovatively developed and immediately populated that British rivals on both sides of the Atlantic recognized it as a major threat to the sustainability of their frontier policies as early as 1766. The French merchants of St. Louis were pioneers of globalization, thanks to the fur "currency" of Indian "bankers," which stimulated economic development and population growth throughout the entire region of Upper Louisiana—one of America's more prosperous areas even before Americans took it over. Despite its small size, St. Louis was a true city by design and function, and both Spanish royalists and American republicans chose it as their regional capital.

While trade made St. Louisans wealthy, their astute diplomacy with native nations provided the personal security and regional peace essential for the enjoyment of such prosperity. Frontiers were meeting grounds of many different worlds, where sincere conversations across cultural boundaries could preclude serious confrontations. The "Middle Ground" frontier of the Great Lakes necessitated negotiations among alien peoples of equal strength, but the "Native Ground" frontier of Missouri required talented, trustworthy, professional diplomats to please the powerful Osages. St. Louis became an *Indian* capital committed to their interests—a rare development in American history—because French traditions of trading had led to the trading of traditions for generations. French-Americans experienced more frequent, consistent, mutually productive and physically intimate relations with a greater variety of Indians over a longer span of time than any other European colonizers. Centuries of extensive and intensive French contacts with native nations influenced the literary traditions of France itself, inspiring an admiration of Indians never equaled by other European empires. Ideas from both sides of the Atlantic reinforced one another, as the colonial-inspired essays of Montaigne, Jesuit missionaries and Enlightenment philosophers encouraged later generations of well-educated Frenchmen, such as Laclède, to explore physical, as well as intellectual, frontiers.[9]

By excelling at diplomacy as well as trade, members of the Laclède-Chouteau family consistently made the city's survival and success their highest priority and most cherished legacy over many generations. Laclède deserves and receives a large share of the attention in this book, which for the first time explores his long-ignored early life in the Pyrenees, his merchant activities in New Orleans and his residence in Illinois. All of those French places influenced his development of a special "spirit of St. Louis" that made the city exceptionally hospitable to Indians. Auguste Chouteau is also a major character, serving as the essential narrator whose words and deeds over a long, eventful life provided continuity in the evolution of St. Louis from 1764 to 1829. His efforts sustained the family alliance with the Osages until the United States expelled those loyal co-founders of St. Louis from the state they had helped create. That was the most historic example of *abandonment*—a sub-theme that permeates every chapter of this book on personal, cultural and national levels.

The key organizing concept in dealing with so many individuals and societies, issues and events, on both sides of the Atlantic, is *culture*, which allows the historian to analyze distinctive, separate hearths and lifeways and to assess the acculturation that occurred when people with different ideas, goals, languages, religions, economies and customs came into close, prolonged contact. Thematically, this book emphasizes the convergence of cultures promoted by the confluence of major rivers, and it adds many new details to the recent inspiring works of Stephen Aron and Jay Gitlin, among others. Based on thorough scholarly research but written as an engaging narrative for general readers, this book further enhances a cultural focus through fifty illustrations, many of them rare—pictorial "artifacts" that truly allow us to visualize the past.[10]

Despite its notable achievements, St. Louis has been overshadowed by other sites that have marketed their French heritage to better advantage, sometimes erroneously. A case in point is Ste. Genevieve, which, contrary to the persistent myth, was *neither* "the first permanent French colonial settlement west of the Mississippi River" *nor* "Missouri's oldest town." Both of those honors belong to St. Louis, for even without historic structures, it has the historical authenticity to refute those claims. "*Permanent* settlement" means continuous residence at one specific location down to the present. St. Louis qualifies as Missouri's oldest permanent settlement because it has flourished on its original site since February 15, 1764, whereas today's "second" or "new" Ste. Genevieve was not built until some thirty years later—after the original "old" Ste. Genevieve of the 1750s became extinct due to devastating floods. In 1814, Henry Brackenridge, a former resident of the second town, observed that the original Ste. Genevieve "was formerly built immediately on the Mississippi, but the washing away of the bank, and the great flood" left only the "ruins of the old town." Almost a century later, Louis Houck wrote that a "new village was founded" after the old one "*disappeared*."[11]

Carl J. Ekberg's *Colonial Ste. Genevieve* acknowledged "the *demise* of the Old Town and birth of the New Town" but then asked readers to accept this obvious contradiction: "the 'Old Town' of Ste. Genevieve, which was located on the Mississippi floodplain three miles below the present site of Ste. Genevieve, Missouri, was the first permanent European settlement west of the Mississippi River." Extinction and relocation do not equate with *permanence*, and a single settlement cannot exist in two places with a physical and temporal break in between. If the second town had adopted a different name, which it did for a while, there would be no basis for confusion.[12]

Longevity to the present is the only characteristic that merits distinction, since colonial America offers many examples of attempts to gain the respectability of a false antiquity by reusing the same name for different places that existed only briefly. Arkansas Post (Arkansas), for instance, claims to be the "first French establishment west of the Mississippi," with a founding date of 1686—but it was not permanent. That site was abandoned in 1749 to establish another fort with the same name several miles up the Arkansas River. A third "Arkansas Post" was built some ten miles from the Mississippi River in 1756 (where Laclède was buried in 1778). Only the *fourth* settlement with the same name, founded in *1779*, was *permanent*.[13]

While other towns came and went, St. Louis endured as the most prominent "Child of the River and Parent of the West"—founding and/

or sustaining satellite settlements throughout Missouri and far beyond its borders. St. Louis's extensive commercial reach along the vast Mississippi-Missouri River system nourished "a boundless region where several millions of the human race are already domiciled, and where countless millions will reside in the future," as Charles Gayarré already acknowledged in 1854. The Chouteau dynasty alone founded trading posts that grew into towns in Oklahoma, Kansas, South Dakota, Nebraska and Montana. In the mid-nineteenth century, a city resident stated that "many of the old St. Louisans are to be met with in every town and county in…California, for St. Louis was the pioneer starting point for all the mountain expeditions up the Missouri to the Yellow Stone, and across to the Columbia River, and to the Pacific Coast and Mexico." While wider recognition of the "Creole Corridor" is admirable, St. Louis deserves more credit as the only dynamic late eighteenth-century French-American city in the region with significant global connections.[14]

Competing and confusing claims of first or oldest settlements symbolize one aspect of the "historian's paradox"—trying to explain, with accuracy and authority, a distant past never actually experienced by modern researchers. In the last half century, scholars have pursued new areas of innovative research that provided refreshing insights about French America. But in that same period, the neglect of local history in many schools has allowed an escalating number of myths and mistakes to prevent accurate knowledge of our own city, which detracts from its historical significance. The city's bicentennial in 1964, for instance, celebrated the wrong founding date (it should be February *15*, 1764), and an award-winning author made the serious error of stating that St. Louis was named for "Spain's [nonexistent] King Louis XIV," instead of French King Louis IX. Few citizens know much about the principal founder because a National Park Service website misstates Laclède's birth date, while Ekberg consistently misdated his death in a recent book. One of Laclède's descendants, John Francis McDermott, confused generations of readers by writing the founder's name two different ways, including the fabricated and inaccurate "LaClède." The "Liguest" that Laclède appended to his surname in signatures has been misinterpreted by scholarly books, public monuments and websites as his middle name, a hyphenated name or an actual surname. One recent author considered it a (nonsensical) "second surname," while a University of Missouri Press book consistently misspelled it with a *q* instead of a *g*. The February 2007 issue of *St. Louis Magazine* stated that Laclède was one of two "Catholic laymen" who "first explored this stretch of the Mississippi in 1673"—which certainly obscures when, why and how St. Louis was founded ninety-one years later. A leading historian claimed that Auguste Chouteau was Laclède's "future son-in-law," rather than his unofficial stepson, while decades ago family members changed the birth date on Chouteau's gravestone in Calvary Cemetery to make him seem twenty-four, instead of fourteen, when he supervised the construction of St. Louis. An even more imaginative manipulation of history was Stan Hoig's book on the Chouteaus, which claimed that Auguste was fifteen when he left New Orleans and turned fourteen after a three-month voyage![15]

There is no excuse for such carelessness about factual accuracy, especially among scholars of French Illinois, French Canada and French Louisiana, who too often reveal their ignorance of French St. Louis. The proliferation of errors that infect historical sources like computer viruses undermine efforts to understand and appreciate the city where we live and work. The present generation must honor that heritage because it contributes more to the dignity of a place and the identity of its people than construction projects and vapid public relations campaigns—or at least it should. Historical amnesia is akin to the confusion experienced when someone overhears only the middle of a conversation without knowing how it began. The most relevant and resonating historical "conversations" are personal and local, creating a geographical connection through time among all people who have lived in St. Louis and those who will do so in the future. Community pride is sustained generation after generation by the process of *remembering*—the greatest honor and most cherished compliment that anyone can bestow on ancestors who helped make the society we live in. Respectful recognition of the debts owed to the past is why people buy tombstones, publish obituaries and name children after relatives or streets after famous citizens. Such remembrance enhances the value of our common humanity, ensuring that our labors in life have created legacies that will survive our deaths.

Part I

Founding St. Louis:

ORIGINS

In all they wrought, the souls of these still live;
Their deeds, their thoughts, each brave word bravely said,
Live past the grave and master it, to give
The living help and strength when life is fraught
With sorest need of courage.[16]

The Pioneer from the Pyrenees

French he can speak, with such an air,
As if the ways of courts he knew;
And if he wore a sword, you'd say,
It was the King who passed this way.
—Cyprien Despourrins

We cannot understand the founding of St. Louis without investigating the formative influences on its founder, Pierre de Laclède (1729–1778). All prior histories of St. Louis have neglected his first quarter century spent in the Pyrenees province of Béarn—more than half of his entire life—leaving a critical gap in our understanding of the man. The personal origins of those who change history are intertwined with their professional achievements in ways that are both evident and intangible. Genealogy, genetics and family relationships are critical aspects of heritage, of course, but distinctive landscapes and regional subcultures are also important for shaping individual experiences, developing personalities and determining destinies. It is particularly important to investigate the background of a native Frenchman who was legally a citizen of France but culturally a product of only one tiny part of that country.

Laclède's heritage and early life were firmly rooted in *Le Béarn*, a small and special world unto itself in southwestern France. That ancient province, now within the French Département of the Pyrénées-Atlantiques, is wedged between the Basque Country to the west and the Pyrenees Mountains on the east and south. Beyond that stoney southern boundary are Spain's historic

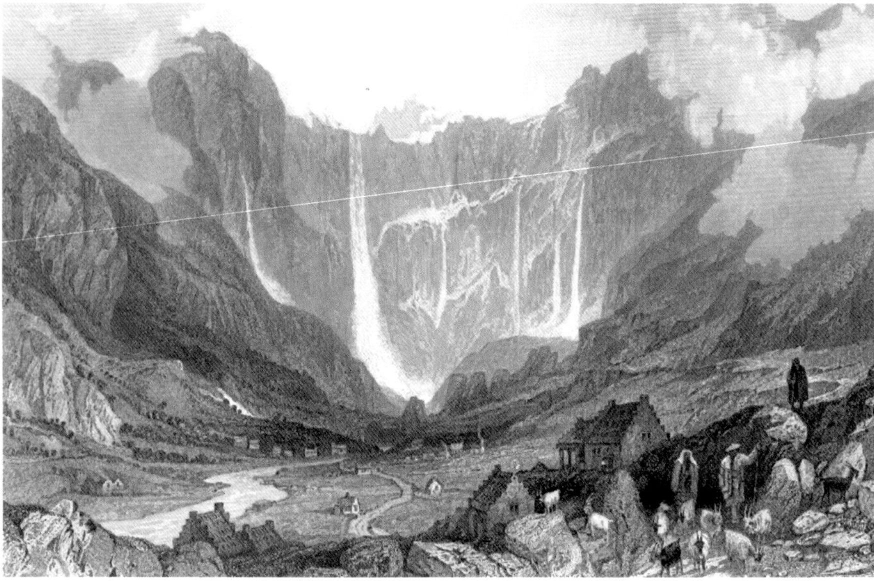

Spectacular Pyrenean waterfalls of Gavarnie with sixteen-hundred-foot drop. *Drawing by Thomas Allom in* France Illustrated *(London and Paris, 1847). Author's collection.*

kingdoms of Aragon and Navarre; the former ruled Béarn until the ninth century, while the Béarnais "kings of Navarre" later lived in Pau, France. Located closer to Pamplona than Paris, Béarn was influenced by the Spanish and the Basques much earlier and for far longer than it was by the French. The Béarnais traded with Spain "since time immemorial," and every year thousands of Béarnais, Basques and Spanish traveled to market towns through the Pyrenean passes that Laclède patrolled as a soldier in the 1750s. Merely exchanging commodities did little to alter varying values, cherished customs, distinctive dress or ancient languages—an important lesson for a future Indian trader.[17]

Béarn's raging rivers, mineral springs, deep lakes and heavy rainfall fully justified its inclusion in Roman *Aquitania*, but political integration was another matter. The variegated topography of Béarn, including both broad, fertile plains and high, sterile mountains in a very small space, created a paradox between multicultural inclusion and subcultural exclusivity. For centuries, a vast variety of peoples—Romans, Visigoths, Franks, Vascons, Muslims, Normans, Spanish, Basques and even Calvinists from Geneva—entered Béarn. But like the pilgrims from around the world who still trek through the province to reach the famous shrine at Santiago de Compestela, Spain, the mere presence of foreigners did not transform local traditions. The choice to accept or reject cultural change remained with the native Béarnais. While the prohibitive highlands provided asylum from invaders, economic independence was sustained well below those snowy peaks by the rich soils and mild climate that nurtured vineyards, grain farms, huge flocks of sheep and pastures filled with Béarn's famous cattle.[18]

The Béarnais, like the Basques, were a tribal "people apart," speaking a unique language while resenting and resisting the imposition of authority by outsiders. Until the nineteenth century, Béarn gave more to France than France gave to Béarn, and the province was not even loosely incorporated into that nation until 1620. As late as 1788, the Béarnais claimed to live "in a country foreign to France" and still regarded Navarre and Béarn as "nations." The French language was only a school subject until the end of World War II, and even today, a large percentage of the native Béarnais prefer to speak their distinctive dialect of the Gascon-Occitan language. Such pride and clannishness, according to Pierre de Marca's 1640 *Histoire du Béarn*, were owed to the "natural fortifications" of the Pyrenees, giving the Béarnais an "elevated" opinion of themselves as "remarkably intelligent, and at the same time, simple in their habits and manners." They cherished Béarn's independence as a "republic of shepherds," gently governed by local counts, princes and kings for half a millennium. The Béarnais expected their rulers to live among them as familiar celebrities, like clan chiefs, whose main concern was their welfare. The most beloved of their rulers, Henri III of Navarre (1553–1610), who would become the first Bourbon king of France as Henri IV, began life with garlic and the local Jurançon wine rubbed on his lips. His grandfather insisted that he be raised as a hardy, outdoor peasant lad rather than as a pampered prince. An expert swordsman and a womanizing playboy, that warrior king was a Calvinist who became a Catholic for his coronation as France's monarch. His Edict of Nantes in 1598 reaffirmed Catholicism as the state religion but also granted freedom of worship to the Huguenots he once championed. "Good King" Henri's concern for his subjects (desiring a "fowl in every pot"), his efforts for religious toleration, his preservation of Béarn's forests and his impressive support of early French colonization in North America made him an excellent role model for a young Laclède. His study of local history surely made him aware that King Henri was descended from Saint Louis IX on his father's side.[19]

Since the Béarnais did not subscribe to the gender bias of France's Salic Law, their province also enjoyed a rich and rare heritage of strong and intelligent female rulers. King Henri's mother was Jeanne d'Albret, queen of Navarre, who promoted Protestantism in her realm, and her mother was Queen Marguerite d'Angoulême de Navarre, sister of King François I of France. Marguerite was a patroness of Rabelais and an accomplished author herself, publishing the popular *Heptaméron* (1559), seventy-two short stories inspired by Boccaccio's *Decameron*. Henri, "the Green Gallant," married Margaret of Valois and then Marie de Medici, and his three daughters from that second marriage were Elizabeth, queen of Spain; Christine Marie, duchess of Savoy; and Henrietta Maria, queen of England.[20]

The attention that King Henri paid to finding excellent mates for his children was a dynastic necessity. But the value placed on family life and the perpetuation and reputation of one's surname was shared by all landowning classes in Béarn, which included most of the peasants. "The single most important social organizing principle in the French Pyrenees is 'the house,' a complex value encompassing dwelling, property and family." The House of Laclède, like the House of Bourbon, sought sustainability and continuity over the centuries through primogeniture—bequeathing all property, as well as "authority, reputation and status," to a single, usually the eldest male, heir in each generation in order to preserve the maximum accumulation of property that symbolized social status. Younger males would receive a small settlement in cash or minor lands for renouncing their claims of inheritance, while women retained their material possessions in a marriage, as was the liberal French practice on both sides of the Atlantic. The so-called stem family tradition of primogeniture in the Pyrenees considered the local reputation of The House and its members to be the truest measure of "wealth," and the mountain topography created the kin-based "neighborhoods" where a "sterling reputation" counted the most.[21]

Ice Age glaciers had carved four major valleys of north-flowing rivers (*gaves*) in Béarn, and since deep gorges and high peaks made overland east–west travel difficult and dangerous, local customs were preserved by upstream or downstream contacts with family and friends. The cultural conservatism of valued traditions that resulted from physical seclusion allowed Béarn to remain relatively unchanged in the eighteenth century. Without serious wars, famines or epidemics to disrupt the region in the 1700s, residents embraced the status quo, which they considered satisfying and already equitable. Even peasants were free farmers who owned their lands, and tenancy was virtually unknown. "Few provinces of Old France," wrote a nineteenth-century Béarnais, "had such liberal institutions as the small independent state of Bearn." A sociologist wrote recently that Béarn "society has always manifested an acute awareness of its values and a strong determination to defend the foundations of its economic and social order." Only gradually, partially and always on their own terms did the Béarnais come to "share a common Atlantic orientation" of commerce and colonization through their proximity to the seaport cities of Bordeaux and Bayonne. There were always some residents who wanted to be involved with the epochal events that transformed the rest of Europe, including Pierre Laclède, who crossed more *gaves* than most Béarnais and would ultimately seek adventure in a much larger, watery world across the sea.[22]

A Life Shaped by Elevated Expectations

Pierre de Laclède was born in the village of Bedous on November 22, 1729, to Magdeleine d'Espoey d'Arance (1697–1733), from a noble family, and Pierre de Laclède Sr. (1690–1776), a prominent, wealthy *avocat* (attorney). Their home was a multistoried mansion of whitewashed stone dating to the seventeenth century. While it lacked the size and splendor of Château Lassalle, owned by nearby nobles, the location of the Laclède house on the outer edge of Bedous and its castlelike tower identified the family as old, respectable and willing to defend the town's two thousand residents. The Laclèdes lived along the small Gabarret River—the first river that Pierre crossed on his way to be baptized in Bedous' Church of St. Michel. His godparents were from nearby villages: Jean Marie d'Arret was a merchant from Accous, and Suzanne de Lamarque was from Athas. At the baptismal font, Father Gabé probably pronounced the baby's surname "Laclayed" in the Béarnais language, rather than the French "Lacled," and certainly not the "Lacleed" that present-day St. Louisans prefer.[23]

The Gabarret River in which young Pierre played was a tributary of the legendary Gave d'Aspe, connecting Urdos on the Spanish border with Oloron (Oloron-Sainte-Marie since 1858), the largest local town. Bedous was within its Roman Catholic diocese, which is famous for its twelfth-century Romanesque cathedral. Oloron grew wealthy and influential in the medieval textile trade with Aragon due to its location at the confluence of the Aspe and Ossau Rivers. Even though the "green, bright and foaming" Aspe River was only about twenty-five yards wide, it was one of those "magnificent torrents" that contributed to "the charm of the Pyrenees, making the country…a scene of beauty and animation…[and] singular grandeur." However, as Laclède learned as a child, the "uncontrolled majesty" of such streams could take an angry turn, creating a horror when summer thunderstorms swelled

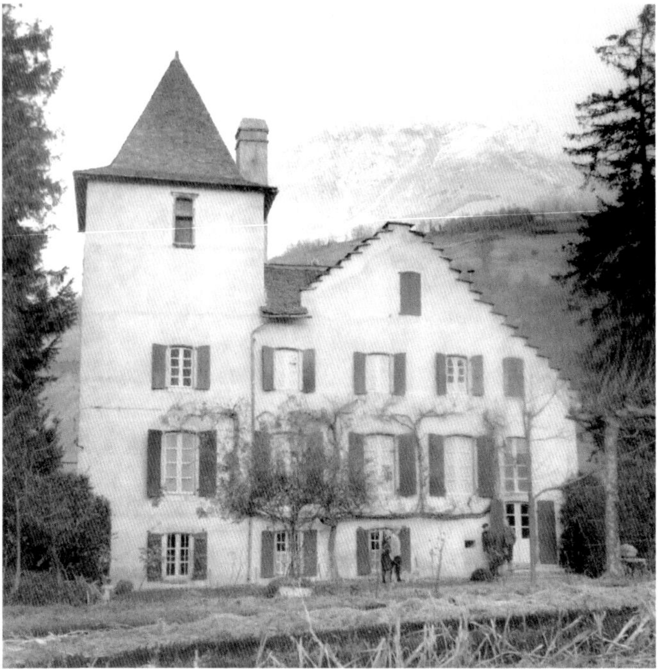

Maison de Laclède in Bedous, where Laclède was born. Photograph by Pier, circa 1960. *Courtesy Missouri History Museum, St. Louis.*

rushing waters from melting mountain snowcaps. Devastating floods did "terrible mischief" in Béarn, as rivers escaped their low and narrow banks to inundate defenseless towns.[24]

At the confluence of the Aspe and Gabarret Rivers near Laclède's home, the landscape was rural and agricultural. Surrounded by forests, meadows and fields, Bedous was centrally located in the "garden of Béarn"—a region of foothills that were fifteen hundred feet above sea level but in sight of mountain peaks that were eight thousand feet higher. "The plain of Bedous" was "highly cultivated and very picturesque"—a beautiful "little Paradise," as one visitor discovered. "I could hardly believe my eyes," wrote Arthur Young, an English agricultural reformer in the late eighteenth century, when he observed the prosperity of even the smallest farms in Béarn. "Neatness, warmth, and comfort" described the bountiful fields, healthy livestock and tile-roofed stone houses he regularly encountered among the peasantry. Adding to the charm of that "happy valley" were several green, conical hills or mounds (called *turons*) that "constitute one of the most characteristic features of the scenery," a microcosm of "the buttresses of lofty sugar-loaf mountains" farther south. Bedous was also surrounded by six other small villages, all located along the Gave d'Aspe. Most notable were Osse (present-

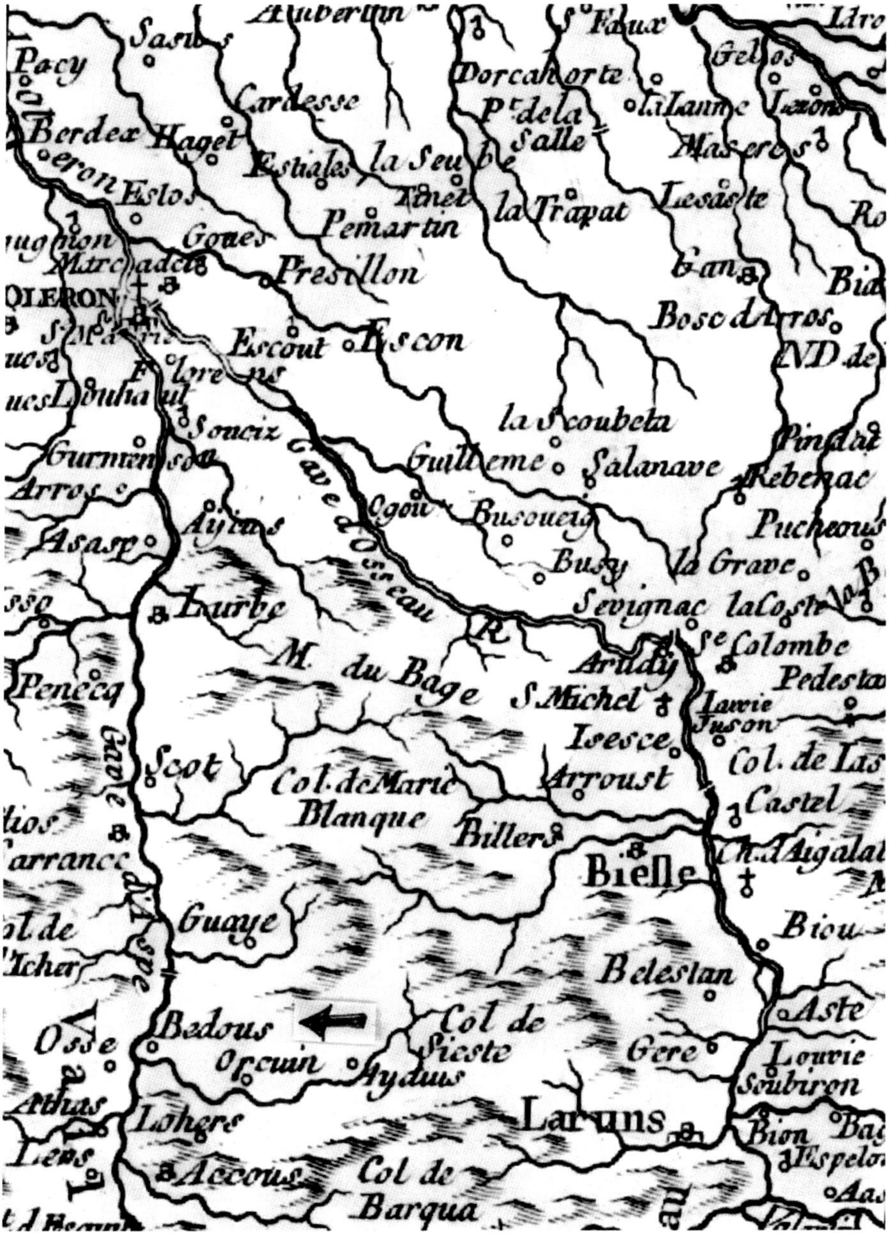

The Aspe and Ossau Valleys, showing Laclède's Bedous and adjoining villages. *Robert (Vaugondy),* Partie Meridi du Gouvernement de Guienne…et Béarn, *1757. Author's collection.*

day Osse-en-Aspe) and Accous. Well into the nineteenth century, Osse had a Protestant church and a thriving congregation, a rare reminder of the Calvinist enclaves that flourished in Béarn, La Rochelle and elsewhere in the sixteenth and seventeenth centuries. Accous, located only a mile and a half directly south of Laclède's home, was "highly cultivated and adorned with the cottages of the peasantry" but was most famous as the birthplace of the popular pastoral poet and swashbuckling swordsman Cyprien Despourrins (1698–1759), who wrote:

The riches of the world bring only care and pain,
And nobles great and grand, with many a rich domain,
Can scarcely half the pleasures, with all their art, secure,
That wait upon the shepherd, who lives content and poor.[25]

Despourrins attracted a new audience in the Romantic Age, especially among English gentlewomen, who fell in love with the Bedous area: "It is scarcely possible to imagine a region more fitted to…poetic feeling than this, or more calculated to give sublimity and power to the…human mind." Despourrins's theme of contentment amid poverty captured the imagination of Sarah Stickney Ellis, who in 1841 commended the Béarnais for "their obliging good nature and the simplicity which characterizes many of their habits"—especially their lack of "pretension: A peasant is a peasant, a shopkeeper a shopkeeper, a gentleman a gentleman…and men are not ashamed to appear what they really are." To her, that represented "moral courage…in daring to be poor—in dressing and living according to their means, when these means are extremely limited." Ellis believed that the "cheerfulness of the Béarnais is that of regularly animated industry, [for] each individual, having his wealth and his power within himself, and no human influence to conciliate or to fear, is able to gather in security and peace the full return of his unremitting activity." She also linked that "almost uniform cheerfulness" to the "delightful climate" of the lower Pyrenees. "There is an effect produced by the clearness of the atmosphere, the brightness of the sunshine, and the elasticity of the air" that enhanced the "sensation of being alive." It was "a perpetual enjoyment" that made "another day welcomed as another blessing."[26]

English writers, who rarely complimented the French, found the Béarnais to be "clean, active, good-natured, and cheerful," having the "general appearance of order, industry, and prosperity" that was "far superior to the inhabitants" of the higher Pyrenees to the east. Physically, the men of the Pyrenean foothills were "a noble looking race"—handsome, hardy and tall, often "above six feet in height, thin, agile, and admirably formed." Visitors commended their white teeth; jet-black, shoulder-length hair; "vigorous complexions"; physical strength; and athletic ability. Shepherd boys were described as "the most beautiful specimens of human nature," brimming with "glowing health and buoyant youth." Outdoor physical activity contributed to the "industrious hardihood" of men who climbed rocks for business or pleasure. Shepherds practiced transhumance, ascending mountains with flocks of sheep to pasture them on elevated grazing meadows (*estives*) all summer long, while the gentry fished for trout and salmon in highland streams and hunted brown bears and wild goats (*izards* or *chamois*) amid the peaks. The young women of Béarn were considered "extremely handsome, too, with dark eyes and fine features," and some were tall enough to be "majestic-looking." Peasant women got their exercise sowing fields and tending crops while male shepherds were far from home. Entire villages of women, wearing "glittering cross[es] of gilt" that accentuated their dark smocks and black hair, could be seen filling "sacks with manure, which they carried on their heads, and then spread upon the land [before] sowing broad cast, with the seed in their aprons."[27]

In Bedous and much of the Aspe Valley, the main grain and "chief article of consumption" was maize long before Laclède's era. The Béarnais cultivated Indian corn "with great industry," relishing its taste and using waste leaves and stalks to feed livestock. In most of eighteenth-century France, food production increased by some 40 percent. But Béarn was a *pain court* (short of bread) place, since the "corn annually reaped is not more than would suffice for the maintenance of the people during six months of the year," despite a "salubrious climate and the indefatigable labor of the occupants." Milling maize into corn flour occurred in most of river-rich Béarn, and Laclède studied the operation of his family's water mill years before he owned one in St. Louis. Maize became a dietary staple, and the Béarnais preferred corn-and-milk porridge to oatmeal for breakfast and baked more cornbread (*mesture*) than wheat bread. They ate heartily in only two meals a day, and whether in the morning or the evening, the fare would include trout, pork, goose, bacon, fried potatoes, boiled cabbage mixed with lard, eggs or omelettes, mountain ewe cheese with a licorice smell, coffee and red wine from either France or Spain.[28]

Pierre Laclède was denied many years of such large family dinners because his mother died before he turned four. She had borne seven children—Marie (1726), Jean (January 1728), Magdeleine (December 1728), Pierre (1729), Vincent (1730), Jean Pierre (1731) and Catherine (1733)—in only seven years and succumbed to complications from the last birth on September 21,

1733. But Pierre grew up "determined, bold and boisterous," nurtured by nannies and numerous aunts in a house filled with other children. He was especially close to his brother Jean and sister Magdeleine, who were only slightly older. When he could be pulled away from watching the water mill or fishing for trout in the Gabarret, young Pierre learned grammar from the parish sexton, studied Latin and history with Father Gabé and took riding lessons from a farmer who worked for his father.[29]

In time, Pierre became aware that he was a member of "one of the most distinguished families" in the Aspe Valley for several centuries. The Laclèdes became landed gentry in 1385, when Count Gaston Phoebus acknowledged their purchase of abbey properties in the villages of Aydius and Osse. Pierre's great-grandfather, Jean de Laclède (born in 1636), had been a notary, and his grandfather of the same name (born in 1660) was both syndic and lieutenant major of the Vallèe d'Aspe, much praised for donating supplies to Louis XIV's soldiers during the War of the Spanish Succession. Like later Laclèdes, his status as a landed gentleman was not diminished by being a merchant, and he earned community respect for his personal integrity, public generosity and ability to father eleven children. His wife was Marie Latourette, who was probably a Calvinist like her father and brother. Historian Alfred Cadier wrote that "never did the protestants of Osse knock in vain at the door of the Laclède[s] of Bedous." Such toleration befitted a family that valued education, collected books and earned professional esteem as lawyers, doctors, priests, merchants and local officials.[30]

Two of young Pierre's uncles, Jean Pierre Joseph Laclède of Bedous and Jean Pierre Soubie of Accous, were physicians, and a great-uncle, Father Jean, was curé at the village church in Escot. Pierre Jr.'s most distinguished relative was Jean Joseph de Laclède (1689–1736), the older brother of his father. He was a celebrated traveler and author (*L'Histoire Générale du Portugal*) and became a good friend of Voltaire, who enjoyed his "lively wit" and shared his interest in Portugal. The famous philosopher mourned Jean Joseph's passing in a February 1736 letter: "I had loaned some money to the deceased Monsieur Laclède but without note. I would rather have lost ten times more [to have him] still alive." Laclède had incurred a debt of three hundred livres to buy books—a family trait.[31]

When Pierre was born, the Laclèdes were linked by blood or friendship to many rich and even noble families of the Aspe Valley. They had enough landed wealth to be considered aristocrats but achieved more regional respect as dutiful professionals of high intellect. Pierre de Laclède Sr. assumed the management of family lands in 1725 during the prolonged absences of his brother, the historian, and inherited the entire estate when he died in 1736. But the law was the passion of Pierre's father. He was educated at the University of Toulouse and served the judicial Parlement of Navarre at Pau for most of his adult life. His eldest son, Jean (1728–1813), studied law at the same university and also argued cases before that parlement. But Pierre's older brother gained fame for his botanical research and the introduction of new tree species in his native province. In 1751, Jean de Laclède became a member of the Academy of Fine Arts and Sciences at Pau, and in 1763, King Louis XV appointed him "Private Master of Waters and Forests in Béarn," awarded him five hundred arpents of royal land and recognized the family's coat of arms. The two large birds on that crest are reputed to be eagles, but they look more like vultures, three varieties of which are native to Béarn.[32]

Long before the king's recognition of their contributions to forestry, the Laclèdes were associated with woodlands and wood products, since *clede* means "hurdle" in Béarnais—a gate placed across the gap in a hedgerow to block livestock from trampling crops. Lashing several of those gates together created a sheep corral, known as a *clédat.* Young Pierre had a personal stake in trees. By family tradition, the second son appended the word *Liguest* to the surname, signifying his rights to revenues from the Laclèdes' grove of willow trees (*ligues* or *saligues* in Béarnais) near the village of Athas, just south of Bedous on the opposite side of the Gave d'Aspe. *Liguest* was similar to the word *cadet* (second son) in identifying birth order in families, and all *cadets* in Béarn were "promised a portion [of property or money] in return for renouncing their rights" of inheritance, according to the principle of The House. But in Laclède's case, Liguest also served to distinguish him from his father and all other Pierres in the family, of which there had been one in every generation since 1570. In St. Louis, Pierre literally made a name for himself

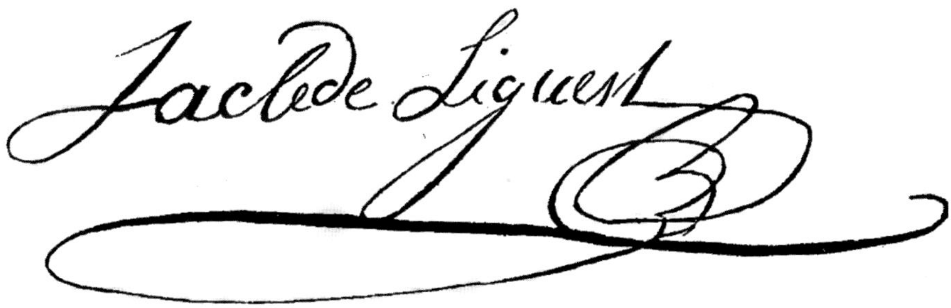

The founder's eccentric "Liguest" signature, although he was always addressed as Laclède. *From Walter B. Stevens,* St. Louis: The Fourth City, 1764–1909 *(1909).*

by signing documents as "Laclede Liguest" in large, bold letters for the rest of his life—although he was always addressed by his surname, Laclède, in conversation. That distinction has confused historians ever since, but there was no possibility of confusing Pierre with other Laclèdes in America, since he was the only one, and the line there ended with his death in 1778.[33]

Expanding Horizons

As a precocious teenager, the latest Liguest fulfilled adult responsibilities by working in the Isseaux Forest with his godfather, the merchant Jean Pierre d'Arret. The French navy requisitioned large trees for ships' masts near the Laclèdes' willow grove, and d'Arret leased ten oxen to Gabé de Sarrance's company of Basque lumberjacks to help haul the huge logs to the small Aspe port of Athas. Pierre helped prepare the trees for rafting downstream, for which d'Arret gave him a pony from Spain. During his days in the forest, young Laclède may have encountered some "Cagots"—discriminated outcasts erroneously associated with goiters, gypsies and/or cretinism—since such "untouchables" were restricted to employment as woodcutters and carpenters far away from most Béarn villages. In the eighteenth century, forests were frightening, forbidding places inhabited by *European sauvages* ("wild people"), such as the Cagots and several famous feral children.[34]

Probably in his early teens, Pierre Laclède left home to begin his formal schooling in the historic provincial capital of Pau, located on the prominent Gave de Pau. He followed family tradition by enrolling as a boarding student at the Jesuit College, founded in the early 1600s by Henri IV. That "large and airy building, without grace or beauty, [and] enclosed in high walls," stood in the Porte-Neuve quarter at the opposite end of the city from the huge, elevated royal château dating to the Middle Ages. That school was the closest academy where a young Bedous gentleman could receive a classical education to qualify for admission to a university. Known for their academic rigor, the Jesuits may have introduced Laclède to the *Jesuit Relations*, the fascinating, but sometimes gruesome, accounts of colonial missionaries who lived and died among *American sauvages*. Father Joseph-Francois Lafitau from Bordeaux (1681–1746) both studied and taught philosophy and rhetoric at that academy before researching the native cultures of North America and publishing his famous, pioneering ethnographies.[35]

The influential city of Pau offered a stimulating secular education to supplement the priests' curriculum. When Laclède lived there, it was not

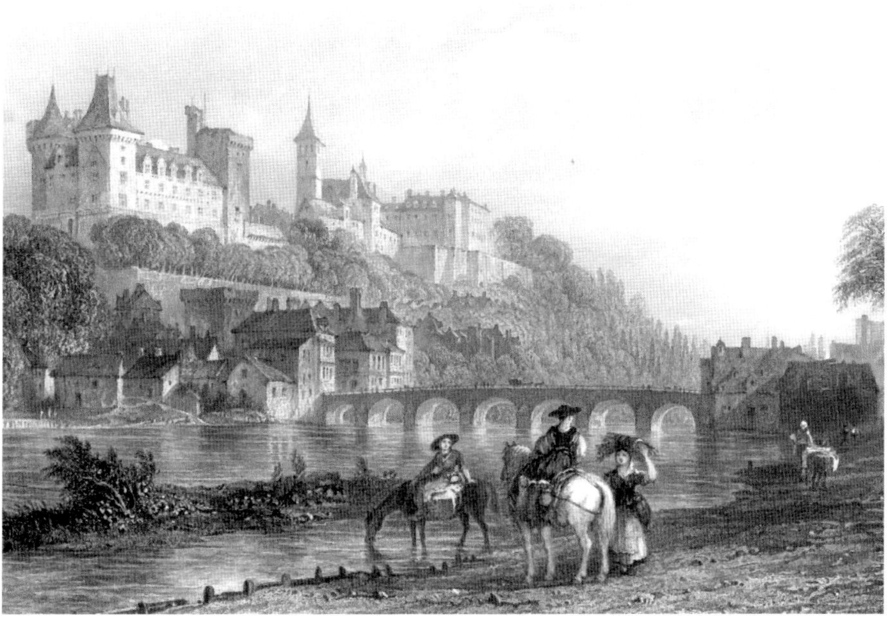

Royal Palace of Henri IV at Pau (dating to 1370) along the Pau River. *Drawing by Thomas Allom in* France Illustrated *(London and Paris, 1847).*

yet the "Little Paris of Southern France" that catered to English tourists in the post-Napoleonic era (with the first golf course on the continent). The boy from Bedous got his first exposure to town planning and modern urban architecture as he walked along the principal boulevard, Rue de la Prefecture, and saw the tangible symbols of religion and royalty. The Catholic establishment was well represented by the Jesuit school; a seminary; Capucin, Orpheline and Ursuline convents; eight churches; and a large cathedral named for Saint Louis. The "noblesse of Béarn" attended the theater in the La Fontaine district, had access to a hospital and lived in fashionable town houses, protected by soldiers in nearby barracks who paraded on the Champ de Mars. Royal power was evident everywhere: in the parlement building; in the provincial mint, whose distinctive coins depicted a fat Béarn cow; and especially in the ancient palace. Located along the river, that was the medieval residence of the Gascon counts of Foix and the birthplace of King Henri. Still on display there is the huge tortoise shell "cradle" used by the future monarch. Pau offered only one sight more impressive than that palace—stunning views of magnificent mountains that appeared to be a single "long chain" of stone gleaming in the sunlight.[36]

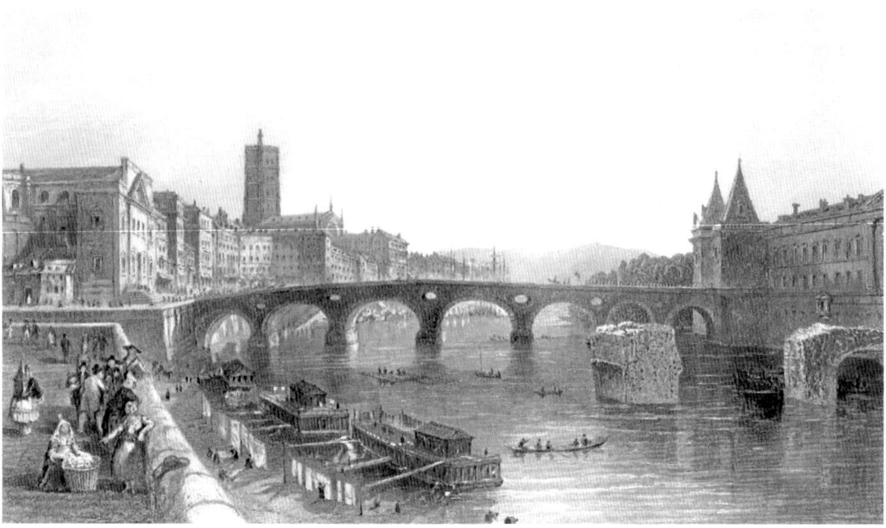

City of Toulouse on the Garonne River where Laclède studied and won his sword. *Drawing by Thomas Allom in* France Illustrated *(London and Paris, 1847).*

By 1746, perhaps earlier, Pierre and his older brother, Jean, moved from Pau to the famous "pink [brick] city" of Toulouse, the larger and grander capital city of the Midi-Pyrénées region on the Garonne River. Both brothers may have read law there, but only Jean was definitely enrolled at the University of Toulouse. Most scholars agree that Pierre attended the Académie d'Armes de Toulouse, where on June 30, 1748, he was awarded an ornate sword—a silver-hilted épée engraved with the coats of arms of King Louis XV and the city of Toulouse—for winning a fencing competition or, less likely, "for his performance as a student." He was still carrying that sword inscribed by Toulouse's "chief magistrates" on the day he died thirty years later along the steamy lowlands of the Arkansas River, so very far from the clear air and lofty mountain peaks of his boyhood.[37]

In his early twenties, Laclède was serving in the thirty-man Compagnie du Vic de Bas (home guard) under the command of a Captain Laaslurbe, patrolling the mountain passes into Spain. Laclède's unit was there to arrest "strange, wild-looking men" and "banditti from the other side of the frontier," since the southernmost Aspe Valley contained the "most daring smugglers." The young fencer from the foothills was now a "Roland" of the high peaks, and he developed a soldier's keen eye for distinguishing cultures by appearance. Spaniards traditionally wore head scarves of printed cotton, wide-brimmed conical hats of black velvet, silk sashes, white leggings, rough cloaks and sandals laced up to their calves, while Béarn's peasants resembled Canadian voyageurs with their homemade breeches, red waist sashes and capote-like woolen cloaks with pointed hoods. Only their brown berets and large wooden shoes would have seemed odd in Indian bark canoes along the Great Lakes. Military service also gave Laclède the opportunity to broaden his linguistic skills. The intersecting ethnicities along the Pyrenees border helped make him at least trilingual, as he added Spanish and perhaps some Basque words to his native Béarnais dialect and the French he learned at school. In his library at St. Louis, Laclède had French, Spanish and English dictionaries.[38]

The most pleasant aspect of Laclède's soldiering was probably the spectacular mountain scenery. He was stationed at both the Col (pass) de Pau and the Col du Somport, at an elevation of over fifty-three hundred feet, but he could also see the Pic (peak) d'Anie at eighty-two hundred feet and the Pic du Midi d'Ossau, one thousand feet higher, with its impressive "cloven crest" that was "often wrapped in mist." Laclède was viewing the "grandeur and sublimity" of the Pyrenees for the last time. He would soon leave that "barrier between earth and heaven" in the "purer atmosphere of another world" to begin a new life in a sordid city below sea level, where he would associate with better-dressed and more respectable smugglers as his future business partners in America.[39]

Making His Way Across the World

As a second son with almost no chance of inheriting his father's estate, and showing little enthusiasm for a legal career, Laclède had decided, by 1755, to move to America. He must have found it intolerable to live in the direct shadow of his very talented, and only slightly older, brother—the honored heir who shared the same professional interests as their father. Those were fairly convincing *push* factors for leaving Béarn, but was Laclède also *pulled* to the Western Hemisphere for some reason? Both his choice of destination—the ill-reputed "Babylon" of New Orleans—and the port he decided to sail from, La Rochelle, suggest that Laclède may have been recruited specifically to fill a key position in Louisiana.

Statistics confirm how unusual it was for anyone from Béarn to immigrate anywhere in North America and rarer still to choose Louisiana as a destination. All of southwestern France only contributed 11 percent of the residents in the better-known and older colony of Canada in nearly two centuries. Louisiana received a mere seven thousand colonists from the entire nation of France between 1700 and 1763—less than half as many who went to Guyana and

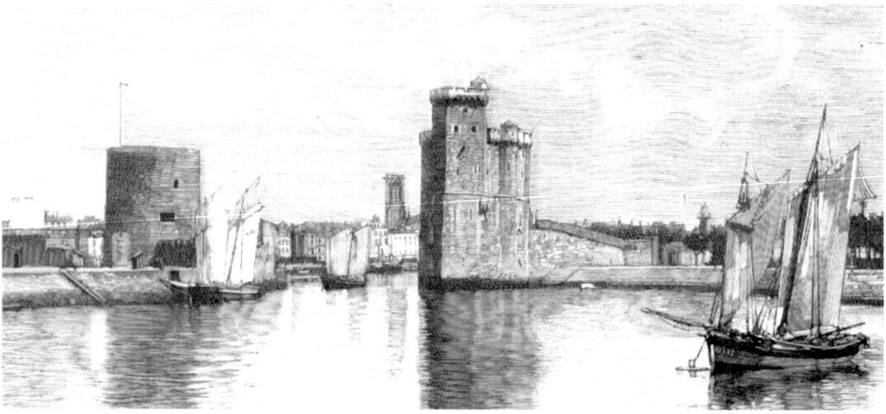

Old Harbor of La Rochelle, the last part of France that America-bound Laclède would have seen. *Engraving from* Le Monde Illustré *(1898).*

three thousand fewer than the French living in the Ottoman Empire! Even La Rochelle, a port with strong trading ties to New Orleans, only carried an average of fourteen passengers to Louisiana and sixteen to Canada per year between 1749 and 1763, compared with ninety-eight people sailing from there to the Antilles on an annual basis. But Laclède chose to depart from that port on the Bay of Biscay, rather than Bordeaux, a larger Atlantic coastal city that was only half the distance from Bedous than La Rochelle. Was it a mere coincidence that Laclède's senior business partner in New Orleans had his closest commercial contacts with La Rochelle and purchased most of the supplies for early St. Louis there? Another related link may have involved Paul Rasteau. He was a La Rochelle native living in the Louisiana capital, while his brothers, Pierre and Eli, dispatched the family fleet to both of those ports, as well as Saint-Domingue and Spanish Veracruz. One of the merchant associates of the Rasteaus was Nicolas Forstall, Laclède's future friend, attorney and perhaps business partner, in New Orleans.[40]

In any case, on Saturday, June 7, 1755, twenty-five-year-old Pierre Laclède boarded François Guillard's ship *La Concorde* as the only one of the two-dozen passengers who was a native of the Pyrenees. *La Concorde* was one of only five ships in 1755 leaving La Rochelle for New Orleans. Laclède probably headed for the capital of Louisiana with some family capital, which was often the case when a bachelor son abandoned The House. He probably packed some of his favorite books, and he definitely took his cherished sword with him—as well as indelible memories of a tiny Béarn valley that would prove relevant to his future in a much larger world.[41]

The Planners in New Orleans

The reputation of New Orleans as a wild town where the rule of law was weak attracted just the right sort of people to keep trade favorable.
—Shannon Lee Dawdy

For the next two decades, Laclède would lead a lucky life, since he always seemed to be in the right place at the right time to avoid danger or to gain an advantage. That streak of good fortune was apparent as he began his odyssey to America. His ship pulled out of La Rochelle only one day before the British navy captured the French ships *Alcide* and *Lys* in the Gulf of St. Lawrence, with 130 of his countrymen killed or wounded and another 2,000 taken prisoner. Laclède left just as British privateers started to intercept French vessels throughout the Caribbean, and transatlantic transportation from the Bay of Biscay would soon cease altogether. If he had delayed his journey, Laclède may never have reached America, since in 1758, 70 of the 76 ships sent from La Rochelle were either captured or destroyed, while 224 vessels in Bordeaux's fleet were lost.[42]

Before *La Concorde* docked in New Orleans, war was raging in Pennsylvania. On July 14, 1755, a force of French Canadians and Indian allies, including some Osages, destroyed General Edward Braddock's British army along the Monongahela River, killing, wounding or capturing eleven hundred men. The first global conflict in history—the Seven Years' War, known in America as the French and Indian War—was underway long before the official declaration of hostilities between France and Great Britain in May 1756. Coming to a continent not in concord, the Pyrenees soldier with a sword at his side arrived just in time to use his military skills.[43]

WARTIME OPPORTUNITIES

Louisiana's oppressive summer heat and humidity must have been a shock to someone used to refreshing mountain breezes, but otherwise, Laclède's background in Béarn prepared him for a career along the Mississippi River far better than most historians have realized. He was ready to be a merchant, as many ancestors had been. He already knew Spanish before he arrived in a polyglot and multiethnic New Orleans near a Caribbean Sea dominated by Spain. He had met at least two black slaves aboard ship, so he was somewhat prepared for the racial diversity of New Orleans, and he shared a fear of flooding with all residents in that port city. Laclède was a good choice to lead an expedition to the Illinois Country, for he found much there that was familiar to him. He had studied with Jesuits before he tried to purchase the property of that order in Kaskaskia. He was familiar with salt extraction from the saline marshlands of Béarn before he ever visited the saltworks near Ste. Genevieve. He had dined on the succulent ham (*jambon*) of Basque Bayonne prior to tasting the famous pork of French Creoles in Illinois. And he knew many Protestants who lived near Bedous prior to dealing with British merchants and army officers along the Mississippi.

"Indian Country" did not surprise Laclède, either. He had grown up amidst extensive maize fields tilled by women before he ever visited an Algonquian village, and he thought it normal for Siouan men to spend summers among buffalo herds far from home—behavior that resembled Pyrenean traditions of transhumance in that season with hoofed animals of another kind. Laclède had already encountered the wolflike dogs that both Indian warriors and Béarn shepherds used to guard their campsites. And he was familiar with hunting bears and deerlike *chamois* before buying such furs from Osage hunters in Missouri.

New Orleans in the mid-1750s offered exceptional opportunities for a French gentleman with a sharp sword seeking to make a killing in commerce. In the Louisiana militia, Laclède found a patron and future partner who would influence the rest of his life. His regimental commander, Gilbert Antoine de St. Maxent (1724–1794), or simply "Maxent," was the perfect role model for combining public service in the military with private profits as a merchant, and he was a master in obtaining the patronage of royal officials to advance both careers. Maxent was born in Longwy, Lorraine, on France's contested northeastern border, and that province would not be incorporated into the French nation until 1766. In 1747, he headed to New Orleans, married Elizabeth La Roche, a wealthy widow born in Montreal,

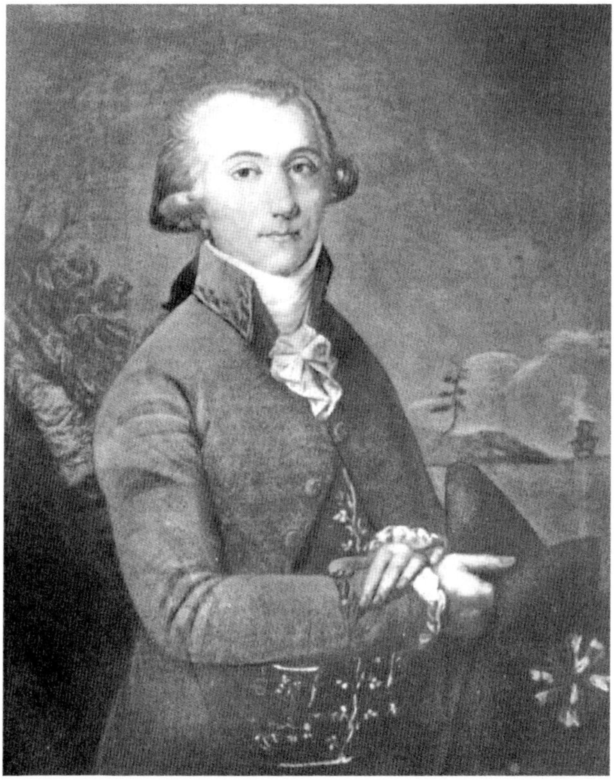

Reputed portrait of Pierre Laclède, circa 1755, in the family collection at Bedous. *From Walter B. Stevens,* St. Louis: The Fourth City, 1764–1909 *(1909).*

and became a successful Indian trader just a few years before Laclède arrived. Maxent probably took a liking to the gentleman from Béarn because both were well-educated émigrés born in France, only five years apart in age, who shared an inquisitive spirit as avid readers and acquisitive ambitions as businessmen—a combination of characteristics that was all too rare in a crude colony of Creoles and Canadians.[44]

One special Creole was Marie Thérèse Bourgeois Chouteau (1733–1814), a woman as unconventional, intelligent and strong-willed as any queen in Béarn, who became Laclède's lover for the rest of his life. She was born in New Orleans when it was "a mere assemblage of a few poor cabins…made of planks and mud," subject to periodic floods and famines. Her parents were Nicolas Charles Bourgeois of Paris and Marie Joseph Tarare, probably from Cambray, although some historians claim that she was Spanish. Young Marie's father died when she was five, and within a year, a stepfather, Nicholas Pierre Carco, was living with her pregnant mother and three younger siblings. On September 20, 1748, at the age of fifteen, Marie married René Auguste

Chouteau (1723–1776), a baker and tavern keeper from L'Hermenault, Poitou, near La Rochelle. Less than a year later, on September 7, 1749, she gave birth to Auguste Chouteau. By 1755, Marie's husband had abandoned them and returned to France. Under the laws of that Catholic country and its colonies, Madame Chouteau could neither divorce her absent spouse nor remarry until his death. Considering herself "widowed" by abandonment, she made the pragmatic but daring decision to take Laclède as her lover without benefit of clergy.[45]

Maxent presumably introduced them, and historians have speculated about how the "polished and self-assured Laclède [may have] favorably impressed" Marie Thérèse, not only with his education and manners but with his looks as well. His reputed portrait shows him formally attired in the royal colors of France, including an elaborately embroidered gold waistcoat. Those fancy clothes, his confident expression and his rather feminine hands all confirmed his status as a gentleman, while his faint but beguiling smile made him seem approachable. Based on family lore and one eyewitness from St. Louis's first decade, Laclède had an olive, almost swarthy, complexion, a broad forehead, a prominent nose and "piercing, expressive eyes" of black or dark blue that "seemed to penetrate." His "commanding presence" was attributed to his height of at least five feet, nine inches—only average for Béarn but considered "tall" among most European-descended men in Louisiana and Illinois. Statistics on 241 French soldiers in New Orleans only two decades earlier reveal that 25 percent were less than five feet tall, and only two exceeded five feet, seven inches. One wonders if Laclède had a voice that was "cracked and hoarse" and very "unmusical" like all too many Aspe Valley men. Whether or not love was blind, or deaf, the romance between Marie and Pierre resulted in the birth of Jean Pierre on October 10, 1758—the first of four children born in only six years, all of whom were baptized Chouteau for the sake of decorum. The pair's twenty-year liaison provided a stepfather for Auguste and would leave a profound genealogical legacy in the history of St. Louis and the American West.[46]

New Orleans was a compact community that compressed 2,500 residents of various cultures, colors and classes (a third of all Louisianans) into a small space, so it is no surprise that the two people who changed Laclède's life—Maxent and Marie—knew each other and lived only twelve houses apart. In the New Orleans census of September 1763, Madame Chouteau's household and Maxent's family of six were living in the Fourth Militia District. That "back of town" neighborhood of taverns and lowly tradesmen contained a total of 160 white adults (93 men, 67 women), 232 white children, 170 adult African slaves, 48 slave children, 37 mulattoes and 6 Indian adults. Maxent was the largest slave owner in that district farthest from the river, with 20 Africans (10 adult males, 3 boys and 7 girls), 6 more than any other resident. He also had 4 "mulattoes," probably "free persons of color" hired as house servants. In 1766, the first city census under the Spanish regime revealed that "Gilberto de St. Maxent, Officer" had moved to the more respectable Third District, nearer the waterfront. He now had some elite neighbors, including Charles-Philippe Aubry, France's last (acting) governor of Louisiana, and Nicolas Chauvin de Lafrénière, the king's prosecuting attorney, who would be executed for leading the 1768 New Orleans Revolt against Spanish rule. That intriguing neighborhood included other military officers, merchants, physicians and an entertainer, "San German, singer." In early 1770, Maxent was living at "house #4 on Conti Street," next door to one of the men in his militia company—none other than forty-seven-year-old René Chouteau, "pastry cook," Marie's runaway husband, only recently returned.[47]

With a Bourgeois mother, whose husband had fled Louisiana for France, and an immigrant stepfather who had left France for Louisiana, Auguste Chouteau quickly learned how to calculate personal losses and gains in adapting to fluid relationships. As an apprentice clerk for a junior merchant, Chouteau worked closely with Laclède, while Maxent taught both of them the delicate diplomacy of dealing with royal governors and Indian chiefs. Our modern perceptions of children make Chouteau seem unusually precocious, but eight- to twelve-year-old boys began military or mercantile careers fairly regularly in French America. As Auguste's guardian, mentor and boss, Laclède became the consummate role model for the young boy, providing personal stability, demonstrating professional responsibility and imparting information about the history and heritage of a France that Chouteau would never visit.

Like Maxent, who amassed a personal library of nearly five thousand volumes, Laclède and Chouteau shared a love of books in that exciting era of Enlightenment literature. Laclède amassed some two hundred volumes, while Chouteau later acquired three times as many, including several that Laclède originally brought to St. Louis. Both became independent, iconoclastic thinkers, collecting many works that were banned by the Catholic Church. Above all, Laclède gave Chouteau the most precious gift that would determine his future destiny—the encouragement and opportunity to fulfill adolescent dreams of performing great deeds like the heroes they read about. "An explorer constantly sees new things," wrote a contemporary in French Illinois, "and he learns to read in the great book of

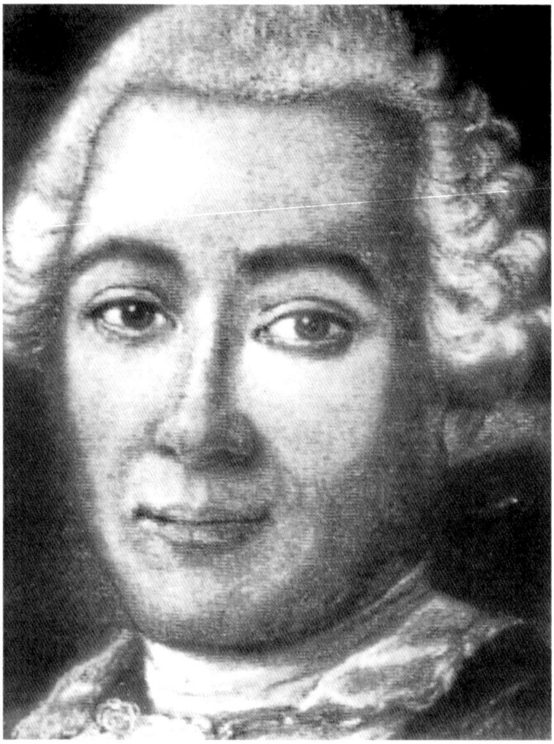

Governor-General and Chevalier Louis Billouart, count de Kerlérec. *From Marc de Villiers du Terrage,* Les Dernières Années de la Louisiane Française *(Paris, 1904).*

the universe what cannot be found in a library." Invigorated by Chouteau's youthful enthusiasm, Laclède gained a devoted friend for life by trusting him to handle adult responsibilities, as he had as a boy in Béarn. Forty years later, the fifty-four-year-old Chouteau would repay that debt of confidence by making Laclède the hero of his "Narrative"—a very personal and respectful memorial that helped rescue the devoted mentor from historical obscurity.[48]

KERLÉREC AT THE HELM

While Laclède and the Chouteaus were enjoying a tranquil family life, their city was in great turmoil during the French and Indian War. The governor-general of Louisiana for that entire period was Louis Billouart, comte de Kerlérec (1704–1770), chevalier of the Royal and Military Order of Saint Louis and captain of the King's Vessels. Kerlérec was born in the famous pottery town of Quimper, Brittany, in June 1704 and lost his mother only two days after his baptism. That westernmost province of France was, like

Béarn, a tribal enclave on the periphery, where natives spoke the ancient language of Breton. In that dialect, Quimper (*kemper*) means "confluence."[49]

Of noble lineage, Kerlérec turned his back on landed estates and looked to the sea that lapped the Brittany coast for his future career. He began sailing at age fourteen, joined the French navy in 1721 and served his sovereign for over thirty years in some of the bloodiest naval battles during that "glorious" era of wooden warships. Kerlérec's bravery and leadership earned him France's highest military honor, the Cross of Saint Louis, in 1746, following campaigns in the Mediterranean, Caribbean and Atlantic, and even on the Mississippi River, where in 1730 he went ashore to battle Natchez Indians. His most notable engagement, however, was the Second Battle of Cape Finisterre on October 14, 1747, aboard the seventy-four-gun *Neptune* in Admiral Desherbiers de l'Etenduère's fleet. Attacked by three British ships, whose cannon blasts had killed both senior commanders and most of the gun crews, shattered the mainmast and started a roaring fire that threatened the powder magazine, the *Neptune* was nearly destroyed when Kerlérec rallied the remaining sailors. But with a right foot mangled to the point of amputation, Kerlérec reluctantly surrendered his ship by hanging a white bedsheet down the side. Thirteen of seventeen officers were killed, including Kerlérec's nephew, who died at his feet with blood gushing from a severed arm.[50]

When Governor-General Kerlérec arrived at New Orleans aboard the frigate *Chariot Royal* on February 9, 1753, he was heavily in debt and in fragile health, debilitated by yellow fever, "intestinal rheumatism" and other ailments, including painful old wounds to his back and both feet. The battle-scarred naval hero would need the resolve and resilience he had displayed at Finisterre and in combat against Barbary pirates to navigate his ship of state through the perilous political waters that engulfed Louisiana. Upon his arrival, Chevalier Kerlérec was disheartened to discover that the capital city lacked food, funding and an adequate fighting force but had plenty of debts and escalating expenses. "Very dishonest" merchants were fleecing residents, many of whom had been displaced by recent flooding, while Capuchins and Jesuits were engaged in a bitter struggle for religious supremacy. New Orleans needed cannons, better barracks, a new hospital and a refurbished residence for the governor, which was so "ready to collapse" that Kerlérec and his wife "spent several nights sitting up during gusts of wind, in order to evacuate at the slightest provocation." To make matters worse, the misnamed "island" of New Orleans was increasingly isolated by navigational problems along the fickle Mississippi River. Kerlérec's predecessor, Pierre François de Rigaud, marquis de Vaudreuil-Cavagnal (1698–1778), departed from the capital on May 8, 1753, but could not even reach the Gulf of Mexico until June 19.[51]

Such impediments to progress symbolized the overall state of affairs in Louisiana. Versailles considered that colony to be a financial sinkhole with few prospects for economic solvency or social stability. France's neglect was symbolized by the failure to conduct a census for twenty-six years and the lack of response to 162 urgent messages sent by Kerlérec in an eighteen-month period. The Ministry of Marine only dispatched ships to Louisiana in even-numbered years during the French and Indian War, so Kerlérec received a mere seven official dispatches from 1760 to 1762. Louisiana was a low priority in the wartime strategy of Versailles. Since France could not defend all of its sparsely populated, widely dispersed American colonies from superior British naval power, royal officials concentrated on protecting the homeland of 23 million people against invasion. Canada received the most soldiers and supplies in order to launch offensives against the British in the East, while the French navy was committed to protecting the lucrative sugar islands in the West Indies.[52]

With such a meager commitment to Louisiana, Versailles at least should have allowed a talented military man like Kerlérec the freedom to make tactical decisions in defense of his colony. However, official policy dictated that he had to limit spending even in wartime. A senior comptroller, called the *commissaire-ordonnateur* in Louisiana and the *intendant* in Canada, scrutinized expenditures and could block even essential military decisions if they were deemed too expensive. Governor-General Kerlérec had to contend with a new, noble ordonnateur, Vincent Gaspard Pierre de Rochemore (1713–1769), son of a Nîmes marquis, who constantly challenged his military decisions. Between 1758 and 1762, Louisiana suffered a crisis of conflicted leadership as those officials each sought complete control in pursuing their very different objectives. As a navy officer used to having his commands obeyed, Kerlérec refused to put his colony at risk due to the arrogant whims of an accountant, however well-connected.[53]

The reputations of both men in that divisive, dysfunctional regime were ruined by the reciprocal charges of malfeasance, corruption and even treason during a decade-long, transatlantic scandal known as the "Affair of Louisiana." That controversy erupted in 1759 with the capture of two British merchant ships, *Texel* and *Trois Frères*, at New Orleans. Kerlérec and Rochemore agreed that the cargoes were contraband, but the ordonnateur confiscated the merchandise in the governor's absence and placed it in the king's warehouse. An incensed Kerlérec removed that property and allowed his merchant friends to profit from its sale. The commander and the comptroller were equally pompous and petty in justifying their impetuous, often clandestine, actions. While the Rochemore faction slandered Kerlérec, writing letters to France that accused him of stealing ten million livres from the treasury, of extorting funds from the Jesuits and of even trying to sell Louisiana to the British, the old combat veteran became a "dangerous man," responding with arrests, intimidation, deportations and physical violence. Although Kerlérec succeeded in removing Rochemore and his cronies, he, too, was recalled to France in disgrace, spent time in the Bastille and did not receive even partial exoneration until September 3, 1770, only five days before his death.[54]

The *Texel* affair played a key role in building a coalition of pro-Kerlérec financiers that would lead to the founding of St. Louis. That Laclède was functioning as an independent merchant favored by the governor's patronage was revealed in a June 25, 1759 public endorsement written and signed by him and eighteen others (but not Maxent). They commmended Kerlérec's "consummate wisdom…which has maintained this Colony in such a situation as to hardly feel the unfortunate results of war, at a time when all others…[are] in the most frightful state of want." They praised him for allowing them to profit from the invitation-only sale of "articles of absolute necessity" from the *Texel* cargo, since the "entire Colony [was] pressed by needs (which have never been so great since the war began)." Those privileged merchants disavowed "the dissension raised lately" against Kerlérec and proclaimed their "fidelity to the King, Our Sovereign, in whose service we would gladly spill our blood to the last drop."[55]

Chevalier Kerlérec counted on such merchant support as he waged war on two fronts, keeping one eye on the British military and the other on Rochemore's "conspirators." Punitive and predatory in what he considered a just cause to preserve Louisiana, Kerlérec became a dictator—"the absolute master of all the civil and commercial operations." Someone needed to act—illegally but realistically—to avert catastrophe, since the idealistic but impractical expectations of distant Versailles could not address the crises at hand. Defense was Kerlérec's top priority, since he was 600 troops short of the minimum 1,800 needed to patrol just one side of the long Mississippi River—with one soldier per mile! The French and Swiss soldiers in New Orleans actually declined from 405 in 1754 to a mere 127 by 1759, and military personnel at Louisiana's fourteen other garrisons was "reduced by at least half" due to desertions, disease and "debauchery of all sorts." At war's end, France sent more troops to dismantle its forts than it had dispatched to defend them. The lack of soldiers was matched by critical shortages of farmers and food, slaves and ships and convoys and cannons throughout the Mississippi Valley. In the later 1750s, even the once-bountiful Illinois Country, caterer to the capital, was deficient in the farm products that Lower Louisianans so desperately needed.[56]

Kerlérec's critics claimed that "the scarcity of food served as a pretext for his ambition," condemning the "insatiability" of his "self-interest" and "uncontrolled thirst for riches" as an alleged war profiteer. Although he left himself open to such accusations by circumventing the ordonnateur's legal responsibilities and did, indeed, "accumulate money without end," Kerlérec redirected those funds to pay for essential, expensive military projects to protect the public. The greatest of his "unexpected and extraordinary expenditures" was the construction of a new stone fortress to guard the valuable but vulnerable Illinois Country—"the keystone of the arch of French imperialism" along the Mississippi River. Costing some 300,000 to 500,000 livres or more, the massive Fort de Chartres was begun in 1753, using locally quarried limestone. Its walls were over two feet thick and at least fifteen feet high, capable of supporting twenty cannons—none of which was ever fired in combat. The fort's two-thousand-foot perimeter enclosed four acres, space enough to house three hundred soldiers, although fewer than two hundred troops of Les Compagnies Franches de la Marine were there during the French

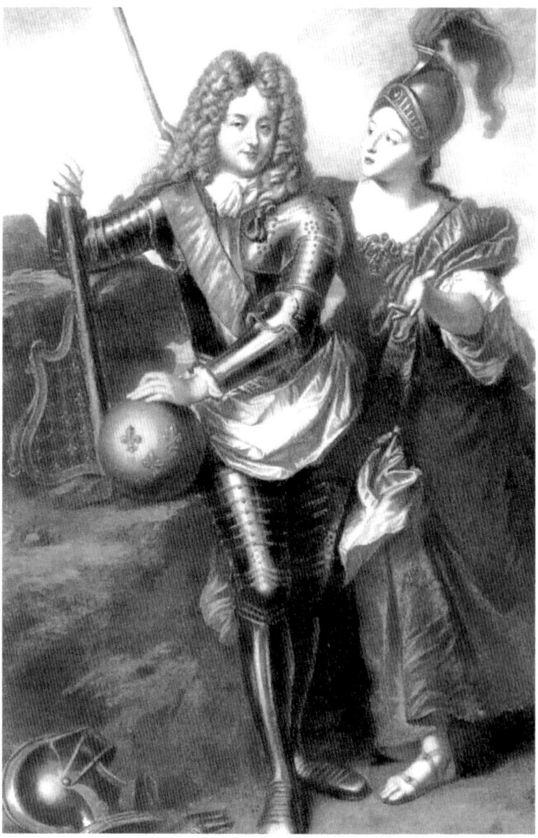

Duke Philippe II (1674–1723), regent of Louis XV and namesake of New Orleans and Fort de Chartres. *From Alcée Fortier,* History of Louisiana *(1904).*

and Indian War. Like the two wooden forts that preceded it, Kerlérec's pet construction project was named for the "Duke of Chartres," a title held by Philippe, duc d'Orléans (1674–1723), the regent for young Louis XV from 1715 to 1723, as well as Philippe's son, Louis d'Orleans (1703–1752). Surprisingly, Kerlérec did not put his own name on the fort, because only his dogged determination got it built. He refused to locate the new facility at Kaskaskia and then ignored a stop-construction order from the Ministry of Marine, claiming that the message arrived "too late," after "the fort was nearly completed" (which it never was).[57]

Fort de Chartres was the military, diplomatic and administrative capital (*chef lieu*) of French Illinois, where the commandant of Illinois resided. That experienced military officer oversaw a huge region, stretching from present-day Terre Haute (Indiana), the southern border of Quebec governance, to the Arkansas River, the northern border of New Orleans's direct control. The fort's *magasin*, which was replenished twice a year by royal convoys from New Orleans, was a magnet for commerce among several nearby French and Indian villages, all of which traded with the troops. Fort de Chartres was most valuable as a center of Indian diplomacy, attracting multiple tribal delegations from Lake Michigan southward for official parleys and the distribution of diplomatic presents. The fort was also France's westernmost garrison to participate actively in the French and Indian War, dispatching marines, militiamen and Indian allies to raid English settlements in Virginia and Pennsylvania and to deliver supplies to Fort Duquesne (site of present-day Pittsburgh). Beginning in 1753, an annual convoy of fifteen to sixteen boats from Fort de Chartres made the three-month trip up the Ohio River, loaded with a vast array of food, ammunition "and other products necessary both for the French who are there and for the Indians who surround them." Thus, military necessity thousands of miles away deprived New Orleans of some desperately needed provisions.[58]

The strategic but exposed location of that Illinois fortress required a commandant who was "wise, capable, vigilant, and of sufficient rank to be respected." The ideal person for that position was Kerlérec's brother-in-law, Major Pierre-Joseph Neyon de Villiers (circa 1718–1779), who would be the trustworthy eyes and ears of the governor after 1760. From a cash-poor noble family in Lorraine, Neyon de Villiers was familiar with intercultural turmoil in that French borderland. He fought on the continent as a captain in the Royal Lorraine Regiment, relocated to Louisiana with the same rank in 1752 and married the widowed sister of Kerlérec's wife. When Neyon de Villiers arrived at his Illinois post, he found it to be the "most embarrassing in the colony," formerly administered by an incompetent commandant who alienated colonists and Indian allies alike. But the two kinsmen, who governed twelve hundred miles apart, worked in close harmony to clean up the mess, for which Neyon de Villiers was rewarded with induction into the Royal and Military Order of Saint Louis with the honorific title of *chevalier* (knight).[59]

The commandant reaped monetary rewards as well, thanks to his brother-in-law's patronage. The "whole Indian trade was so much in the power of the commandant that nobody was permitted to be concerned in it, but on condition of giving him part of the profits." Those could be immense, given the value of the Illinois fur trade, but Neyon de Villiers and his senior officers also allegedly helped themselves to forty-six thousand livres' worth of the king's official merchandise, including gunpowder. With Kerlérec determining the composition of convoys to Illinois and Neyon de Villiers deciding how the goods would be distributed upon arrival, those military leaders blurred the line between public service and private profits. But if the governor-general in Lower Louisiana and the major-commandant in Upper Louisiana monopolized "all matters concerning trade with the savages…without any care for the interests of the King," it was largely because Louis XV took no interest in Indians or frontier defense at all.[60]

Because Kerlérec had discovered the "secret of changing everything" through his "intrigues, schemings, and emissaries," he came to epitomize the concept of "rogue colonialism" that Shannon Lee Dawdy analyzed in her book, *Building the Devil's Empire: French Colonial New Orleans*. She identified a coalition of profiteering "military entrepreneurs" and favored merchants who, as "self-interested agents," employed illegal—but socially acceptable—means (for that time and place) to bring some stability to a dysfunctional colony long ignored by Versailles. An oligarchy of self-made men and impoverished aristocrats brought a bit of order to the chaos, using earned wealth, not inherited pedigree, to determine social status. Historians trace official "corruption" (our term) to the frontier roots of New Orleans, and that pattern was established long before Kerlérec's tenure. When he succeeded in building the first fortifications around the city in 1760, which took nine months and cost one million livres, bureaucrats in France belatedly realized that his "predecessors had never built the fortifications represented on the dozens of maps sent across the Atlantic in the 1720s and 1730s, and that the funds sent over for these projects had suspiciously evaporated." Lack of oversight and erratic funding by Versailles created a perfect environment for private entrepreneurs to engage in smuggling, but New Orleans could not have functioned at all without contraband commodities. "Commercial

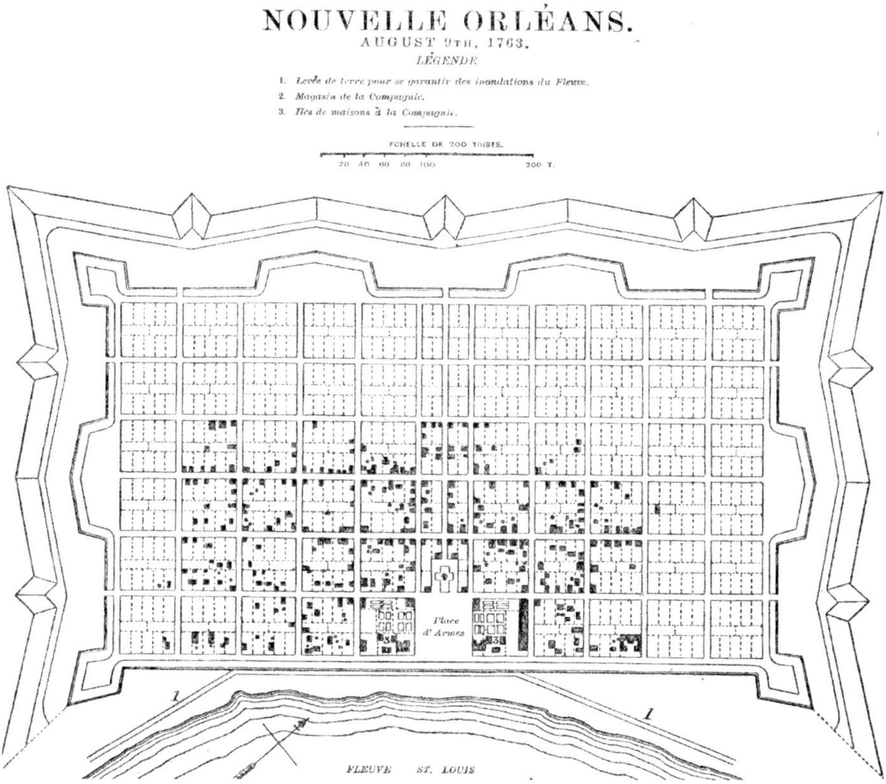

New Orleans as it appeared when Laclède left for Illinois. *Nineteenth-century print of "Plan et Projet de la Nouvelle Orléans" in the author's collection.*

development" of all sorts increased tenfold under Kerlérec, from 672,000 livres in 1755 to 6.6 million livres by 1762.[61]

Even without royal apathy or wartime opportunism, merchants would have dominated the political economy of New Orleans because of its strategic location. It was the "last stop" for cargoes moving down the Mississippi from Canada and all settlements in between, as well as the gateway to the Caribbean Sea, a multinational commercial zone that encouraged mixed motives in trading virtually anything with almost anybody. Dawdy identified four categories, or "tiers," of New Orleans merchants: those involved with a local urban-rural exchange of products; Indian and Illinois Country river traders; agents of intercolonial commerce along coastal waterways; and major transatlantic shippers. Legal and illegal commerce of all varieties made New Orleans a cosmopolitan city with international connections, despite its small size, and promoted the growth of a multicultural population, from 519 residents in 1721 to at least 2,524 forty years later—35 percent of whom were "people of color." Despite its crude conditions and wartime vulnerabilities, New Orleans survived because local merchants filled the gap between the infrequent delivery of government supplies and the daily consumption needs of the populace. Major merchants became the dominant decision-makers in the city and Governor Kerlérec's strongest supporters—most of whom brazenly admitted to being smugglers.[62]

On April 29, 1763, Maxent joined Laclède and many of the same merchants who had publicly backed Kerlérec four years earlier in issuing a second signed memorial. Twenty members of the chevalier's favored inner circle again praised his "sage and prudent administration" for relieving the suffering of needy residents—but especially "for the advantages which have resulted for each of us." That was a very frank summary of how merchant oligarchs made private profits on public services, but what prevented a totally ruthless exploitation of the weak by the rich was the permanent residence of those elites in the same community. Unlike royal appointees, colonial capitalists planted roots in Louisiana, dealing with the duality of greed and generosity as they redistributed resources and contributed more to local development in a unique environment than distant, distracted officials at Versailles.[63]

Kerlérec expressed a similar commitment to the colonists under his care during his decade in office. He was particularly astute in recognizing Indians as the greatest asset, as well as the greatest threat, to the survival and success of Louisiana. In his first week as governor, he met with seven Choctaw chiefs, who gave him "nine Chickasaw scalps," for which he "paid the customary rate," and held an impromptu two-day parley. Kerlérec "assured them" that he "would not fail to go to Mobile every year…to give each one the justice due him." At those huge, annual assemblies of southern tribes, lasting one to two months, the "supreme commander over Native alliances" delivered and heard diplomatic "harangues," resolved intertribal disputes and distributed mandatory presents to leading "medal chiefs" and their retinues of warriors and dependents. Official alliance certificates depicted Kerlérec holding a large white feather fan of friendship. He regarded Indian allies as "thoughtful men" who "have only the name and color of savages. They are like us, capable of reason, and know how to make use of it." He valued their advice, acceding to Choctaw demands not to execute deserting soldiers they had captured, and he proposed to have his troops carry tomahawks instead of bayonets.[64]

But the most tangible, traditional symbols of respect, gratitude and concern for native allies were abundant, often lavish, official gifts. In a single parley, Kerlérec distributed twenty-four thousand feet of limbourg cloth, forty-three hundred wool blankets, thirty-four hundred cotton shirts, forty thousand pounds of gunpowder and seven hundred muskets, plus many smaller items. Acculturated frontier diplomats like Kerlérec regarded such presents, which were separate from purchases of furs, as annual "retainers"—regularly renewable rewards for the "generous service" of Indians as troops and trading partners. European bureaucrats, however, denounced such expensive diplomatic gifts as wasteful bribes and "shameful tribute to savages" that demeaned the power and status of Christian kings.[65]

Critics who charged Kerlérec with "unnecessarily squander[ing] new gifts upon the savages" and "increas[ing] the profit of the traders" on "the pretext of taking care of the savages" ignored the invaluable role of Indian allies in defending the colony. Kerlérec reported in 1760 that gifts and gunpowder had encouraged the Cherokees and Alabamas to divert British attention away from a sea campaign against French forts in the Gulf of Mexico. "We came within two inches of losing this colony," he wrote, giving all credit to Indian assistance. But the tribes that "have served us so well are going to turn to us to meet their needs, now that we have put them in the position of being unable to obtain anything from the English." The "salvation of this colony is in the hands of the Cherokee and the Alabama Indians. Would it be right to expose them to their enemies and ours?" In another 1760 letter to the Ministry of Marine, Kerlérec observed that those tribes "were completely bereft of merchandise which I have been promising them for four years and which I have requested from you for the same length of time." His persistent lack of Indian presents, coupled with the aggressive encroachment of British agents and fur traders along the lower Mississippi, had precipitated a ruinous civil war between pro- and anti-French factions among the indispensable Choctaws, and alliances with other key tribes were in a precarious state as the war wore on.[66]

The demand for, and cost of, Indian gifts escalated, and the supply diminished due to the wartime difficulties of transatlantic shipping. Officially, presents for Indians cost the Louisiana government seventy-five thousand livres in 1744, which declined to sixty thousand livres in 1752 (then 7 percent of the annual budget). But in 1756, Indian gifts represented only 4.8 percent of Kerlérec's official budget, because private merchants often supplemented deficient royal supplies "off the books." At the 1760 multinational parley in Mobile, Kerlérec had to scramble at the last minute to provide red and blue

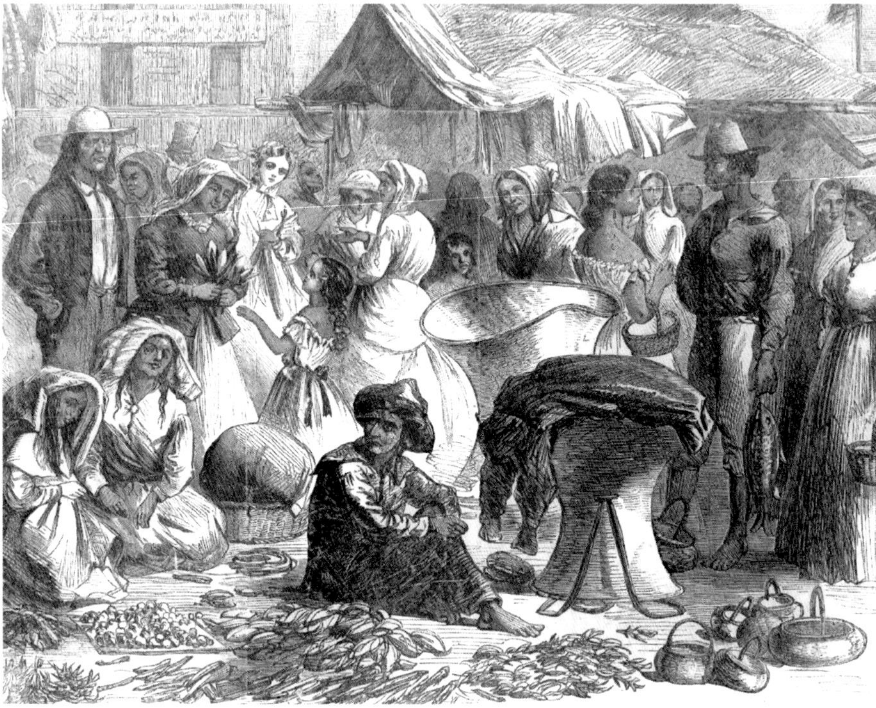

A multiethnic street market in New Orleans. *From* Harper's Weekly, *August 18, 1866. Author's collection.*

limbourg cloth for twenty-five hundred assembled Indians and paid a huge sum of seventy thousand livres to get it from local sources. Such emergency expenses were not budgeted, but they could be foreseen as the war progressed. Affluent city capitalists with transatlantic trading connections were as essential to colonial defense and Indian diplomacy as any military force. With widespread commercial contacts from La Rochelle to Caribbean islands of every nationality, Maxent grew increasingly wealthy as a war profiteer who specialized in supplying *fusils* (trade muskets) to friendly tribes and flour to hungry citizens at huge markups. Kerlérec was credited with being a master of Indian relations, who "kept the Native alliance system…intact," only because Maxent and other merchants extended him credit.[67]

Private financing could not solve all the many other severe problems that threatened New Orleans, however. As the French and Indian War wound down, Kerlérec's capital was in a desperate condition, having suffered greater hardships during that conflict than any city not actually invaded. Lower Louisiana was mired in a long economic depression, barely kept afloat by shrinking royal subsidies in a rising sea of red ink. That colony had cost France over 70 million livres in the previous six decades, and by 1762, annual expenses were running 1 million livres per year. But the king pledged more financial support than he paid, for royal accounts were seven years in arrears. New Orleans was drowning in over 3 million livres worth of dubious paper currency, which contributed to rampant inflation and exorbitant prices for everything. The Crescent City was "in the most unfortunate position in the world," with "no troops, no money, no commerce," according to a senior official. "Peace and harmony, which lend happiness to life, have been banished from this country for quite some time." As usual, the king's storehouse was "quite empty," and New Orleans was more acutely and accurately deserving of the epithet *pain court* than St. Louis would later be. A British blockade had increased the cost of food, including the French dietary staples of bread and wine. The price of flour more than doubled between 1757 and 1762, while a cask of wine that cost 400 livres in that former year had escalated to 3,500 livres by the latter date. That was a particular hardship in a town where each adult consumed an average of 416 pints of alcoholic beverages per year.[68]

A New Beginning at the End of Empire

Residents would soon have more reasons to drink heavily. Great Britain defeated France most decisively in the Seven Years' War, and diplomats of England's "Britannic Majesty," France's "Most Christian Majesty" and Spain's "Most Catholic Majesty" met from March 1761 to February 1763 to determine how much territory would be taken from Louis XV. Canada was lost, as was Cape Breton Island (Île Royale) and its magnificent fortress of Louisbourg. The much-bloodied trans-Appalachian frontier, including the Illinois Country, would also be excised from France's empire. Gone, too, were the islands of Grenada, Saint Vincent, Dominica and Tobago in the Caribbean sea of sugar, the West African slaving center at Saint-Louis, Senegal, and outposts in Asia.

While Versailles was relieved to shed some of the enormous expenses and distressing debts of empire, French-Americans condemned the "shameful treaty of peace [that] inconsiderately ceded to Great Britain one of the finest regions on the habitable globe, the possession of which had been obtained after nearly a century of efforts and discoveries, and at the sacrifice of much blood and money." In 1929, the Catholic bishop of Peoria, Illinois, was still angry that "the dissolute and wretched Louis XV, whose reign disgraced France for fifty-nine years, took little interest in the colonies" and thus destroyed a huge empire and dismissed a precious heritage. The white Bourbon flag that had flown above French global garrisons symbolized only ignominious surrender when the Treaty of Paris was signed on February 10, 1763. Many observers assumed that once the Canadian "head" of France's American territories had been lopped off, the small, dispersed southern settlements, stretching down the long, twisting "spine" of the Mississippi, would wither and die. "France could not have aimed at such a power [in Louisiana], so long as she was in possession of Canada," wrote Joseph N. Nicollet, "but she ought to have thought of it the day when she surrendered that great colony" in the north.[69]

Several people—in New Orleans, not France—were already addressing that issue as early as 1762, and the lead planner was Governor-General Kerlérec, who sought to reenergize Louisiana and empower it to fill the void created by the loss of Canada. Because of all the crises facing Louisiana, he saw a prime opportunity to seize the initiative and turn military defeat into a commercial victory. The governor was in a perfect position at an ideal time to act because New Orleans assumed new importance as France's last capital city in North America following the British conquests of Quebec in 1759 and Montreal in 1760. Now that New Orleans was free of the oppressive dominance of those older, more affluent Canadian cities, it might realize its economic potential under innovative local leadership. During the French and Indian War, the British sought to eliminate French commercial and cultural influence across a wide swath of Native America by capturing trading posts east of the Mississippi. In addition to Quebec and Montreal, they included Louisbourg, Fort Frontenac, Fort Duquesne, Crown Point, Fort Niagara, Detroit, Presque Isle, Miami, Ouiatanon, Sault Ste. Marie, Michilimackinac, Green Bay, Fort St. Joseph, Chequamegon, Mer d'Ouest, Le Boeuf and Venango. With the St. Lawrence River now closed to French shipping, the ice-free port of New Orleans along the Gulf of Mexico would be indispensable to France and fur-trading Indians as the "Cybele of the western waters, rising in pride with her shining crescent of ships."[70]

In 1762, the English provided a positive example to Louisiana merchants by trading some £135,000 worth of their popular merchandise in Indian Country and then doubling that sum in profits from the sale of American furs throughout the world. Britain's need for large quantities of woolen blankets and metalware in the Indian trade helped stimulate its industrial revolution and invigorate England's domestic economy. Trade goods and gifts for

Indians more than paid for themselves, as Kerlérec had preached endlessly to his superiors. But the British also provided the Louisiana governor with a negative example—and an unrivaled opportunity—by suddenly changing their trade policies in postwar America, refusing to "bribe" Indians with expensive presents once their military services were no longer needed. That would backfire, of course, since European gifts had always been the key to earning Indian respect, which was essential for gaining their commercial cooperation and/or military support. Kerlérec cautioned Versailles not to make the same mistake, since "such…thinking can only be adopted by persons without knowledge of the situation and who are unwilling to plan…for the future." For the feisty governor, that future included renewed combat with Britain—or at the very least, a trade war—so he was passionate about keeping key Indian allies loyal to France.[71]

In the spring of 1762, Governor Kerlérec was years behind in providing presents to the Choctaws; in 1760, he had given them gifts he owed for 1757 and 1758, and he still needed to cover 1759 and 1760 at least. He was optimistic about retaining their allegiance, however, because he learned that a royal convoy was finally en route with abundant merchandise. That all-too-rare shipment represented Kerlérec's last chance to encourage Indian allies to "redouble their hostilities…against the English," which in turn might convince King Louis to resume the war. But when that small fleet finally arrived, Kerlérec experienced "cruel despair," as he unpacked merchandise so deficient in quantity and quality that it was "not of a kind to be given to an Indian"—especially the most trustworthy warriors who "have suffered…for my sake for so long." The blankets were of the wrong type, and the shirts were "only useful for making sacks." He could not go back on his promises to the Choctaws, given "the rebellious state of this nation," so to save face (and scalp), Kerlérec placated those warriors with over 850 shirts designated for French troops.[72]

That was the last straw for a proud, energetic leader isolated from royal officials in France, alienated from rivals in New Orleans and now embarrassed in his dealings with Indians he needed to impress. Kerlérec's latest frustration with royal indifference occurred in the same month that he deported Rochemore and several of his supporters. He had hoped for unimpeded progress on several fronts with his old adversary out of the way and new supplies on the way, but once again, his hopes were crushed by incompetence abroad. On June 24, 1762, Kerlérec wrote an angry letter to Étienne François, duc de Choiseul, the minister of marine, condemning the Bordeaux supplier, who had treated Louisiana as if it were a "plaything"—just the latest example of "wise projects for the good of the State" being aborted "as soon as they are formed." Since royal officials had made such a mess of the war, Kerlérec was ready to turn his attention to a new and ambitious "wise project" to stimulate commerce in peacetime Louisiana, using only local talent and capital.[73]

New Orleans needed private enterprise, expanded exports and new markets to revive its economy and reverse its fortunes. Large, lucrative harvests of sugar cane and cotton were years in the future, so in 1762 Lower Louisiana's main cash crop was tobacco, with exports of 160,000 pounds worth 3.6 million livres. Indigo was next in value at 410,000 livres. All furs, "cured and uncured," ranked third among exported local products, worth only 250,000 livres, with animal byproducts, such as oil and suet, bringing in another 25,000 livres. But the fur trade had the greatest potential for future growth with substantial profits, both immediate and longterm, given the elastic demand throughout the world. Furs were tangible, transportable "currencies" that could be "cashed" almost anywhere on the planet. Given the declining value of paper currency in postwar New Orleans, where a 4,000-livre treasury note was required to purchase a letter of exchange worth only 1,000 livres, furs were appealing because they were nearly inflation proof. Although Lower Louisiana was too far south to yield the most valuable beavers, the "furs of Upper Louisiana were far superior," and present-day Missouri represented a barely tapped pelt paradise with a vast variety of all marketable mammals. In particular, Missouri River "deerskins were larger and more valuable" and "kept better than those from the south."[74]

While "nearly all the known fur country in North America was within the British Empire" following the recent war, that did not include the trans-Mississippi West, which Kerlérec knew more about than any senior official in France. The governor's 1758 *Memoir on Indians* revealed his expertise regarding the Missouri River tribes that could contribute to "the flourishing advancement of this colony." All of the Indians in Upper Louisiana combined had never received more than 12 percent of annual gifts from New Orleans, but Kerlérec realized that he "could not afford to alienate" the strategically located Osages now that their terrifying cavalry controlled "500 miles of the Arkansas River Valley" and could move even closer to his capital. The chevalier knew the "great importance to show consideration to this nation" because the Osages were central to his plan to expand trade in the north. Those equestrian warriors had traded with visiting Canadians since the late 1600s and fought as French allies at Detroit in 1712 and near Fort Duquesne in 1755. But the war had prevented the Osages from receiving the muskets they desperately needed to defend their extensive territory filled with furs. In 1757, the Osages had traded only eight thousand pounds of deer leather and bearskins—a mere fraction of their fur harvests after St. Louis was founded—and Kerlérec had to secure a long-lasting commercial alliance with them now that many of the traditional "French tribes" in Lower Louisiana lived in British territory and were being lured away by English traders. Just as New Orleans assumed new importance after the fall of Canada, the populous and powerful Osages came into their own because the British were coming to Illinois.[75]

Displaying the same determination he had demonstrated in building Fort de Chartres, Governor-General Kerlérec made the bold decision to create a commercial colony twelve hundred miles upriver. The initial step in that plan was granting an old friend's new venture—"Maxent, Laclède et Compagnie"—the "exclusive trade…with all [Indian] nations residing *west* of the Mississippi," up to present-day Minneapolis and St. Paul, for a period of six years, with the fur rich Missouri River Valley being the prime objective. Maxent had been the most prominent Indian merchant in New Orleans for several years, and his company "alone had the capital to undertake expeditions" that would make St. Louis "the preeminent trading center of the Mississippi Valley." Such an expensive, expansive enterprise would necessitate the building of an actual town filled with supportive laborers, which would replace Fort de Chartres as the center of French fur trading in the Illinois Country. Chouteau reflected the urgent need to found that settlement before the British army arrived on the east bank, stating that "as soon as the terms and conditions were signed with the government," Maxent "arranged to import from Europe all the merchandise necessary to sustain their business on a large scale." The senior partner determined that Laclède had the necessary experience and talents to lead an expedition upriver, found a trading town near the mouth of the Missouri River and direct field operations for a quarter share of the profits from furs.[76]

Chouteau's "Narrative" has confused generations of historians by crediting Kerlérec's successor, Director-General Jean-Jacques Blaise d'Abbadie (1726–1765), with granting Maxent's monopoly "in 1762," even though that new official would not arrive in America until the next year. Writing in 1804, Chouteau remembered the right date, and his memory was sharp enough to recall d'Abbadie's personal connection to his stepfather—which is why he received top billing. The director-general was a native Béarnais nobleman, born at the Château d'Audoux near Navarrenx, Béarn's only *bastide* (fortified town), just fifty miles north of Laclède's birthplace. In 1744, when d'Abbadie was a clerk at the Rochefort naval base south of La Rochelle, he visited the Laclède home in Bedous to discuss the procurement of masts for the French navy, with which Pierre was directly involved. Those personal ties were important for d'Abbadie's sustained support of Laclède's town, but in 1762–3, timing was more critical.[77]

Only Kerlérec possessed the power, patronage and perceptive vision to sponsor Maxent's enterprise, and he had to have issued the trade license in 1762 to give the new company time to obtain Indian trade goods from the merchant house of Le Leu in La Rochelle. The sailing time from that French port to New Orleans ranged from fourteen to twenty-one weeks, so Maxent and Laclède needed as much advanced notice as possible in order to outfit an expedition to the Illinois Country by early August 1763, when the regularly scheduled royal convoy had to depart due to river conditions. D'Abbadie did not reach Louisiana until June 29, 1763, and he immediately came under the influence of Kerlérec's strong will and vast experience. D'Abbadie quickly *reissued* or merely confirmed Maxent's monopoly on July 6, only one week after his arrival but barely a month before Laclède's departure. D'Abbadie worked *under* Kerlérec until October 23, when, as he wrote in his journal, "Kerlérec remitted the colony's government to me."[78]

If Kerlérec, the flamboyant navy captain, was the innovative "father" of St. Louis, d'Abbadie, a cautious naval accountant, proved to be its nurturing "uncle." The new director-general was Louisiana's first chief administrator without military rank or experience, having spent his entire career on shore as a financial bureaucrat. The only times that d'Abbadie went to sea (as a passenger), he was captured by a British ship. When he finally reached New Orleans, he faced a daunting challenge, since he combined all the governmental functions that had been divided so disastrously between Kerlérec and Rochemore. The king ordered the director-general to establish administrative efficiency, to bolster public confidence, to evacuate all French garrisons east of the Mississippi and to surrender that territory to British forces. He was to "avoid the problems which a change of domination could occasion," while also giving "the greatest attention to maintain good relations with the tribes." And he was expected to accomplish all of those tasks as cheaply as possible.[79]

Despite their different personalities and abilities, Louisiana's top officials demonstrated rare administrative cooperation that reflected the compelling merits of Maxent's ambitious project. Resembling the garrisoned ports and interior *bastides* of France, which combined urban commercial functions with a strategic military purpose, Maxent's corporate colony near the mouth of the Missouri River and west of the new international boundary line would control a huge territory through trade, not troops. Neyon de Villiers was confident that a new French settlement so close to Fort de Chartres would be a popular refuge for Illinois residents fleeing from an army of British Protestants. Private profits, rather than public subsidies, would fund the gifts to gain the cooperation and retain the loyalty of Indian trading partners. Since those hunter-warriors would be the defensive "ramparts" and protectors of the new settlement, there would be no need for expensive fortifications or soldiers—which had cost Kerlérec about 950 percent per year more than the 62,000 francs allocated for tribal gifts. Only a trade war was planned for now, but Kerlérec expected to renew combat with Great Britain "sooner than we think." Laclède's partnership with mounted Siouans who intimidated British infantry would "perpetuate the French name among [native] nations that we shall be very glad" to have as military allies when "France…restored by force what we have been obliged to yield by misfortunes."[80]

Although Dawdy did not mention the founding of St. Louis in her book, that project was a particularly ambitious example of "rogue colonialism"—an alliance of daring individuals who were "most likely to propose bold new schemes and…personally oversee their implementation in new territories" without approval or assistance from France. For New Orleans capitalists to sponsor their own satellite colony in Upper Louisiana was a fitting climax to Kerlérec's roguish regime. He alone possessed the rare combination of military expertise, administrative audacity, obsession for Indian alliances, proclivity for profiteering and a sea captain's courage to best his old British enemies through the shipment of furs rather than the maneuvering of ships. He was the linchpin connecting all the other participants in his innovative scheme. His friendship with Maxent recruited Laclède and Chouteau, and they would receive essential assistance from the governor's brother-in-law at Fort de Chartres. Commandant Neyon de Villiers' most accomplished officer, Captain Charles-Philippe Aubry (circa 1720–1770), had built Fort Massiac along the Ohio River, carried supplies to Fort Duquesne and helped defend Fort Niagara. Shot twice in the head at that New York site, he was captured and tortured by British Indian allies, which earned him the coveted Cross of Saint Louis. He became d'Abbadie's chief infantry commander (and Maxent's neighbor) when Laclède and Chouteau headed to Upper Louisiana. After Kerlérec left for France in November 1763, d'Abbadie assisted Laclède's colony, and when the director-general died of a stroke on February 4, 1765,

Aubry became the last (acting) French governor of Louisiana until 1769. His greatest contribution to St. Louis was transferring the Fort de Chartres garrison under Neyon de Villiers' replacement—Captain Louis Grotton, Saint Ange de Bellerive (circa 1700–1774)—to the new town in 1765. He served as commandant until 1770.[81]

It was significant that those planners and promoters of St. Louis showed little respect for Versailles bureaucrats because all of them came from peripheral areas of France. Maxent and Neyon de Villiers grew up in the borderland of Lorraine, while Laclède and d'Abbadie were born into the subculture of Béarn, first learning a language other than French, as did Kerlérec, the Breton, who spent more time at sea than in France. Aubry was a native of Bordeaux, near Béarn, which was even farther from Paris than Brittany. Neither Saint Ange (as he signed his name), a Montreal native and lifelong resident on Indian frontiers, nor Chouteau, the New Orleans Creole, ever saw France. With such tenuous ties to the French capital and a roguish disregard for its king, the men behind the "St. Louis Project" cared less about legality than practicality as they envisioned a cathartic, commercial offensive against the British—the common enemy of them all. Those perennial foes in four intercontinental wars with France had imprisoned Kerlérec, Aubry and d'Abbadie and severely wounded the first two in combat. Kerlérec, Neyon de Villiers and Aubry all wore the Cross of Saint Louis, and their military valor inspired the militant merchants of St. Louis. Kerlérec's coalition was a brilliant adaptation to postwar realities. While the diplomatic efforts of d'Abbadie and Aubry in New Orleans and Neyon de Villiers and Saint Ange in Illinois complied with treaty terms by convincing eastern Indians not to attack the British, the aggressive French fur traders of St. Louis attracted Indian business from both banks—"depriving us," a bitter Englishman admitted, "of the chief benefit of our new Country, namely the Indian Trade."[82]

The Harsh Reality of Royalty

Kerlérec and d'Abbadie were well aware of Versailles' strict policy of free trade, but there were plenty of precedents for royal approval of monopolies. The Compagnie d'Occident and Compagnie des Indies controlled Illinois between 1717 and 1731, and Kerlérec's predecessor in Louisiana "granted (without ministerial approval)" a six-year fur trade monopoly (1744–50) to operate Fort de Cavagnal near present-day Leavenworth, Kansas. French officials responded to that violation of free trade by promoting Vaudreuil-

Cavagnal to the governorship of Canada. That earlier trading license, like Maxent's and most subsequent ones, was designed "to extend commerce…to keep the Indians favorably disposed, to establish good order among the traders, to carry out the police regulations, to assure provision of the colony with the merchandise needed to carry on trade, and to reduce transport costs…for the government."[83]

A fur trade monopoly required more than large investments, for trustworthiness was as critical as wealth, and to be successful the grantee(s) had to be sensitive, solicitous and respectful regarding individual Indian cultures and interests. As earlier Canadians and later U.S. citizens discovered, a truly free trade open to all in Indian Country often created competitive chaos that alienated native hunters and increased frontier violence. Acting Governor Aubry would later report to the Ministry of Marine that d'Abbadie had "considered the precautions that this branch of [fur] commerce requires," and he regarded Maxent's monopoly "as an almost foolproof means of maintaining liaisons with the Indians," while policing the frontier and generating income for Frenchmen. Extensive consultations had occurred between Kerlérec, Neyon de Villiers and "many other colonists who were in a position to be able to compare the advantages of exclusive and free trade" before they unanimously approved Maxent's project.[84]

Throughout French America, rival merchants always protested the exclusive trading privileges bestowed on more politically astute competitors, and the pros and cons of commercial monopolies would become a recurring theme in the history of St. Louis. Unlike Kerlérec's other schemes, however, Maxent's monopoly was *too* exclusive, and because it did not involve enough of his fellow merchants, competitors complained to officials in France. Versailles cancelled the grant to Maxent on January 18, 1765, which he only learned about the following July, and severely censured Director-General d'Abbadie, who never learned of it because he died in February. D'Abbadie's reputation bore the brunt of vicious royal criticism, largely because he had reported everything in a letter to the Ministry of Marine on October 1, 1763, even before Laclède and Chouteau arrived in Illinois. It was not until April 30, 1767, that a civil court in New Orleans ordered Maxent to pay damages to aggrieved merchants in Ste. Genevieve, but by then, St. Louis was a growing town with a booming economy, prospering due to local leadership and supportive Indian alliances rather than any assistance from France.[85]

The hostile response of Versailles to the "Maxent matter" was related to a far more serious issue that placed St. Louis in legal limbo. Royal officials were most concerned about a powerful merchant cartel acting independently in Upper Louisiana because France had already ceded all of its territory west of the Mississippi River, plus New Orleans, to Spain in the November 1762 Treaty of Fontainebleau. Three months before the definitive Treaty of Paris officially ended the French and Indian War, Louis XV had secretly "donated" his namesake colony to his Bourbon cousin, King Carlos III of Spain, to keep it out of British hands. It was so secret that not even the senior administrators in Louisiana learned of the transfer of one million square miles until September 9, 1764, twenty-two months later. That example of France's indifference to Louisiana interests was only surpassed by the king's selfish determination to get rid of "a Colony with which we are unable to communicate by sea…and which costs France eight hundred thousand livres a year, without yielding a sou in return." He was so anxious to be rid of that "devil's empire" and "useless wilderness" that he threatened "to evacuate the whole of Louisiana," even if the Spanish refused to accept his "gift." After a long, disastrous and expensive war, France and Spain were far less optimistic about the economic potential of the trans-Mississippi West than they had been many decades earlier. King Carlos grudgingly accepted that dubious donation only because of its "negative utility" as a defensive buffer to protect Spain's most valued possessions in Mexico, the Southwest and the Caribbean from commercial intrusion and military invasion by the British. King Carlos stated that "without the hope of some day showing the same courtesy to France [by giving Louisiana back], I would always have opposed the cession."[86]

Spanish resentment of France's arm-twisting was reflected in their slowness to take control of the region on a permanent basis, which did not occur until July 1769 in Lower Louisiana and May 1770 in Upper Louisiana. That procrastination was a boon for the development of early St. Louis, which did not have to deal with strong royal interference in its first six years. The times were tailor-made at the end of France's New World empire for innovative entrepreneurs and energetic colonists who wanted to chart their own course in a remade America. The vast majority of the seventy-five thousand Canadians, fifteen thousand Acadians and ten thousand Louisianans whom Louis XV abandoned in his cession to Spain in 1762 and his surrender to Great Britain in 1763 remained in the only homeland they knew, pulling together even after their king had pulled out. Numbering only one-sixth of the 1763 population of Paris, those "orphaned" French-Americans seized unparalleled opportunities once they were freed from the clutches of an ungrateful monarch. Decisive actions in America had more of an immediate impact than treaties negotiated in Europe, and if all went

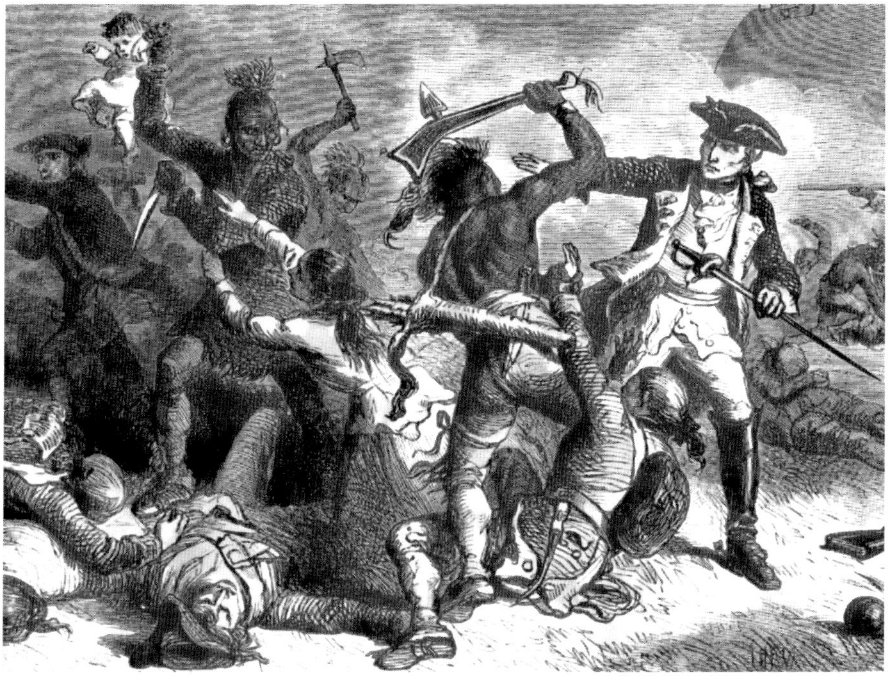

St. Louis was founded during Pontiac's War and survived another thirty years of frontier violence. *Nineteenth-century print in author's collection.*

as planned, French merchants from New Orleans and French colonists from Illinois and Canada would create a new community in St. Louis that was French in conception, culture and citizenry, reaping personal profits from the Indian trade even if France, Spain or England did not.[87]

Just before Pierre Laclède launched his expedition to the Illinois Country, shocking news reached New Orleans of widespread Indian attacks against British troops and Anglo-American settlers from present-day Michigan to Pennsylvania. That "War for Indian Independence" was initiated in May 1763 by the Ottawa leader, Pontiac (he preferred "Pondiak"), and his alliance of Great Lakes Algonquians. For another two years, his forces demonstrated how outnumbered but determined Indians fighting for their homelands could bring chaos to the American frontiers of Europe's largest empire. When Neyon de Villiers' urgent dispatch from Fort de Chartres arrived in the Louisiana capital on August 2, Pontiac's warriors had already captured seven British forts, besieged Fort Detroit and Fort Pitt for months, killed 450 soldiers, forced some 4,000 colonists to flee their homes and plundered "not less than one hundred thousand pounds" of English merchandise, including an alarming amount of ammunition for Indian flintlocks. Neyon de Villiers urged Kerlérec and d'Abbadie not to recall his troops until the crisis passed, but plans proceeded to "evacuate the outposts, thus reducing [his] garrison to minimal size." Louis XV was adamant about avoiding any further involvement with Indian issues—even military victories by native allies loyal to the French.[88]

Despite the potential danger of heading to a region of "bloody tragedies which are a horror to humanity," Laclède kept to the schedule for the royal convoy's departure. On Wednesday, August 10, 1763, he left his power of attorney with Judge Nicolas Forstall (1727–circa 1805), a Martinique-born merchant with commercial connections from La Rochelle to Veracruz and perhaps Béarn as well. Many weeks later, Jean Laclède in Pau received a moving letter that Forstall (whom he called Pierre's "partner") had sent from New Orleans on August 11, "expressing the feelings my brother had for me." The pleasant boyhood they shared in the peaceful Aspe Valley may have been on the mind of the younger Laclède, since he would be traveling on the river claimed for "Louis the Great, King of France and Navarre"—the Bourbon descendant of Béarn's beloved King Henri. Saying farewell to Marie Thérèse, who was pregnant again, Laclède perhaps recalled the following passage from the song "Adieu to Navarre" in the Béarnais language of his birth:

Cuando lous mountagnos seroun loën,
When the mountains are far away,
Ho lou cor attendri, Thérèse, Thérèse.
My heart will be heavy, Thérèse, Thérèse.
Rosa de mi bodro, adious, adious!
Rose of my soul, adieu, adieu![89]

A VOYAGE INTO THE FUTURE

As they embarked on the adventure of their lives at the risk of their lives, Laclède symbolized the mature wisdom of Enlightenment Europe, while thirteen-year-old Auguste Chouteau represented the youthful vitality of frontier America. St. Louis would reflect that combination of traditions for years to come. This would be the first, most momentous and only recorded long journey that those partners from opposite ends of the Old French Empire ever took together. Nothing in cosmopolitan New Orleans could have prepared either one for the dangers and demands of fur trading on a distant frontier, but the rigors of an exhausting and hazardous upriver voyage came close. No one in his right mind looked forward to the alternatingly tedious and treacherous Mississippi boat trip from the Crescent City to the Illinois Country. The voyage required 90 to 120 days to cover twelve hundred river miles against the current—a longer time than an Atlantic crossing from France to New York and more risky.

Due to the sponsorship of Kerlérec and d'Abbadie for their semiofficial mission, Laclède and Chouteau traveled with the royal convoy of "five ships [that] departed" from New Orleans in "the first days of August [1763]," carrying "various provisions" for Fort de Chartres. The "ships" were actually river *bateaux*, plank boats of shallow draft that were capable of hauling up to forty tons. Laclède may have needed two bateaux for his cargo—one owned by the colony and the other by Maxent, perhaps the fifty-foot long, ten-foot wide *berge* (barge) named *L'Esperance* (Hope) that Laclède later used in St. Louis. The typical crew of each "king's boat" consisted of a *patrone* (experienced skipper), a "royal slave" as an expert pilot and at least twenty well-armed marines, who rowed and defended the convoy. Such precautions against attacks by Indians or pirates would have been comforting to the junior merchant and his clerk, since they were transporting Maxent's La Rochelle merchandise valued at nine thousand livres, which, in 1770, was enough to provide lavish presents for twenty Indian nations.[90]

Contrary to an old, persistent myth, Laclède and Chouteau did *not* take colonists from New Orleans, friends from Béarn or family members with them on that initial voyage. Chouteau's "Narrative" named the earliest colonists, and genealogical research has identified all of them as veteran Creole or Canadian residents of Illinois—the most desirable and experienced settlers, already acclimated to the region, far superior to southern city dwellers or recent immigrants from France. Other than Laclède, only four documented natives from the Pyrenees lived in early St. Louis, and all arrived after 1763. Madame Chouteau and her four youngest children (one only five weeks old) did not leave New Orleans until June 12, 1764, and did not arrive in St. Louis until September 1764.[91]

When Laclède and Chouteau pulled away from the wharf in New Orleans, they faced twelve weeks of persistent discomfort and periodic danger. Large freight boats loaded with tons of bulky cargoes were as agile as tractor-trailer trucks. The "teamsters" in that era operated on water, not land, propelling vessels upriver at the typical pace of one mile per hour by rowing, poling, sailing and/or cordelling with ropes pulled from shore against a current two, four or even six times faster. Navigational expertise was required to avoid river debris of every kind—innumerable islands of shifting sand (*batture*), virtual forests firmly anchored to the river bottom (planters) and swaying trees in mid-channel, called "sawyers," which rapid currents would bend down and then flip up in a sawing motion that could rip apart a wooden boat. Even in the steamboat days of Mark Twain's comical character Tom Sawyer, 156 of those technologically advanced watercraft still sank due to such treacherous river obstacles.[92]

Travelers were willing to endure the enervating heat and humidity of an August trip in order to avoid winter ice from the northern Mississippi, which could have *Titanic*-like consequences, or spring flooding. "In the Spring the Mississippi is very high," wrote a traveler in the 1760s, and the "current, at this season, runs at the rate of six or seven miles an hour, [while] in autumn, when the waters are low, it…does not run above two miles an hour." To avoid the fast mid-channel current on the upriver route, patrones sought slower water in eddies or crosscurrents, called *remoux*, near either shore. But that delayed the trip, as they had to zigzag back and forth between alternate riverbanks almost four hundred times before reaching Illinois. And if a boat got too close to shore, mudslides could be catastrophic. In 1766, an eyewitness reported that entire riverbanks of mud or clay, up to thirty feet high, would suddenly crash into the water along with dozens of trees. The depth of the Mississippi also represented a trade-off between speed and safety, since a lower water level reduced the frenetic pace of the current but exposed boats to more hazardous obstacles. On downriver voyages to New Orleans from February to May, rapid terror replaced slow tedium. The swollen river thrust boats southward so fast that they could reach the capital in less than a month, but when the Mississippi flooded, the journey became a gut-wrenching log flume ride taking as little as two weeks.[93]

Although experienced boatmen described the first 275 miles between New Orleans and Natchez as a "piece of cake," with few navigational hazards, that stretch of river was infamous for Indian attacks on vessels that ventured too near the shore. One such assault altered the course of history. On March 20, 1764, at Roche à Davion (present-day Fort Adams, Mississippi, south of Natchez), France's Tonica/Tunica allies and other Indians ambushed the large convoy of ten bateaux and two pirogues (log canoes) carrying Great Britain's Twenty-second Regiment of Foot to take possession of Fort de Chartres. The initial volley of massed musket fire from the riverbank, only twelve yards away, killed six and wounded at least four of the fifteen redcoats in the forward canoes, and as those blood-soaked vessels careened toward the main convoy, terrified oarsmen lost control of the bateaux. The strong current swept the British boats downstream so fast that they covered in only three days the same distance it had taken three weeks to advance upstream. Despite having 360 veteran troops and two swivel cannons, Major Arthur Loftus, the intimidated commander, returned to New Orleans and made no further attempt to reach Illinois. Months later, a British general criticized Loftus for not taking "the Precaution to pave the Way with Presents [to the Indians], which the French have always done, [since] you can't be always in a Condition to force your Way." It would be another year and a half before English troops reached Fort de Chartres via the Ohio River rather than face hostile southern Indians along the lower Mississippi. That fortuitous delay allowed St. Louis to mature without interference.[94]

Laclède and Chouteau were not attacked by Indians, but they had to contend with hostile insects and the burning rays of a late summer sun on a boat that offered only a tent for shelter and no amenities for travelers. A typical day on such a voyage began at dawn and ended in darkness, with insatiable mosquitoes, howling wolves and soaking thunderstorms making a restful night's sleep impossible. During a five-month voyage upriver in 1765, a traveler reported heat so intense that rowing began at 3:00 a.m., stopped at 9:00 a.m. and began again at 4:00 or 5:00 p.m. "Efforts to stretch the morning stint proved catastrophic," as the rowers "suffered forty cases of heat prostration" and one died. Rowers received short "pipe" breaks every two hours or so and a long midday lunch of stored beef or salt pork (fresh venison or buffalo if the convoy had hunters), along with rice, maize and biscuits. Boatmen would wash that down with a *fillet* (a few ounces) of *eaudevie* (brandy) or *tafia* (sweet, semidistilled rum from the French Caribbean). One British convoy carried over five thousand gallons of brandy "to sustain the rowers and placate the Indians," and it is likely that the Laclède-Chouteau voyage allowed extra rations of liquor for toasting the Feast Day of Saint Louis on August 25.[95]

Impatience with the slow progress of a "laborious" voyage, "subject to a thousand inconveniences," was tempered by the realization that the greatest navigational challenges lay farther upriver on the final leg of the journey. The Mississippi was at its worst between the mighty Ohio River and the miniscule Kaskaskia River, the "most dangerous and fatiguing" part of the trip. A variety of ever-mutating obstacles created especially capricious currents, ranging from six to nine miles per hour. Avoiding sand islands in mid-channel and tumbling trees closer to shore, even the best rowers quickly reached their physical limits in such speedy waters. They could not stay at their oars "more than a quarter of an hour without resting," so boats made only one mile in two hours. Going ashore was not an option in that stretch of the river because of deadly quicksand and "vagabond" Indians, who posed a threat into the 1790s. Some twenty miles north of where Jean Baptiste Girardot had a trade outpost in the early 1730s (the future site of Cape Girardeau), Laclède and Chouteau would have spotted the landmark known as "The Tower." Surrounded by swirling birds of every description, it was the tallest of the many rock formations, called "chains," in that area. Farther north, the expedition passed the four Isles à la Merde (Dung Islands)—one of the "disgusting appellations" that "characterize the state of the people," according to a Parisian traveler. Once the bateaux passed the mouth of the Kaskaskia River, it was a mere fifteen miles to Ste. Genevieve, then the only port in the Illinois Country located on the west bank of the Mississippi.[96]

The People and Prospects of Illinois

The French familiarized themselves with us,
Studied our Tongue and Manners, wore our Dress,
Married our Daughters, and our Sons their Maids,
Dealt honestly, and well supplied our Wants,
Used no One ill, and treated with Respect
Our Kings, our Captains, and our Aged Men;
Call'd us their Friends, nay…their Children,
And seem'd like Fathers anxious for our Welfare.
—Pontiac's address in the play *Ponteach* (1766)

Laclède and Chouteau finally stepped ashore on Thursday, November 3, 1763, after eighty-five days on the river. They found themselves in a strange new world shaped and shared by a physical and cultural mixture of Algonquian Indians and French colonists. The new arrivals missed the annual "great fires" that natives traditionally set to burn off forest undergrowth and summer prairie grass, which grew twenty feet high. Such Indian land management over many centuries helped make Illinois "the finest Country in the known world," considered "superior…for local beauty, fertility, climate, and the means of every kind which nature has lavished upon it." Most impressive were maize plants twelve feet high, "tobacco as fine as in Virginia" and verdant pastures covered with the "greatest quantity of black cattle." Its "appearance is truly delightful, and some are of the opinion that this is the spot…called by French writers the Terrestrial Paradise." Although in decline a decade before 1763, Illinois had served as the breadbasket of

New Orleans since 1732, providing residents of the capital with wheat and flour, "fruit…as good as that grown in France," bear oil shipped in deer heads, salt from local saline springs, hams as fine as "those of Bayonne," buffalo tongues and beaver tails. The immigrant from Béarn would have appreciated such agricultural abundance in a farmer's paradise with a milder climate than New Orleans.[97]

The Special World of Illinois

The French explored more of eastern North America than any other Europeans, and their diverse colonial subcultures were connected by a network of intersecting waterways unimpeded by large mountain ranges. The Mississippi linked the cold Canadian Great Lakes of extensive fur trading to the hot Louisiana Gulf Coast of intensive plantation farming, and midway between those two extremes was the temperate climate and mixed economy of Illinois, which French residents, like Goldilocks, found to be "just right."

The original Canadian colonists in Illinois had left the St. Lawrence Valley due to limited arable lands, a short growing season and often-oppressive obligations imposed by secular and religious authorities. Those émigrés would make the mid-Mississippi a productive cultural hearth with the most diversified economy of any French colony by combining African slavery, wheat cultivation and commerce in furs, lead and salt. According to Carl J. Ekberg, "The Illinois Country was unique among French regions of colonization anywhere in the world, for it was the only one…well suited for producing large quantities of cereal grains." The small, long-lot fields of free farmers and village common lands recalled medieval life in northern France and contrasted with the separated *seigneuries* (landed estates) stretching between Quebec and Montreal and the dispersed plantations surrounding New Orleans. There was no comparable large city in Illinois, even after fifty years, since residents preferred tiny, compact, rural towns to enhance community cohesion. The commitment to preserving the traditional language, laws, customs and Catholicism of France in a comfortable, kinship society of prosperous farmers emerged from origins that were anything but conservative or conventional. French Illinois began as a squatter society of illegal immigrants who were invited to live among native Algonquians in *their* country—*Le Pays des Illinois*—without initial approval or financial support from Versailles. The independent initiative of colonists seeking personal

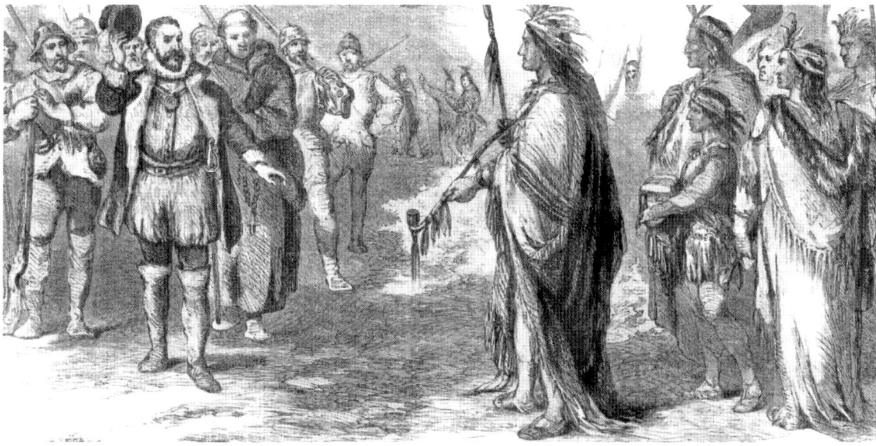

Illinois Algonquians offer the calumet of peace to a representative variety of Frenchmen who would live among them. *From* Ballou's Pictorial, *Boston, April 19, 1856.*

profits in an isolated, self-governing frontier society made those residents ideal recruits for the rogue settlement of St. Louis.[98]

Illinois became French after a quarter century of religious, commercial and military contacts with the Illiniwek Indians, who were essential to the enterprises of acquisitive fur traders and inquisitive missionaries. By the mid-1600s, both types of French frontiersmen were well ensconced throughout the western Great Lakes (*Le Pays d'en Haut*) and soon sought new customers and converts farther south. In 1673, Jacques Marquette and Louis Jolliet left the Jesuit mission of Saint Ignace at the Straits of Mackinac and reached the Mississippi (then called the "St. Louis River"), becoming the first known Europeans to pass the site of the city that would make that name famous in American history. Their explorations established the prime routes of trade between Canada and St. Louis that Auguste Chouteau was still using as an old man. Marquette and Jolliet found friendly Illinois Algonquians living in twelve communities south of Lake Michigan, then known as the "Lake of the Illinois." The most familiar of those tribes were the Kaskaskias, Peorias, Cahokias and Tamaroas, which were heavily concentrated along the Illinois River, not the Mississippi.[99]

The explorations of René-Robert Cavelier, sieur de La Salle, and his Italian compatriot, Henri de Tonti, followed in the 1680s, reflecting French interest in the Illini Indians when they were most vulnerable to outside influences. In 1680, the Iroquois League of Five Nations attacked huge villages of those Algonquians from the Kankakee River to Peoria, leaving "copper kettles full of half-eaten arms and legs," houses and fields "burned to the ground" and "charred lodgepoles decorated with human skulls." La Salle constructed Fort Crevecoeur in 1680—the first European garrison in Le Pays des Illinois—in a vain effort to protect those French allies. Two years later, Tonti, an amputee, used his iron fist, literally and figuratively, to construct an elaborate fortress atop Le Rocher (Starved Rock), a 125-foot-high sandstone boulder. Between 1682 and 1691, that settlement in the sky, also known as Fort St. Louis des Illinois, was home to the first large multicultural community south of the Great Lakes. With merchandise provided by Montreal merchants, that site attracted thousands of Indians and elevated expectations for future mixed settlements based on commerce and cooperation against common foes.[100]

Invading native enemies and invasive European epidemics near the end of the century finally forced the depleted but still-populous Illini to move south. Three simultaneous events in the late 1690s helped determine the timing of that diaspora. The Chickasaws launched large slave raids, capturing over one hundred Cahokias in a single day to sell to English traders from South Carolina. Those white men introduced smallpox to the banks of the Mississippi, a disease that caused a higher mortality than Indian raids. And then in 1696, Versailles suspended the fur trade in Canada, encouraging French *coureurs de bois* (unlicensed roving traders) to exploit the mammal wealth of present-day Illinois and Missouri on a year-round basis. In 1700, the Kaskaskias, the first of the Illiniwek tribes to embrace Catholicism twenty-five years earlier, settled with Jesuit missionaries along the Des Peres River, Missouri. But after three years there, they moved across the river and founded the town and mission of Kaskaskia. Cahokias and Tamaroas were already living in the fertile flood plain of the "American Bottom" between the Illinois and Kaskaskia Rivers. Declining numbers of Indians and increasing numbers of Canadian fur traders and farmers created innovative "dual settlements" with "domiciled" Algonquians, making multiethnic cooperation, mutual acculturation and mixed marriages important features of the Illinois Country.[101]

According to historian Joseph Zitomersky, the "establishment of new French places generally presupposed the existence of Native settlements either in their near vicinity or in their more general area. The one does not seem to have developed without the other." Those "Native settlements continued to be recognized as functional components of the core area, contributing to its food supply and part of its outer defense." Symbiotic bartering of local products among French, Indians and Africans resembled the "frontier exchange economy" in Lower Louisiana. The sharing of space in contiguous bicultural villages in Illinois "generally persisted throughout the French regime in those areas where the structure was first developed. It underwent a decline or a change in its form only at locations where either the French settlement itself failed to persist or where the Native population died out or dispersed." Zitomersky's revisions of the flawed 1752 Illinois census revealed that at least 1,315 "domiciled" Algonquian Indians, plus another 149 slaves from other native nations, outnumbered the 443 white adults and 446 African slaves.[102]

Most of the inhabitants of European descent in that small-scale, mixed-race society shared a common commitment to French customs, Catholicism, multicultural coexistence and agricultural productivity, but only the oldest towns—Cahokia and Kaskaskia—were centers of both commerce and Indian conversion. Cahokia was founded in 1699, and its strategic location a few miles south of the vital Illinois River route to Canada attracted a variety of merchants, voyageurs and habitants from that northern province—plus Catholic missionaries from the Seminary of Foreign Missions in Quebec. Those priests established the Holy Family Parish, which thrives to this day, and named the settlement Sainte Famille de Kaoquias ("Caos" or "Caho" for short) after the Cahokia Algonquians who already lived there. Neither those Indians nor their town should be confused with the ancient Mississippian Mound Builders of the famous "City of Cahokia." Since scholars do not know what those architects of monuments called themselves, they named that site after a small group of Cahokia Algonquians who lived with Catholic priests atop Monk's Mound from 1735 to 1752. Compared to the 15,000 to 20,000 Indians who thrived at that aboriginal capital a thousand years ago, "French Cahokia," located about eight miles from that site and only four water miles from St. Louis, had a tiny population of 90 whites, 24 black slaves and 23 Indian slaves in 1752, plus some 350 Cahokia and Peoria Indian neighbors.[103]

Sixty miles south of Cahokia, Jesuits founded Kaskaskia (Kaw) in 1703 as Notre Dame de Cascasquias. Fifty years later, that town had the largest population in French Illinois, with 352 whites, 246 black slaves and 75 Indian slaves of every age, and cultivated the greatest acreage with an unusually high African population of 40 percent. Some 670 Kaskaskia Indians lived in their own village three miles away, and they were the great success story of France's *mission civilatrice* in Illinois. In the late 1600s, Marie Rouensa, daughter of a Kaskaskia chief, embraced Christianity so intensely that she married a "wild" Frenchman to save *his* soul. She became the Pocahontas of French Illinois, enriching many notable colonial families with her numerous descendants.

An equally famous "princess" from the Missouria tribe was living with the Kaskaskias in the 1750s and still had the "fine repeating watch set with diamonds" she had received from Louis XV—*Onontio*—on a visit to France with several regional chiefs in 1725. She was baptized at the Cathedral of Notre Dame and married two French soldiers. An old Illini man claimed to have made that trip, too, describing the Paris Opera and the king's impressive "huts" at "Versailles and [the] Louvre," containing "more people than there are in their country."[104]

By the late 1740s, the Kaskaskia French had a need for new fields, and they founded the first satellite settlement across the Mississippi in what was still considered "Illinois" (as well as western Louisiana). That town was Ste. Genevieve, named for the patron saint of Paris. When Laclède and Chouteau arrived there in November 1763, it had a total population of 460, including Indian and African slaves, and was still dominated by French Canadians, whose children born in Illinois would be called Creoles. Wealthy merchant

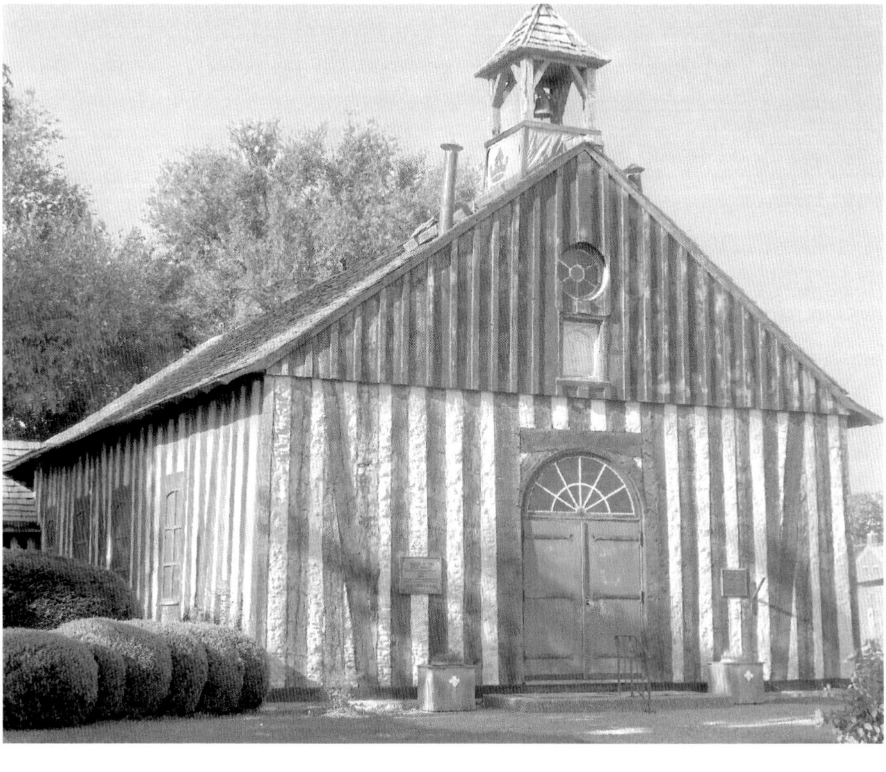

Holy Family Church (1799) in Cahokia, Illinois, as it appears today. It is an excellent example of French vertical log construction. *Photo by Jeanette Fox Fausz.*

families, such as the Vallés, were at the top of the socioeconomic ladder due to their merchandizing of local lead, salt, crops, furs and livestock, but Laclède could not find a building large enough in that small village to store even one-fourth of his valuable trade goods. In searching for a storage facility, he certainly would have noticed the distinctive local architecture. Illinois colonists constructed most of their early buildings out of vertical logs hewn flat on two or four sides, either set directly in the ground (*poteaux en terre*) or placed on sills to retard rotting (*poteaux sur sole*). They filled the space between the timbers with a mixture of clay and grass (*bouzillage*) or rubble stone and clay (*pierrotage*). Those houses, when plastered and whitewashed inside and out, roofed with cedar shingles and surrounded by airy galleries (porches), had a more refined appearance better suited for town living than crude, horizontal-log cabins in a solitary forest.[105]

Laclède probably regarded the Norman trusses in Ste. Genevieve attics as quaint holdovers from medieval France, and he was certainly surprised that old European grain farming in long-lot parcels and village common lands for grazing livestock were thriving in America. But his experiences in the Pyrenees made him wary of the regular flooding of low-lying fields by the "American Nile." Such torrents threatened expensive merchandise, as well as lives and houses, and the standing water they left behind spread a variety of waterborne diseases. Although Ste. Genevieve may have had old-fashioned buildings and a vulnerable location, Laclède was probably impressed with how Canadians, Creoles, métis, Africans and Indians lived together without serious violence. That would have been reassuring to someone who was about to gamble his life and that of his stepson in such a multiethnic society.

The Kerlérec Coalition in Action

The tour of Ste. Genevieve was short-lived, since a soldier from Fort de Chartres approached Laclède and Chouteau on November 3 and informed them that Commandant Neyon de Villiers was willing to store their cargo in his fort, eighteen miles upriver. Chouteau's "Narrative" did not explain how the senior officer in Illinois "learn[ed] of Laclède's predicament" almost immediately or why he offered his assistance at a critical time. But we now know why—and, of course, Chouteau did, too. Although he sought to portray his stepfather as a heroic, decisive leader favored by providence in the founding of St. Louis, it was Kerlérec's elaborate planning and manipulation of events that were critical to the success of Laclède's mission. The governor-general's brother-in-law at Fort de Chartres controlled all affairs in Illinois, so that region was as much "Kerlérec Country" as New Orleans. With two royal governors and one very prominent merchant pulling strings from the south, and successive Illinois commandants pulling rank in the north, few events related to the creation of St. Louis were accidental or coincidental. Kerlérec and d'Abbadie determined when the royal convoy would depart and where it would land in the Illinois Country, but on August 5, they also sent an urgent dispatch by an overland courier named Berqueville, who reached Neyon de Villiers on October 25. It was certainly prearranged that the new arrivals would proceed to the fort because d'Abbadie had "loaned" Laclède some three hundred pounds of the king's gunpowder, and the only safe place to store that precious commodity was in the powder magazine of a fort guarded by soldiers. In the first week of November, Etienne Marafret Laysard—"attorney of the King, storekeeper of His Majesty, and treasurer of the King's treasury in Illinois"—placed Laclède's valuable cargo in the limestone powder magazine of Fort de Chartres, which survives as the oldest French structure in Illinois. A gabled roof covers an interior loaf-shaped stone vault designed to absorb much of the force from an explosion.[106]

Neyon de Villiers went out of his way to assist the New Orleans merchants, even though it was an especially hectic time for him. On November 2, just

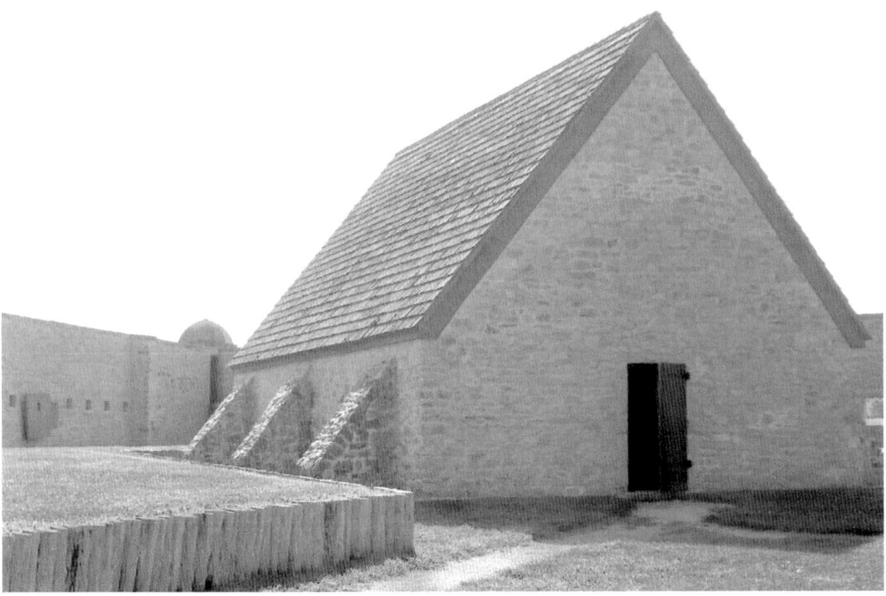

The old powder magazine at Fort de Chartres that once held Laclède's merchandise, as it looks today near Prairie du Rocher. *Photo by Jeanette Fox Fausz.*

one day before Laclède and Chouteau docked at Ste. Genevieve, he held an important parley with "Chief Wolf" and two warriors, who brought messages from Pontiac's allies. They presented the commandant with twenty English scalps, pledged their undying love for the French and requested "guns, powder and [musket] balls" to continue the war against the "wicked" redcoats, "whom we scorn." However, Neyon de Villiers had to deny them ammunition, declaring that the war was over. He expected France's Indian children "to be peaceful, for the great emperors [in Europe] desired…the happiness of both the whites and the redmen." The confirmation that Frenchmen and Englishmen were again "brothers" by treaty trumped rampant frontier rumors, some generated by Kerlérec himself, that King Louis had "got upon his legs again" and would soon send a new royal army to help the Indians battle the British. The commandant underscored the finality of the peace settlement by telling Wolf that Fort de Chartres would soon be occupied by English troops, and he advised the Indians to "bury your tomahawks" and "retreat under French wings to *the other side of the Mississippi River*."[107]

As the commandant was well aware, Laclède's new settlement would be the place to which they could "retreat"—the one hopeful aspect of a depressing situation in which French military officers had to refuse assistance to Indian allies, engaged in a cause they supported, without alienating them forever. Neyon de Villiers may have had compelling personal reasons for helping Laclède over the next several months, probably angling for a profitable role in Maxent's new trading town. The commandant was only a few months away from losing his position, power and profits as the unchallenged master of Illinois fur trading. Even before Laclède and Chouteau left New Orleans, Villiers had tried to extend his stay at Fort de Chartres. But d'Abbadie vetoed that idea and wrote in his journal that the commandant "wanted to call attention to himself and prolong his sojourn in Illinois." In a March 13, 1764 letter to the director-general, Neyon de Villiers stated that he and "commissioner" Jean-Baptiste-Claude Bobé Desclosseaux (whose family had long supported Kerlérec) were assisting Laclède—but he reminded the director-general "that we were waiting for your response to the plan that we had the honor to present to you jointly."[108]

The paper trail of that ambiguously worded document ends there, so it is hard to know if the "we" included Laclède and whether Neyon de Villiers' "plan" involved a partnership in the St. Louis enterprise. Even though that was not to be, the commandant, to his credit, rendered invaluable assistance to Laclède, even after Kerlérec sailed for France on November 17, 1763. He or another officer from the fort probably escorted Laclède to the November 6 auction of Jesuit properties at Kaskaskia. Kerlérec had disbanded the Society of Jesus in Louisiana and ordered the priests to evacuate Illinois by November 24—very convenient timing for Laclède, as planned. On Maxent's behalf, he bid thirty-nine thousand livres on Jesuit lands and buildings—prime investments that his senior partner most likely intended to sell or lease to the British. Laclède was outbid, but obtaining Kaskaskia property was a separate issue and a secondary concern unrelated to his main mission.[109]

Less than two weeks later, Neyon de Villiers found Laclède an ideal property for his home and company headquarters a short walk away from the fort. Laclède paid a mere seventy-five hundred livres to Jean Girardin, a marine private at Fort de Chartres, for the former property of merchant Jean Prunet (*La Giroflée*, "wallflower") and his Pawnee wife, Veronique. The commandant may have coerced the soldier to sell to "Monsieurs Maxant, Laclede and Co." for half the price he had paid just a year earlier because there was no deed and a foreclosure was imminent. The commandant's storekeeper, Laysard, witnessed the transaction, which procured for Laclède a well-situated *poteaux sur solle* house of two rooms with double closets, a barn "covered with straw," a small shed, a "pigeon house," a wooden well and "other conveniences"—including furniture, seventeen cattle, twenty hogs, 150 fowl and one thousand pounds of stored tobacco on a lot enclosed by a cedar palisade.[110]

Storing his cargo in Fort de Chartres had placed Laclède in the commandant's debt, but locating the first branch office of Maxent's company in the adjoining town of Nouvelle Chartres gave Neyon de Villiers direct oversight of all his future activities. Popularly known as *L'Établissement* (the Settlement), Nouvelle Chartres was a small but bustling commercial center, where its population of 250 whites, 100 black slaves, 50 Indian slaves and 300 nearby Mechigamea Algonquians sold crops, bear oil, native crafts and game meat to the 160 or so royal marines and civilian officials in the administrative capital of French Illinois. Laclède's property occupied a prime location near the Church of Ste. Anne and at least one billiard parlor along the King's Road (*Le Chemin du Roi*) that connected Kaskaskia, about eighteen miles away, with Cahokia, forty miles farther north. Along that dusty lane of constant traffic, Laclède conducted business with his neighbors and probably had some contacts with the additional 123 whites, 85 black slaves and 15 Indian slaves who lived in the nearby farming communities of St. Philippe and Prairie du Rocher. Laclède also "sent his merchandize for the Indian trade up the Missouri, as well as up the Mississippi," hiring local

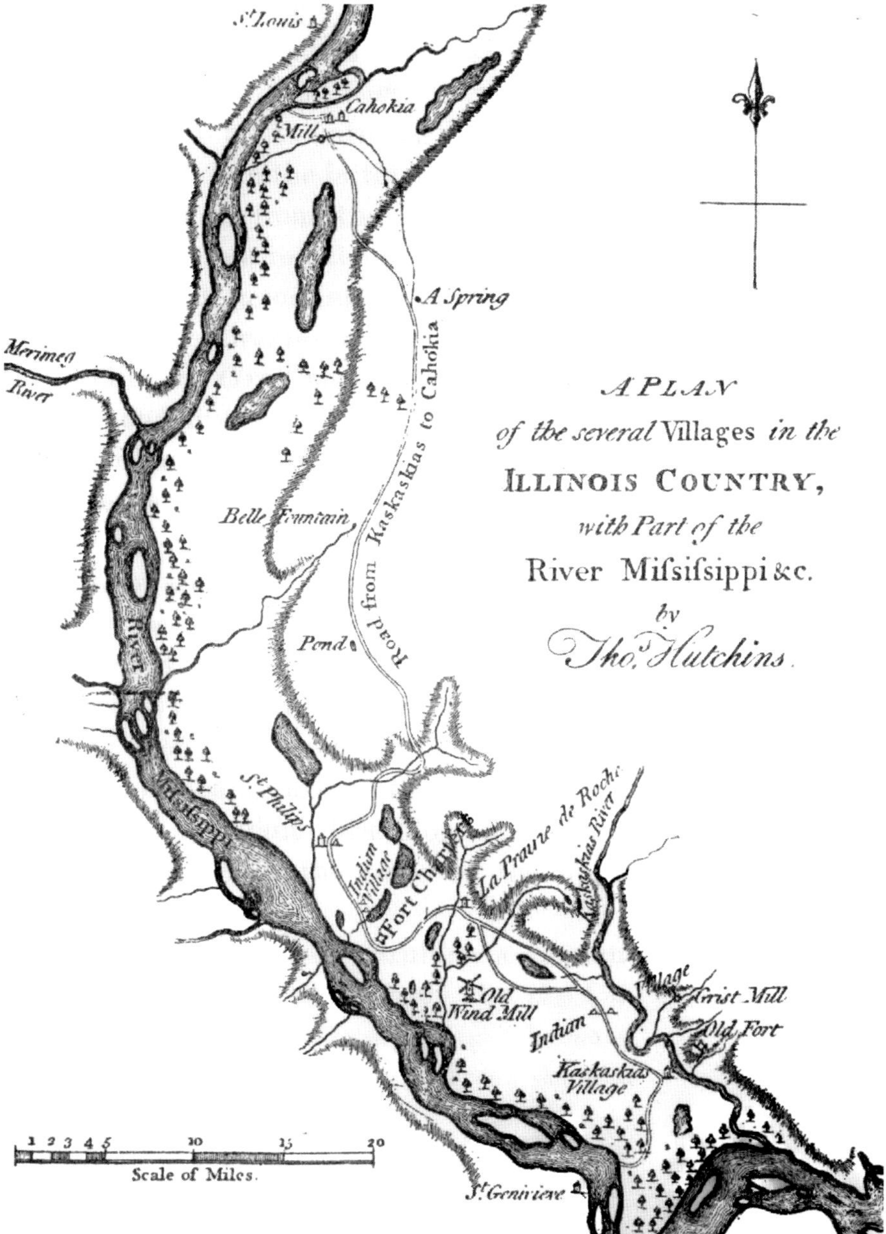

Thomas Hutchins's map of French Illinois settlements as they appeared in the late 1760s. *Published in London, 1778; 1904 facsimile in author's collection.*

voyageurs to spread the word that an affluent new trader was in the area. Archaeological excavations at the Laclède house site by Dr. Robert Mazrim of the University of Illinois have revealed the expensive merchandise that could have come from Europe via New Orleans, including British creamware, Spanish majolica earthenware and lead seals from bales of men's hosiery.[111]

By December 1763, Laclède was anxious to find the ideal site for his settlement, so in winter weather "severe in the extreme, cold, wet, and windy," he and Chouteau traveled almost sixty river miles up the Mississippi in an open dugout before reaching the mouth of the Missouri River. After viewing the torrent of mud gushing forth from that western river, they headed downstream about twelve miles to take a closer look at an impressive landmark. It was a two-mile-long limestone ledge perched high above the Mississippi, and rising thirty-two feet higher was a large earthen mound that beckoned them ashore like a beacon. That man-made mound, later named *La Grange de Terre* (Barn of the Earth), and some two dozen smaller mounds resembling Béarn's *turons* were the only visible remains of a Cahokia "suburb," where some ten thousand Mississippians had lived several hundred years earlier. (There were also two human footprints on the riverfront, eerily embedded into limestone by an ancient resident.)[112]

According to Chouteau, "Laclède was delighted to see the location [and] did not hesitate a moment to make the settlement there that he envisioned." The man from the mountains admired the stony elevation, which solved the problem of flooding. But in walking beyond that riverside ledge, Laclède was equally impressed by the "beauty of the site," which contained mature trees and limestone for building homes; freshwater springs for drinking, cooking and milling grain; and grassy prairies for farming and pasturing livestock. In short, it was an ideal site, containing "all the advantages that one could desire in a settlement, which might in the future become very large" and qualify as "one of the finest cities of America." Laclède notched some trees with an axe to stake his claim and told Chouteau to return with a work crew "as soon as navigation open[ed]" on the icy Mississippi to "have this place cleared according to the plan I shall give you."[113]

What made the site of St. Louis truly incomparable for commerce was its proximity to the confluence of North America's two longest rivers, what is now called the Mississippi-Missouri River System—fourth largest in the world—encompassing nearly four thousand miles and draining parts of thirty-one states. When combined with the Illinois River, only 30 miles to the northeast, and the Ohio River, about 150 miles to the southeast, St. Louis was the major river capital of mid-America, capable of linking Canada to the Caribbean and the Great Plains to Pittsburgh. That centrally located inland port of continental commerce would quickly become the dominant and most affluent city for one thousand miles in any direction. In 1796, Victor Collot predicted that St. Louis was destined to be the "source of inexhaustible riches for more than a century," able to reach the Far West "with more facility, more safety, and with more economy…than…any other given point in North America." Twenty-three years later, Henry Rowe Schoolcraft envisioned that stratrategic crossroads of a continent as a "future seat of empire," because "no place in the world situated so far from the ocean can at all compare with it for commercial advantages." A decade after that, two different visitors referred to St. Louis as the "Queen of the West" and the "Lion of the West." In 1988, the *Dictionary of Louisiana Biography* was still praising Laclède because "few men in American history have made as wise a choice of a settlement site as he did."[114]

But Laclède did not accomplish that alone. He had help from a knowledgeable commandant who knew why such prime real estate was uninhabited and "still available." French Illinois was overwhelmingly agricultural, and few farmers would have regarded the elevated site of St. Louis as preferable to their lowland fields regularly fertilized by flooding. The Illinois French also valued the security provided by their clustered villages, and before 1763, few of them would have risked living so close to the Missouri River, the fluid highway crowded with western Indian warriors. Many Illinois residents also had doubts about how profitable Laclède's new enterprise would be, since Fort de Cavagnal, located about 350 river miles up the Missouri, had been trading with nearby Kaws, Osages, Pawnees, Otos and Missourias since 1744. But that suddenly changed when Neyon de Villiers closed that fort in late 1763 or early 1764. He was not required to do so by the Treaty of Paris, since the site was outside of British boundaries; however, d'Abbadie ordered him to recall the French troops there as part of the cost-saving military evacuation. Civilian traders could have stayed and operated that post—if Kerlérec had not given Maxent a trade monopoly encompassing that site, and if Neyon de Villiers had not been involved with the "St. Louis Project." With Fort de Cavagnal emptied of competitors, Laclède truly had an *exclusive* trade of the Missouri River, which considerably enhanced the value of a town near its mouth. Next to location, the success of St. Louis depended on impeccable timing, and Laclède built the first and last European city on that perfect site at the precise moment in five hundred years when circumstances were ideal for his commercial enterprise.[115]

FULFILLING A WESTWARD VISION

Recently, Carl Ekberg claimed that Laclède "had no preconceived master strategy to establish a new outpost near the mouth of the Missouri River" because he had tried to buy property at Kaskaskia. The idea of a west bank location "came to him belatedly sometime during his reconnaisances of that bitter winter." That ridiculous statement confuses cause and effect, because Laclède and Chouteau would not have endured frigid weather on a boat cruise unless they were determined to locate, as quickly as possible, a settlement site that *had to be* on the west bank near the mouth of the Missouri River. That was their prime objective, not an accident, entirely *preconceived* because of the advanced planning in New Orleans and the specific terms of Maxent's monopoly, which Ekberg ignores. That grant from a French royal governor would have been worthless on the British east bank, which is why the shivering boaters from New Orleans did not stop for hot chocolate and set up shop at nearby Cahokia, directly across the river from later St. Louis. Neither that nor any site in Illinois—certainly not Kaskaskia—would fulfill the objectives to create the first postwar French settlement that was *west* of the Mississippi, *new* (built from scratch) and *novel* (corporate sponsored and entirely devoted to Indian commerce). Although Ste. Genevieve was on the west bank, it was too far from the mouth of the Missouri, and in addition to being small and flood-prone, it had too many well-established, kin-connected merchants who would (and did) compete with Laclède.[116]

Conclusive proof that Maxent intended to create a town across the international boundary line from British Illinois was revealed by his actions in New Orleans. In January 1764—one month before the construction of St. Louis began—he negotiated a contract with British military officials in the Louisiana capital to build ten bateaux to transport their troops to Fort de Chartres as quickly as possible. That was designed to spook the Illinois French and immediately spur their frantic exodus to Laclède's new cultural refuge across the Mississippi. Representing two parts of the same company, Maxent sought to profit by *means* in Lower Louisiana, while Laclède would have benefited from *ends* in Upper Louisiana by the summer of 1764—if attacking southern Indians had not prevented the Loftus expedition from reaching Illinois as scheduled.[117]

Even without such manipulations, the area of present-day Missouri became increasingly irresistible to French settlers because the Illinois Country was collapsing—politically, economically, militarily and environmentally.

"I am in a post at the end of the world without any resources," observed the commander of Fort de Chartres as early as 1751, and it soon became apparent that the old "Creole Corridor" was suffering from economic decline and ecological degradation that only a mass evacuation could address. In the first thorough environmental history of colonial Illinois, M.J. Morgan noted the declining habitat for large deer herds, especially the depletion of oak trees and their essential acorns, due to decades of French land clearing, village building and cutting of firewood. In a nutshell, acorns provided almost 80 percent of the stored nutritional content for winter deer diets, and Illinois could not sustain an adequate supply of those animals for food or furs. By comparison, the west bank of the Mississippi offered a perfect habitat for deer. "Miles of forest, a blend of deciduous and conifer, coated the unglaciated southern Missouri hills south of St. Louis," while the vast quantities of acorns in the Ozarks "had no parallel by the 1770s in the Illinois Country." In addition, the Mississippi River was intruding increasingly into the arable bottomlands of Illinois by the 1760s, with even firewood becoming scarcer. Illinois farmers also "decrease[d] their sowings" because they lacked "plows and teams" and did "not have people to harvest their crops, which often sprout in the field and make very bad flour." In 1752, an official report painted an especially grim portrait of deteriorating agricultural conditions:

> [T]*the drought…caused the loss of the greater part of it* [corn], *which is a great misfortune…for feeding animals. I do not foresee how much salt meat can be prepared this winter, especially in view of the mortality among the pigs….The wheat harvest would have been very good if the rust had not got in part of the wheat….As a result part of the flour will be black.*[118]

Even worse crises soon followed, as the once-rosy future of Illinois became tainted with dark stains of blood. The intersecting waterways that had facilitated French exploration, trade and settlement in mid-America became warrior routes for carrying carnage throughout a vast region during a turbulent era of frontier combat after 1752. Friendly "domiciled Indians" in Illinois were at risk from raids by Britain's native allies because local French marines were often engaged in the East, and military forces in Illinois were weakened by the "ill-timed parsimony" of Versailles. Officers at Fort de Chartres were ordered "to avoid all Indian wars as far as possible without compromising the dignity of the king's name." That garrison also averaged an annual desertion rate of about 23 percent and lost seventy soldiers between 1752 and 1756 alone. A disaster was always looming given those circumstances, and a catastrophe occurred even before the start of the French and Indian War. While the marines were scattered in private homes as far away as Kaskaskia during the construction of Kerlérec's new stone fort, hostile Indians twice attacked Illinois. The most serious raid occurred when French and Indian residents were celebrating the Feast of Corpus Christi on June 6, 1752. Some six hundred Sauks, Mesquakies (Foxes), Chippewas and Sioux swooped down the Mississippi in sixty bark canoes and attacked the Mechigamea village, killed or wounded eighty of their men and captured another thirty women and children, leaving severed limbs and decapitated heads scattered in the cornfields near the Metchys' burned lodges. A French officer reported that when the brazen attackers passed by Cahokia on their way back to Lake Michigan, they "hoisted the French colours" on a canoe and fired an insulting musket "salute." The commandant eventually ransomed most of the captives with the king's merchandise because the Mechigamieas had been one of the "best behaved" Indians in Illinois for "thirty years."[119]

Jean-Bernard Bossu, a Fort de Chartres officer who witnessed that attack, observed that the "Illinois were formerly the most formidable in Louisiana, but the continual wars…[with] the northern nations have reduced them to a very small number." But the French suffered, too, and their tiny towns could hardly absorb the tragic toll. In 1759, six officers and thirty-two marines from Fort de Chartres, plus fifty-four French Illinois militiamen, died defending Fort Niagara in an expedition led by Captain Aubry (of later New Orleans fame). The only comparable loss for the region had occurred in a bloody battle with the Chickasaws on Palm Sunday, March 25, 1736, when the commanders of Fort de Chartres and Vincennes, along with dozens of marines, militiamen and perhaps one hundred Algonquian allies, were cut down by musket fire or burned alive near present-day Tupelo, Mississippi.[120]

The French and Indian War did not end for Illinois residents in 1763; it merely began a new phase. The stunning successes of Pontiac's warriors in the summer of that year could not be sustained, but hostilities continued until 1765. *Because* the sieges of Fort Pitt and Detroit were unsuccessful, "Miamis, Kickapoos, Mascoutens, Weas, Piankashaws, Shawnees, Potawatomies, Ottawas, and others" visited Fort de Chartres in ever-growing numbers more frequently to seek support from Commandant Neyon de Villiers—"their first Father who always treated them with gentleness and [for whom] they continue this war only to save him." Pontiac's envoys brought Neyon de Villiers a six-foot-long wampum war belt and more English scalps, while d'Abbadie in New Orleans received a similar belt, displaying the "47 villages [of Indians] who want to die attached to the French…until the last drop of their blood." Calling himself "French Pontiac," that great leader could usually be found at Fort de Chartres between April and July 1764, when Chouteau claimed that he coerced the Peorias and Mechigameas to support his cause by threatening to "destroy" them "like the fire that passes over a prairie." Losing Indian allies and lacking French support, Pontiac finally agreed to peace, which permitted British troops from infamous Fort Pitt to occupy Fort de Chartres in October 1765.[121]

Many Illinois Algonquians feared the arrival of the redcoats even more than the French did, since native prophets had warned them that "if you suffer the English [to come] among you, you are dead men. Sickness, smallpox, and their poison will destroy you entirely." That prophecy was being fulfilled in Pennsylvania, as British soldiers and Anglo-American settlers revealed their "sinister hearts," with the former deliberately infecting Indian villages with smallpox, while the latter massacred at least twenty defenseless Christian Indians. Recent research has revealed that the terrors and traumas of the French and Indian War solidified anti-Indian attitudes into a malevolent, united "white" racism among normally feuding, culturally diverse European populations in Pennsylvania.[122]

Indian issues had an impact on all aspects of life in Illinois, but Illiniwek lives were in especially short supply. According to anthropologist Helen Tanner, the domiciled Algonquians "most closely attached to the French through intermarriage, Christianization, and commerce declined dramatically." Zitomersky estimated that the Illini lost 78 percent of their population, dropping from 10,600 in 1677 to 2,300 in 1763—almost 5 percent between 1750 and 1763 alone. That tragic decline disrupted fur trading, as the Philadelphia merchant firm of Baynton, Wharton and Morgan discovered while failing to establish profitable Indian commerce in British Illinois from 1765 to 1770. Even a decade earlier, it was evident that a few hundred Illinois Algonquians on foot in a depleted hunting territory without nearby bison could not compete with thousands of western Siouans on horseback who harvested every type of mammal in the fur-rich Missouri Valley. By 1752, Illinois traders were sending "their best goods to the Missouri tribes" and getting "much peltry" from across the river—"twenty-five canoes…loaded with beaver and deerskins" in that year

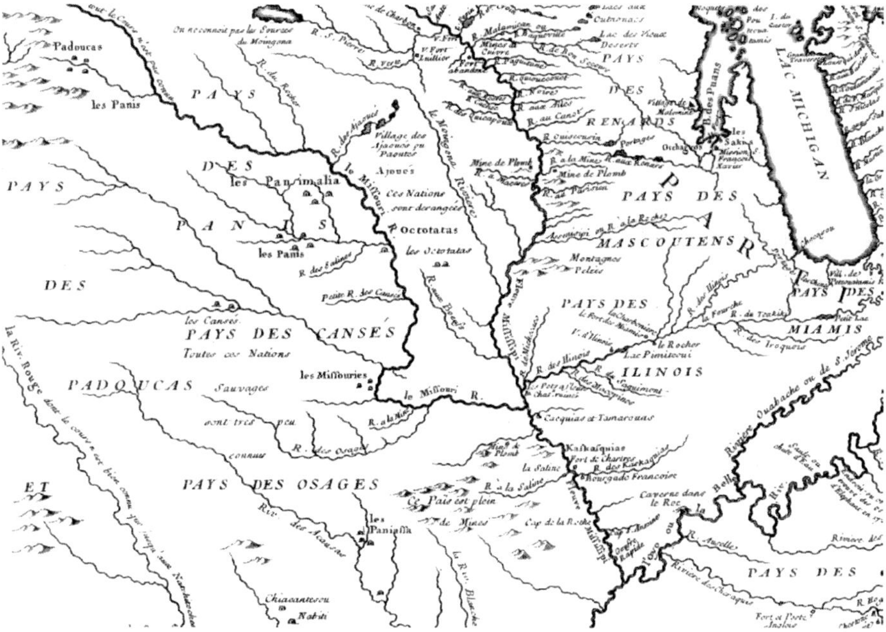

Osage Country, a hilly land cleared of enemies, on Nicholas Bellin's "Carte de la Louisiane" *(Paris, 1744)*. Note the blank area where St. Louis would rise.

alone. The trans-Mississippi West—"an Infant Country that should be the nurse of several others"—was already in play, and Laclède would depend on discontented and disheartened French and Indians alike in the Illinois Country to make his new settlement successful.[123]

Negotiating a Lease on the Land

French-Americans were notable in respecting the sovereignty of Indian homelands, and before the construction of St. Louis could begin, it was essential that Laclède obtain permission to use that Native Ground as the site of his trading town. Although St. Louis is one of the few U.S. cities that did not displace any Indian residents, Kerlérec and Maxent would have convinced Laclède to acknowledge Indian ownership of that place and to negotiate fur trade alliances that gave it value. Algonquians of Illinois and the Great Lakes were particularly sensitive to land issues in 1763, warning British officials not to regard the French surrender as conveying sovereignty over *their* territory, which they had neither sold nor given away.[124]

Once again, Neyon de Villiers proved to be indispensable, since he had the knowledge, authority and respect to serve as a diplomatic go-between on behalf of a recently arrived stranger. The commandant informed d'Abbadie that he had served as Laclède's tutor by including him in a "council of the Shawnees" held in his quarters with "all the officers who compose this garrison." But he was acutely aware that "the government of the Indians is the most extensive, the most difficult, and the most essential part of the command at the Illinois," and he had honed the diplomatic skills of the frontier that Laclède was still learning. Neyon de Villiers was described as "a cold man" but also "gentle and firm," having "studied deeply the nature of the different tribes and…gained their confidence." In December 1763, he reported that Indians were "happy to see me still here"—telling him to "take courage, my Father, do not abandon thy children; the English shall never come here while a single red man lives."[125]

That month would have been an ideal time for calling together the leaders of the Kaskaskias, who were the respected grandfathers of the domiciled Illini; the Peorias, considered the fiercest of that confederation; and the Cahokias, who lived closest to Laclède's future settlement. But it was probably the battered Mechigameas who had the most influence regarding Laclède's lease on the west bank. The familiar, faithful Metchy living near Nouvelle Chartres had always been hospitable and accommodating, and Laclède would have known more of them personally than any other Indians in 1763. The Mechigameas were major producers and peddlers of bear oil, the desirable frontier substitute for olive oil and essential for preventing muskets from corroding. The Mechigamea condiment manufacturers were only partially Christianized, but they had completely converted to European merchandise, investing in huge metal kettles for processing bear carcasses and eating "domestic dog on French faience plates." Most significantly, Metchy merchants "maintained a particularly close connection" with the Osages, receiving "horses and peltries" from them in exchange for lobbying on their behalf with French officials and fur traders. Until 1721, more Mechigameas lived in the Arkansas River Valley than in Illinois, trading with the Osages and Quapaws and learning the Dhegihan Siouan language of both nations. As valued middlemen between multiple cultures, the Mechigameas had the influence to host a parley with the Osages in late December 1763 or early January 1764, after both groups had returned from winter hunting.[126]

The success of Laclède's enterprise depended on an alliance with the Osages, whose many formidable hunter-warriors represented the greatest asset for a fur trading town, as well as the greatest threat to any unwanted intruders on their lands. The Grand Osages were long considered imperious and indomitable, "fastidious and sensitive in their dealings with others"—excepting the friendly, helpful Mechigameas. The Osages were as proud as they were powerful, especially after their Chief Boganienhin accompanied Chief Chicagou of the Mechigameas to France, on the "other side of the sun," in 1725. *Onontio*—King Louis XV—graciously received and generously entertained them at his Fontainebleau and Versailles palaces, giving them precious gifts that indicated his great respect. The Osage leader returned with "a complete French outfit that included a blue dress coat, silver ornaments, and a plumed hat trimmed in silver," plus "a royal medallion on a gold chain, a rifle, a sword, and a watch"—all of which "became instrumental in creating authority" within his own nation. For the next four decades, the Grand Osages demonstrated their "greed for honors" and the "desire that they be regarded with distinction and respect, basing this on the dominion of their lands, and allowing us to enter them, not because of any right, but because they wish it."[127]

Laclède also may have "wished" to give those proud people what Kerlérec called "a pure gift," a rare symbol of special affection and/or charitable compassion that had a greater impact because it was an unexpected display of generosity. But Laclède also possessed impeccable credentials and social status to make a favorable first impression. He was a rare native-born Frenchman of cultural refinement with an aristocratic bearing not found among the rude frontier *coureur de bois* the Osages had seen most often. Laclède was a New Orleans *negociant* (wholesale merchant), used to negotiating, and came with the backing of Onontio's highest royal officials in that capital city. He also had the support of two familiar and trusted commandants in Illinois and substantial funding from a business partner who was known to many tribes as Louisiana's official purveyor of Indian presents. The Grand Osages considered the French to be "the first white men" they had met—"our first father," a "real father," whom they "had the misfortune to lose" during the war of the 1750s. But now, that "father" was back in the person of Laclède, who promised to build an unprecedented, permanent trading town to expand transactions at a most opportune time of international transitions. Speaking to him in the regional trade language of French, the Osages pledged their cooperation and granted the Laclède-Chouteau family "most favored trader status" as junior partners in an ambitious commercial alliance. As the experienced Old Grandfathers of Missouri fur trading, the Osages were clearly the senior, dominant partners in that relationship. But they and all other Indians who traded with French St. Louis accepted the diplomatic designation of "children." That was not demeaning, since it meant only that French "fathers" with the right attitude and proper merchandise would nurture Indian "family members" with generosity and respect. Since the Grand Osages were patriarchal and patrilineal, even symbolic "fatherhood" conveyed a special meaning, and they expected Laclède to be paternalistic, concerned for their welfare and solicitous of their affection.[128]

The detailed planning by Kerlérec's circle of Indian experts in Lower and Upper Louisiana proved to be pivotal, since they advised Laclède that the Osages were very "vulnerable to flattery" and supplied him with new muskets to complement the bravery of their warriors. Guns were meaningful symbols of trust in bicultural friendships, since Indians regarded them as the tangible "indications of attachment" that had "opened our ancestors' eyes" to the practical benefits of trade and military alliances with French "fathers." For decades, warriors from the West had trekked to Fort de Chartres seeking muskets, and Director-General d'Abbadie reminded an Indian delegation in 1763 that "the French" allowed you to become "free men" by teaching "you to use the gun" and "furnishing you punctually with powder, bullets, axes, tomahawks, and knives to defend yourselves against your enemies and to make a living for yourselves." The Mechigameas, who had suffered more losses from recent violence than any other Illini tribe and had fewer than fifty warriors to defend themselves, wanted to "make a living," too, and they "crossed the Mississippi to Spanish Missouri" after the founding of St. Louis to enjoy the fruits of their diplomacy.[129]

Recruiting Prospective Settlers

Having secured the essential trade alliance and a "lease" on the land, Laclède and Chouteau must have been filled with anxious anticipation during the two-month wait before they could begin building their settlement. During that winter interlude in Illinois, they used their time well in meeting, evaluating and recruiting Nouvelle Chartres neighbors to be the first settlers of St. Louis. Even though Laclède and Chouteau were strangers, their purchase of a residence and the public support they received from Neyon de Villiers helped them gain the confidence of residents in that close-knit community. The free-spending outsiders may have alienated some hardworking habitants and underpaid soldiers, but the quality and quantity of their imported merchandise reassured more affluent community leaders that Laclède had the resources and the business acumen to follow through on his promises.

"The rest of the winter," Chouteau wrote, Laclède "busied himself in procuring all things necessary for the settlement—many men, provisions, etc.," since St. Louis was going to be built by free Frenchmen, not slaves or conscript laborers as New Orleans had been. On page eight of his handwritten "Narrative," Chouteau scrawled a list of the full names, just surnames or merely nicknames of thirty men, whom most historians have *assumed* represented his work crew of "thirty men—nearly all mechanics [laborers]," who constructed the first buildings in St. Louis. Even though Chouteau was not conclusive about that, there is enough information on twenty-one men from his list to make a strong case for their participation in the construction phase:

Nicolas Beaugenou Sr. (b. 1710, Canada; d. 1770, St. Louis) married Marianne Jenrion and fathered seven children.

Nicolas Beaugenou Jr.—"Fifi" (b. 1741, Canada; d. 1826, Florissant)—wed Catherine Gravelle in 1775 and fathered four children.

Jean Baptiste Becquet (1723–1797), a blacksmith, married Marie Francoise Dodier (1744–1785) at Fort de Chartres in 1762 and fathered four children.

Joseph Chancellier (b. 1750, St. Philippe; d. 1784, St. Louis), the elder son of Therese Larin and Louis Chancellier Sr., "Surgeon Major of the Marines at Fort de Chartres." Moving to St. Louis as a teenager, he married Elizabeth Becquet (b. 1753, Nouvelle Chartres) in 1772 and fathered five children.

Louis Chancellier Jr. (b. 1752, St. Philippe; d. 1785, St. Louis), the younger son of the surgeon major. His marriage to Marie Louise Dechamps produced three children.

Alexis Cotté (b. 1743, Quebec) married Elizabeth Dodier at St. Louis in 1768 and fathered eleven children.

Gabriel Dodier (b. circa 1740; d. 1805, St. Louis), son of the late "interpreter of the Indian languages" at Fort de Chartres. He married Marie Marguerite Becquet in August 1764 (her brother would marry his sister), and they had seven children. His mother and her married African slaves, Jacques and Frances, plus three married sisters, also moved to St. Louis.

Jean Baptiste Gamache (b. 1733, Quebec; d. 1805, St. Louis) married Charlotte Louviere D'Amours at St. Louis in 1767 and fathered four children.

René H. Kierserau *dit* (known as) Renaud (b. circa 1723, Port Louis, Brittany; d. 1798, Florissant), a church chorister, officiated at St. Louis religious functions in the frequent absence of a priest. He fathered six children with his wife, Madeleine Marie Robillard.

GREGOIRE KIERSERAU (b. 1752, Nouvelle Chartres; d. circa 1805) came to St. Louis as a teenager with his father (above). He married Magdalein St. Francois in 1774, and they had ten children.

PAUL LABROSSE (b. circa 1726, Montreal; d. 1804, St. Louis) was a carpenter and "master cabinet maker."

JOSEPH LABROSSE (b. 1737, Canada; d. circa 1798, St. Louis), an Indian trader in Illinois, married Marie Therese D'Amours Delouviere at St. Louis in 1771 and fathered two children.

JOSEPH MAINVILLE *dit* DECHENES (b. 1740, Canada; d. 1795, St. Louis), a carpenter, married Josette Anne "Nannette" Chancellier in 1770 and fathered nine children.

LOUIS MARCHETEAU *dit* DESNOYERS (b. Montreal, d. 1773, St. Louis), a farmer from Nouvelle Chartres, fathered four children with Francoise Leduc before she died about 1761.

ALEXIS PICARD (1711–1781), a Nouvelle Chartres farmer, moved to St. Louis in his fifties. He and his wife, Marie LaRoche, had one child born in St. Louis in 1772.

LOUIS RIDE SR. (b. circa 1730, Canada; d. 1787, St. Louis), a Cahokia resident, married Veronique May Marcheteau (Desnoyers) at Fort de Chartres in 1759 and fathered eight children.

ANTOINE RIVIÈRE *dit* BACUNÉ (b. 1706, Canada; d. 1816, Florissant) married Marie Francoise Barbe Eloy (b. 1726, New Orleans; d. 1786, St. Louis) at Kaskaskia about 1744 and fathered seven children. He was the cart driver who transported Madame Chouteau and her four young children from Laclède's house in Nouvelle Chartres to Cahokia in September 1764.

JULIEN ROI (d. 1793, St. Louis), a builder/contractor at Nouvelle Chartres, married Marie Barbe Saucier at Mobile in 1755 and fathered nine children.

JEAN BAPTISTE SALÉ *dit* LAJOIE (b. circa 1741, Saintous, France) married Marie Rose Devial-Pande in 1770 and fathered five children.[130]

In addition to those nineteen men, Laclède appointed two "trustworthy" older leaders to assist his stepson because they would have had greater influence over their neighbors than an inexperienced fourteen-year-old from New Orleans. Chouteau did not name those supervisors, but the most likely candidates from his list were Joseph Michel Tayon or Taillon and Jean Baptiste Martigny/Martigné—mature, transplanted Canadians, long resident in Illinois, who would receive prime town lots closer to Laclède's home than any other charter colonists. Tayon, at the top of Chouteau's list, was a fifty-year-old builder and miller who had resided in the Fort de Chartres area for many decades. He married Marie Louise Bosset in 1748, fathered seven children and died at the age of ninety-two in Florissant/St. Ferdinand, a farming suburb north of St. Louis. He built and operated the first water mill in St. Louis, which Laclede would purchase; his son, Charles, became the commandant of St. Charles; and a granddaughter married Chouteau's half brother, Pierre. Similarly well connected was Martigny, a fifty-two-year-old Quebec-born militia officer, wealthy merchant, real estate investor and co-owner of a billiard parlor, well known in St. Philippe, Nouvelle Chartres and Kaskaskia. In 1745, he married Marie Hebert, daughter of a militia captain whose land adjoined Laclède's in Nouvelle Chartres, and fathered twin daughters. The stone house that Martigny erected in 1766 at St. Louis became the second Spanish "Government House," where the United States formally took possession of Upper Louisiana in March 1804. Martigny was still serving in the St. Louis militia in 1780 and died a dozen years later at the age of eighty.[131]

Twenty of those twenty-one identified men lived in, or very near, Nouvelle Chartres, and the other came from Cahokia. They included masons, carpenters and a blacksmith, and two men were described as "builders." Merchants outnumbered farmers, which reflected the "urban services and functions" of Nouvelle Chartres. At least twelve of the men had been born in Canada and two in France; four were Creoles, and the origins of three are unknown. (In the 1752 Illinois census, 58 percent of the French population was of Canadian origin, with Montreal natives outnumbering those from Quebec.) When construction began in February 1764, the known ages of nineteen men ranged from 12 (two boys) to 58 (a man who lived to be 110). Three of Chouteau's workers were also in their teens, while six men were in their twenties, three in their thirties, three in their forties and four in their fifties. Nine of the twenty-one men were married and had already fathered thirty-one children when work commenced, and just four of those would father nineteen more children after 1764. Ten men would marry for the first time within the next ten years and father sixty-five children in their lifetimes. Everyone on the list made St. Louis their new home within two years, with most claiming town plots almost immediately.[132]

The founding of St. Louis did not destroy French Illinois, but it did give residents a new option as they pondered their futures after New France had fallen. The willingness of so many substantial residents, young and old, to follow Laclède across the river was indicative of crisis conditions. During its golden age between 1732 and 1752, *Le Pays des Illinois* played a significant role in French colonization, prospering from a commercial economy based on agricultural abundance and desirable natural resources. Habitants as free as the peasants of Béarn lived in well-furnished houses, farmed an average of forty acres and had sufficient income to import their clothes from France. But the record harvest of 800,000 pounds of flour in 1748 was a one-time bonanza, and some years only produced 40,000 pounds. Warfare between 1752 and 1764 disrupted, and ultimately destroyed, the fragile frontier economy that had been too dependent for too long on huge government subsidies to pay for expensive royal convoys and the costly consumer goods stored in the royal magasin of Fort de Chartres. Illinois was "destitute of everything" by 1762—including writing paper for the commandant—while some residents in New Orleans itself were "naked and dying of hunger."[133]

Failing to reach its full potential in population and productivity even in the best of times, French Illinois declined far faster than it had developed, and it was doomed when an expanding English East engulfed the old Creole settlements. All of the leading officials in New Orleans between 1753 and 1769 were associated with the "St. Louis Project," and when they withdrew monetary support of the east bank and gave moral support to Maxent's privately funded new town on the west bank, they recognized the hopelessness of the former and the hopefulness of the latter for preserving French colonial culture. St. Louis was a lifeline extended to a place that was already sinking—literally in the case of Fort de Chartres when it began to tumble into the river in 1772. Laclède's corporate colony sealed the fate of the Illinois towns by relocating their best traditions and most adventurous people to a preferable location on a frontier of the future. Only a few river miles separated a defeated, depleted land under a humiliating British occupation from the Missouri Valley of unlimited potential and very limited interference from outside authorities.

Part II

Fashioning St. Louis:

OPERATIONS

America is the only country in which it has been possible to witness the natural and tranquil growth of society, and where the influence exercised on the future condition of states by their origin is clearly distinguishable.[134]

Constructing a Wilderness Civilization

Man's mind is generally expanded or contracted in proportion to the objects around him, and shaped or molded to the narrow or extended limits he has to move in.

—Zadok Cramer

St. Louis was a vital link between the past and future of French life in America, representing historical continuity and geographical proximity in the Illinois Country. Bound by a common cultural inheritance from their European homeland, which was stronger than regional variations from Canada to Louisiana, the French had always used the Mississippi River as a boatman's boulevard to connect their settlements on both banks. Even though France did not control either side of the Mississippi after 1763, the French were everywhere, displaying even more cultural tenacity because they lived as orphans without a country. The British in Illinois gave a push to the creation of St. Louis by providing a sense of desperation for French residents, but Laclède in Missouri supplied the pull factors of aspiration, offering new solutions for all their old problems—virgin soils for farmers, huge profits for fur traders, safety from flooding, an escape from eastern Indian wars and the perpetuation of cherished customs with enhanced prospects for sustainable prosperity. While the French reconstructed their lives in a familiar, congenial community, many Indians reportedly crossed the river as well, to enjoy a nostalgic reaffirmation of their traditional ties to French "fathers," who once again lived near them on a permanent basis.[135]

Chouteau Constructs His Future

As Chouteau wrote in his "Narrative," once navigation was possible on the wintry Mississippi, he left Fort de Chartres with a party of laborers on February 10, 1764, and landed at the site of St. Louis on Wednesday, February 15, to begin building the town. That is a day later than the popularly recognized founding date celebrated at least since the city's bicentennial in 1964. All historians acknowledge Chouteau as the sole eyewitness who documented the details of the founding, but for 150 years, they have been evenly divided on the dating issue. Supporters of February 15 actually investigated Chouteau's original manuscript and noted his oddly shaped numeral "5," while the defenders of the erroneous February 14 largely rely on flawed secondary sources, whose authors either did not see, or misread, Chouteau's handwriting. Ironically, those current St. Louisans who are most committed to honoring "French tradition" continue to defend the wrong date, despite conclusive and well-publicized visual evidence of Chouteau's intentions.[136]

Chouteau's work crew from Nouvelle Chartres began clearing trees and constructing a fifty- by thirty-foot "shed" (warehouse) before building cabins for themselves. That followed traditions of the Canadian fur trade, as voyageurs at each new encampment sheltered the valuable trade goods for Indian consumers as the first priority. A resident who moved to St. Louis in June 1764 described those original cabins as "huts" and claimed that "the greater part of the settlers lived for a time on scaffolds, elevated six or seven feet above the ground, to protect themselves from the wild beasts which abounded" at the site.[137]

Until September 1764, Laclède spent far more time in Nouvelle Chartres than he did in St. Louis, protecting the company's costly assets and continuing to conduct business and recruit residents. So the naming of the town had to wait until Laclède first visited the building site "around the early part of April," after the storehouse had been completed. "St. Louis" was hardly an original name; the Mississippi River had been called that since the days of LaSalle, and it was being used as early as 1659 in Senegal for "the first permanent French establishment in Africa," where "whites, blacks and mulattos lived and worked side by side." But Laclède had more of a personal attachment to that name than most colonizers, because Louis IX, the famous crusader-king who reigned from 1226 to 1270 and was canonized by Pope Boniface VIII in 1297, was a direct ancestor of Béarn's King Henri. Laclède sought to flatter Louis XV by

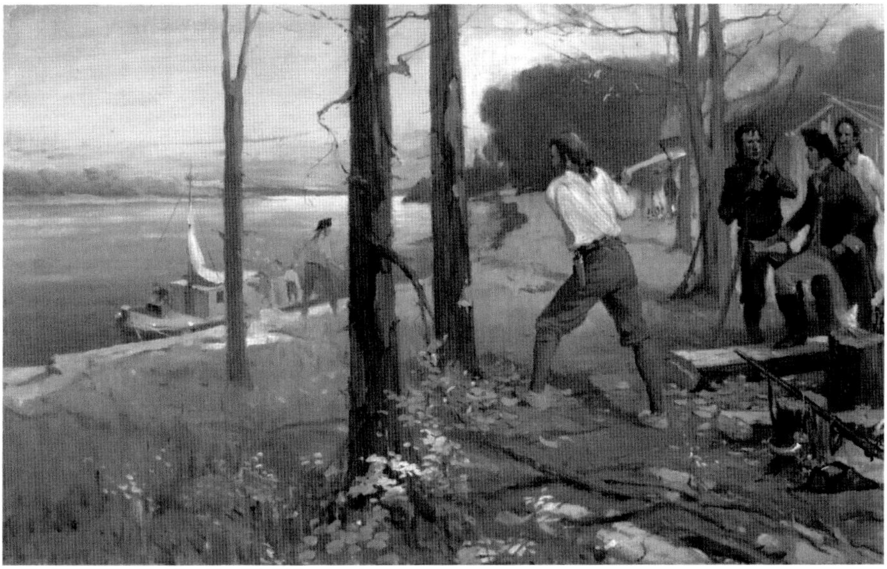

Laclede Landing at Present Site of St. Louis (detail) by Oscar Edward Berninghaus (circa 1914). *Courtesy Saint Louis Art Museum. Gift of August A. Busch Jr.*

honoring his patron saint—before he learned in December 1764 that "his king" had given western Louisiana to Spain two years before. The famous name remained, however, because eighteenth-century Frenchmen still considered Saint Louis to have been a model ruler, praised for "his kindnesses to the poor, his patronage of the arts, his founding of the Sorbonne…and his zeal against corruption in government."[138]

During his April visit, Laclède also "made a plan of the village" now that the land had been cleared of trees and undergrowth. Presumably, it was a sketch map, which has never been found. Before he returned to Illinois, Laclède directed Chouteau "to follow the plan exactly," which he claimed to have done "to the best of my ability and used the greatest diligence to hasten the building of the house" that his stepfather, mother and younger siblings would occupy. That well-conceived town design integrated various elements of earlier colonial French settlements in order to accommodate a combination of commercial and agricultural functions. Obviously modeled on the grid pattern of Laclède's New Orleans, a merchant metropolis facing the same river, St. Louis also reflected an Enlightenment-era sense of order. That design was superior to the chaotic thoroughfares in the medieval French cities that Laclède knew or the tiny,

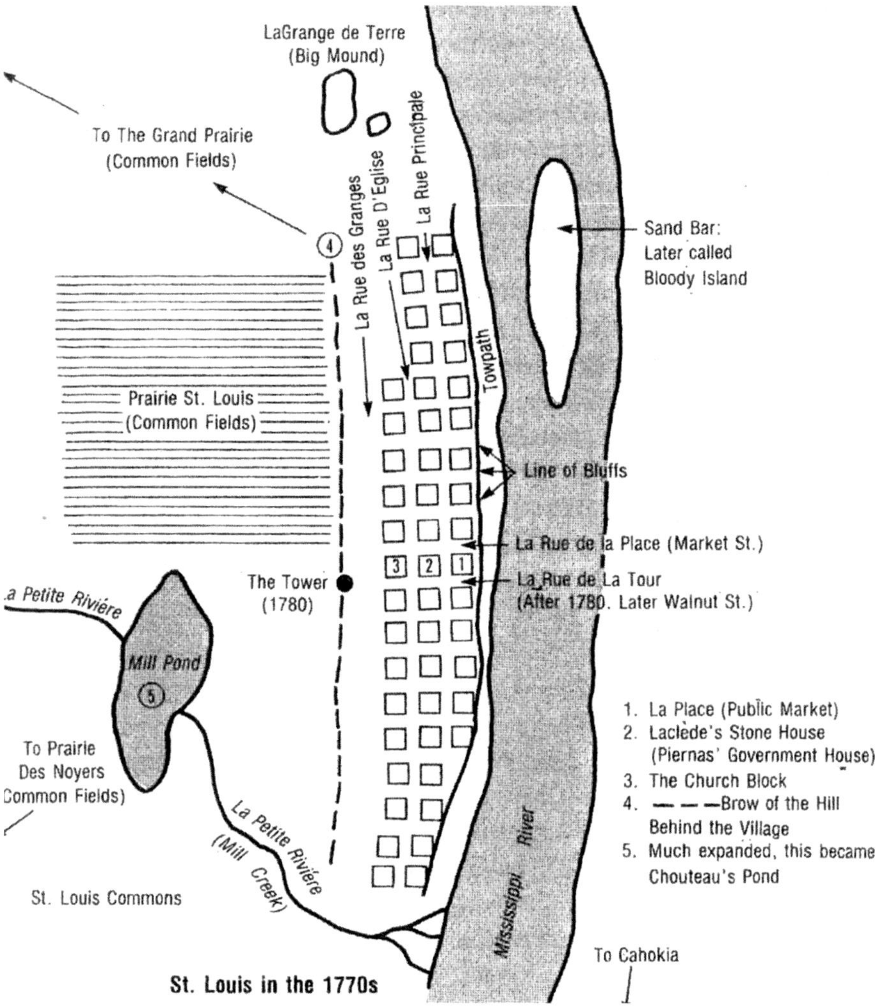

"St. Louis in the 1770s," by James Neal Primm, showing the symbolically significant Market Street and other landmarks. *Courtesy Missouri History Museum, St. Louis.*

irregular roads in the small farming villages of Illinois. Ekberg observed that "St. Louis was the most rigorously planned community in the Illinois Country," the only one "in which residential properties were measured with some care," leading to a "configuration of residential property… quite unlike that used in any other community in the region, on either side of the Mississippi."[139]

The one departure from an ideal design was necessitated by the landscape. The first row of houses was situated on the lip of the limestone ledge and did not have a true street in front of it. Initially, St. Louis had two very long, 38-foot-wide, north–south streets running parallel to the Mississippi: La Rue Principale or La Rue Royale (later, Main/First Street) and La Rue d'Eglise (later, Second Street). Another street behind the others, La Rue des Granges ("Street of Barns," later Third Street), was shorter and only partially built at first. Expertly surveyed, 30-foot-wide cross streets intersected them at right angles to form forty-nine residential "blocks" that measured 240 by 300 feet but were often divided into halves or quarters. Historian James Neal Primm estimated that the average home-lot dimensions of the earliest residents were 120 by 150 feet, while a more recent city historian, Frederick A. Hodes, wrote that "most of the residents were given a quarter of a city block." Irrespective of property size, the key word was "given," since Laclède adhered to "the Illinois Way" in doling out residential lots free of charges, rents or taxes, provided that each recipient "improved" the parcel by building a house of vertical logs or stone within a year and a day. When virtually all of the town lots were allocated by 1770, St. Louis stretched sixteen blocks north to south, occupying an area five times longer than it was deep, in contrast to the compact villages in old Illinois.[140]

In addition to the residential lots, Laclède and Chouteau created three three-hundred- by three-hundred-foot "squares" in the center of town that were dedicated to specific purposes, with commerce being dominant. Closest to the river was the Place d'Armes, a block for public functions, markets, militia drills and official ceremonies, similar to the one in Pau. Behind it was "Laclède's Block," the center of commerce, which contained the founder's first residence, doubling as Maxent Company headquarters, and his fur trade warehouse—a nonmilitary "magasin." Last in the line of squares was the Place d'Eglise, reserved for a Catholic church and a Catholic cemetery. Four churches were built there (in 1770, 1776, 1822 and 1834), including the surviving "Old Cathedral" named for "Saint Louis IX, King of France." Behind that area in the back of town were the long, narrow "ribbon fields" typical of medieval France and colonial Illinois. Those long-lot plots were allocated to every household and proved to be reassuringly traditional for the many Illinois residents who resettled in St. Louis. Also adopted from French village life on the east bank was the "Commons"—a large plot of land measuring 4,500 French arpents, or 3,830 English acres, where all residents could graze their livestock and collect free firewood.[141]

THE OSAGES AS CO-FOUNDERS

While New Orleans and Illinois influenced the physical form of St. Louis, it was the Osages who gave the town its commercial prosperity, protected its residents and inspired progressive intercultural relationships. Many scholars recognize that "towns were the spearheads of the frontier," but fewer acknowledge what Pierre Laclède and Auguste Chouteau took for granted: the most critical "spearheads" in the West were the impressive, productive *Indian* towns that predated, and often determined the survival of, later European ones. St. Louis would never have been founded when and where it was if the Osages had not already demonstrated that they were "masters of the hunting country" and the "best fur producers" in the region, who had been "far more successful than either France or Spain at building a mid-continental empire." As Kerlérec, Maxent, Neyon de Villiers and Laclède all realized, the Osages were the raison d'être for the existence of St. Louis, since their initial and long-lasting support of French objectives was essential for the town's physical safety and economic success.[142]

The Osages were the indispensable co-founders of that one-industry town because they had the largest and most diverse animal empire in the region, a superior and intimidating warrior force to defend it, expertise in harvesting and processing every type of marketable mammal and the willingness to supply that valuable bounty to a single site of trusted traders. The Osages were the most populous and productive Indians between the lower Missouri River Valley and the lower Arkansas River Valley in the eighteenth century, with eight to ten thousand people controlling a 100,000-square-mile hunting domain that extended across three distinct ecological zones of different animal habitats. That huge homeland, which represented nearly one-eighth of the Louisiana Purchase Territory, included most of present-day Missouri, the eastern third of Kansas and about two-thirds of both Oklahoma and Arkansas. Male hunting skills were complemented by the expert fur processing of Osage "career women," who worked in open-air "factories" manufacturing thousands of pounds of soft, supple, shaved and brain-tanned deer and bison leather every year. Thomas Jefferson told naturalist William Bartram about their admirable preparation of pronghorn skins as well, noting that "the Osage Indians shewed me a specimen of its leather, superior to any thing of the kind I ever saw. Their manner of dressing the leather…[prevents] injury from being wet."[143]

The Osages were also known as the *Niukonska* (Children of the Middle Waters), but Europeans called them Osages (pronounced "Wah Sha She"), Eaux, Os or Oz. Their fifteen hundred to two thousand warriors made the Osages more aggressively expansionistic than the other Dhegiha (Tay Gee Ha) Siouans in the central prairie plains: the Quapaws of present-day Arkansas, the Omahas and Poncas of Nebraska and the Kansa/Kaws of Kansas. Although President Jefferson called the Osages the "great nation south of the Missouri," they were never a single, unified entity with centralized governance. For most of the eighteenth century, the Osages were divided into two branches living in separate locations. The *Petit* or "Little" Osages were "lowland dwellers," residing along the Missouri River two hundred miles west of St. Louis. The more populous *Grand* Osages (also called "Big" or "Great") were known as "elevated mound people" because they resided in four large, contiguous villages on defensible hilltops at Marais des Cygnes ("Marsh of Swans") near the confluence of the Osage, Little Osage and Marmaton Rivers, over three hundred miles southwest of St. Louis. With about 75 percent of the total Osage population, warrior strength and hunting capacity, the Grand Osages were the most feared, formidable and affluent, but the Laclède-Chouteau family found them more cooperative and less troublesome than the Petit Osages. In the late eighteenth century, several breakaway bands of the Grand Osages, collectively known as the "Arkansas Osages," moved to present-day Oklahoma and Arkansas.[144]

Long before those diasporas, however, the Osages divided power among numerous leaders with varying responsibilities at different organizational levels. None "ruled" by coercive means, but there was a sort of "nobility" because the Osages adhered to a patrilineal system of inheritance, with qualified sons following honored fathers in office. In a system of dual chieftainship, equal in status and authority, a Tsi-zhu *Ga-hi-ge* (leader) represented the Peace and Sky clans in diplomatic functions, while a Hon-ga *Ga-hi-ge* headed the War and Earth clans in other affairs. Both, however, were subordinate to the *Non-hon-zhin-ga* (Council of Little Old Men), which contained wise, respected warriors from every clan and had the sole responsibility for major tribal policies, such as conducting war on a "national" level. Rapidly organized "minor" raids by individual bands, clans or renegade groups occurred on the village level to circumvent that authority, and senior Osage leaders could legitimately claim that such violence was neither authorized nor controllable.[145]

The Osages lived in fixed towns with farming fields—"large, densely populated centers with over one hundred lodges and a thousand or more inhabitants." One Grand Osage site was occupied by as many as three thousand people for almost a century, with substantial mat-covered longhouses, up to one hundred feet in length, reflecting ancient woodland roots east of the Mississippi. The Osages were not nomadic, endlessly on the move; they did change locations for seasonal subsistence but always returned to their main towns for at least half the year. The increasing demands of commercial fur harvesting, however, made long-distance "commuters" of male hunters, who were absent several weeks at a time for up to eight or nine months a year.[146]

The Osages prospered through a diversified economy that included male-dominated communal hunting organized by tribal leaders, female-dominated fur processing and horticulture based on family units and extensive foraging by everyone. Women planted about a half acre of maize, squash and beans, plus small plots of pumpkins, gourds and melons for their families in fertile, well-watered fields reserved for each household. After planting, adult women left their crops to join the men on the Great Plains for the summer bison hunt, where they skinned and tanned hundreds of huge and heavy hides. Buffalo "robes" (with the hair on) were used as warm blankets, as "carpets" for earth floors and as "siding" for lodges, and they formed the roof and walls of the large, rectangular, fifteen- by seven-foot hunting lodges (not teepees) used on the trail. Returning to their towns in August, women harvested fifteen to thirty bushels of vegetables per family. Whatever was left after harvest-festival feasting was dried and buried in underground caches before departing for the autumn hunts. They were the most important and intense of the year, since the kills included more bison, some beavers and especially large quantities of whitetail deer, the main "cash crop" for trade. February was the cruelest month, when family groups dispersed to small forest camps that could support the subsistence needs of humans and horses. Despite a homeland crisscrossed by rivers, the Osages did not like to eat fish, preferring to supplement meat with wild fruits, roots, nuts and berries "in astonishing abundance," especially water lily roots, acorns and persimmons.[147]

The French learned of the Osages in the 1670s and 1680s, coinciding with the Mississippi River explorations of Marquette and Jolliet, LaSalle and Tonti. French-Canadian coureurs de bois were making annual visits at least by 1696, the date of Quebec's trade embargo, and they supplied the Osages with metal blades and large-gauge, smoothbore flintlock muskets—*wa-ho-ton-the* (that which causes things to cry). As one of the earliest native nations to adopt both guns and horses, the Osages had an early advantage over Quapaws, Caddos, Pawnees, Wichitas, Kiowas, Comanches and Plains Apaches, with whom they frequently clashed and usually defeated. Early eighteenth-century French maps depicted Osage territory as a large circular area without any near neighbors, indicating that their musket-wielding cavalry had pushed other

TABLE A

OSAGE CALENDAR OF SUBSISTENCE AND COMMERCE

Given their economic dependence on the Grand Osages, the French merchants of St. Louis adopted their calendar for commerce. The Osage Year began in April, not January.

SPRING {***Be-in*** in Dhegihan Siouan} Season of Sunrise/Dawn=Human Birth
Late April–Late May: Women plant maize, squash, beans, pumpkins (half acre per woman). In this season, Chouteau traders purchase and transport furs to St. Louis, resupplying the Osages with necessities for a new year of hunting. Delegations usually parleyed at St. Louis in this season.

SUMMER {***Do-gé***} Season of the High Midday Sun=Human Adulthood
Early June–Late July: **Large Summer Bison Hunt on the Great Plains**
Everyone returns to villages in August to harvest crops (fifteen to thirty bushels per family) and to celebrate an abundance of both meat and vegetables.

Autumn {***Ton***} Season of the Lower Sun=Human Old Age
September–November are the months of especially active hunting of diverse species: **Autumn Deer Hunt, Second Bison Hunt, Beaver Hunt and Killing of Migrating Waterfowl**

WINTER {**Bá-the**} Season of Sunset/Night=Human Death
Late December–Mid-January are spent in permanent villages, along with Chouteau "winterers"
Late January–Mid-February: **Black Bear Hunt in Ozark Mountains**
February and March: **Dispersed Winter Hunting for Small Game by Kin Groups**
Late winter is the "Lean Time," when residents leave villages to establish small, separate hunting camps for greater efficiency in procuring a variety of small mammals for sustenance, finding sufficient firewood and locating grasses for grazing horses.

In April, residents reassemble at their permanent villages to prepare for planting and to complete the processing of deer leather and the hides and pelts of other species before the French traders arrive.

Hunting and horticulture were supplemented year round by season-appropriate foraging for nuts, roots, tubers, berries, water lilies and other wild plants. As the fur trade intensified in the late eighteenth century, Osage warrior-hunters were spending at least eight months per year away from home in commercial mammal harvesting

Sources: Garrick A. Bailey, "Osage," in William C. Sturtevant, ed., *Handbook of North American Indians*, vol. 13, part 1: *Plains*, ed. Raymond J. DeMallie (Washington, D.C.: Smithsonian Institution, 2001), 476–96; Willard H. Rollings, *The Osage: An Ethnohistorical Study of Hegemony on the Prairie-Plains* (Columbia: University of Missouri Press, 1992), 71–79; Carl Haley Chapman, "The Origin of the Osage Indian Tribe: An Ethnographical, Historical, and Archaeological Study," in *Osage Indians* III (New York: Garland Publishing, Inc., 1974), 14–29.

tribes to the periphery. The development of the American Bottom increased the power and prosperity of the Osages, as they became mobile middleman traders who transported horses and hides, mules and meat—as well as many Indian captives—between Spanish Santa Fe and French Illinois, enriching both groups of European colonists.[148]

The Osages treated fur trading as an essential component of national security, with mammal harvests purchasing the muskets that allowed them to extend and defend their territorial hegemony. But as they expanded

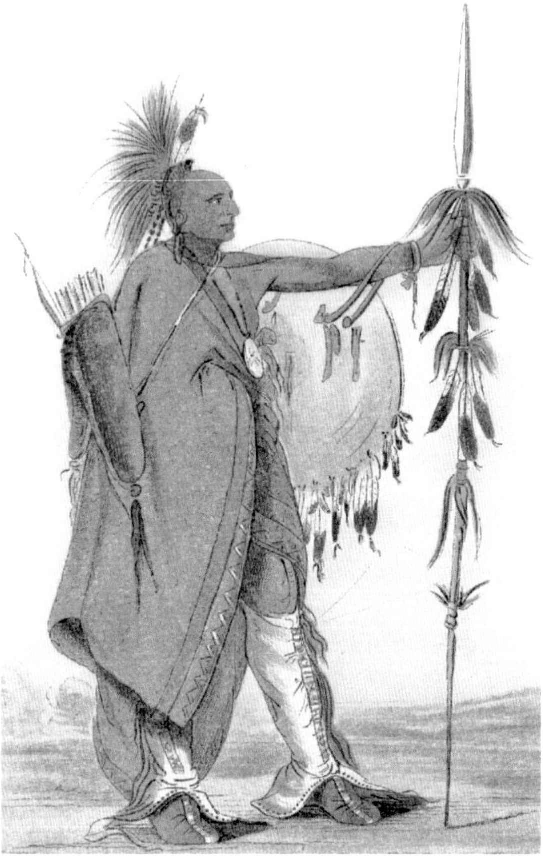

Osage Chief Tah-hah-ka-he (Tallee), painted by George Catlin in 1834. Note his height in relation to his seven-foot lance. *1866 print in author's collection.*

to the boundaries of Indian enemies, poaching increased. That was a very serious offense because it deprived the Osages of food, as well as furs. The punishment for such "commercial crimes" was decapitation, with the offender's head placed in a copper trade kettle or on a pole where his tribe would see it. Since the Osages needed ever-increasing numbers of firearms, they treated white poachers more gently, as they could not risk alienating the fur merchants and royal officials who provided those weapons. European interlopers were rarely killed, just beaten, stripped naked, deprived of their possessions and sent back to their homes. Similarly, the Osages modified their sacred mourning ritual to accommodate the presence of whites. In seeking the requisite fresh scalp to accompany a relative's spirit to the afterlife, warriors headed away from the riverside towns of their French friends in the east and went west to kill an Indian, since almost all area tribes were enemies of the Osages.[149]

The large parties of mounted warriors who hunted mammals on two or four legs could be seen a long way off because the Osages were "the tallest race of men in North America, either of red or white skins," according to artist George Catlin, who visited them for many years. "Very few" adult warriors, he wrote, were "less than six feet in stature, and very many of them six and a half, and others seven feet"—such as Chief Black Dog, who was seven feet tall and weighed three hundred pounds when Catlin painted his portrait in the 1830s. Enhancing genetics and a high-protein meat diet, the Osages bound male babies to cradle boards to create "more than a natural elevation of the top of the head," which produced "a bold and manly appearance in front." President Jefferson, who was over six feet, two inches tall, called the Osages "the most gigantic men we have ever seen" when they visited him in 1804. The Osages appeared even taller and more intimidating because they wore five-inch-high roaches of porcupine quills and deer tails atop bald heads glistening with red vermilion (mercuric sulphide); carried seven foot lances; and towered above the backs of their small female ponies. In 1835, Washington Irving described the "giant" Osages as "the finest-looking Indians I have seen in the West," awed by their "noble Roman countenances" and physiques that "would have furnished a model for a statuary."[150]

While they could be as intimidating as charging medieval knights, the Osages revealed their "civility" and the maturity of their foreign policy by the mutually beneficial commercial partnership with the Laclède-Chouteau family. It was one of the strongest, longest and most significant intercultural trade alliances in North America, and both groups enjoyed a golden age in the last third of the eighteenth century. Those St. Louis merchants grew rich, and their settlement prospered, while the Osages became the last surviving indigenous nation in Missouri—the only one to have interacted with all area Europeans from the 1600s to the 1800s. Such interethnic interest group alliances did not make fur trading perfect, but by demonstrating that toleration and peace produced prosperity, they avoided atrocities based on racial or religious prejudices.

The Significance of Symbolism for the Osages

According to an Osage historian, "symbolism played a large role in their lives, [and] any symbolic article was held in awe and veneration" as "a very special honor [and] a token of the Great Creator's esteem." The "Osages had a greed for honors," and "it mattered not what source the symbol came from, for the Great Creator often used unusual means to reward his favored ones." While Laclède chose his elevated settlement site for practical reasons, the Grand Osages more likely admired it because of tribal heritage, since the surrounding mounds of ancient Mississippians made them feel at home. The Osages were at least the commercial heirs of those premier traders of "medieval America," but some anthropologists claim that the Osages also shared cultural traits with the Cahokia civilization and perhaps a genetic inheritance as well. Most scholars agree that the Osages migrated from the ancient mound-building areas of the Ohio Valley to those of Missouri, and in 1995 anthropologist Garrick A. Bailey stated that the Osages had "Mississippian forebears" and "were the products of the shared cultural influence of the Mississippi peoples." Several eminent authorities agree with him. Anthropologist Robert L. Hall observed that "a division of the Siouan family that is more likely to have included actual participants in the Cahokia development is the Dhegiha Sioux," with "the Osage being closest geographically to Cahokia." The Grand Osages revered the sacred Blue Mound near their Marais des Cygnes homeland, and they continued to bury important chiefs there as late as the nineteenth century. In July 2009, the Osage Nation, headquartered at Pawhuska, Oklahoma, purchased Sugar Loaf—the last surviving ancient mound in the city limits of St. Louis—and have acknowledged Osage ties to the Mississippians by planning to open a cultural center there to honor that heritage.[151]

The arrival of the first French fathers who would permanently occupy that significant site at the convergence of strategic rivers may have made the Grand Osages keenly aware of other symbolic associations. The prominently displayed fleur-de-lis, the "royal lily" of France that honored the Virgin Mary and was stamped into French trade blades, closely resembled the Osages' beloved wild water lily, or "American lotus" (*Nelumbo lutea*), found throughout their marshlands. The delectable roots (*macoupins*) were a favorite food, but the entire plant with beautiful blooms "was considered sacred and had a place in the tribal rites," being gathered by men as well as women with great "ceremony" as "a prayer to the earth." Laclède and the Osages also shared an appreciation for carnivorous birds of prey, especially eagles and vultures. The Laclède family coat of arms featured two such aggressive-looking raptors—large, flesh-ripping aerial predators much admired by Osage warriors for their fear-inspiring ability to swoop down to kill unsuspecting victims and/or to mutilate their corpses. An 1806 portrait of an Osage warrior by the French artist Charles Balthazar Julien Fêvret de Saint-Mémin (see color insert) shows him wearing a traditional bird-beak "crown." The artist described it as a "vulture's beak with other waterfowl beaks and hummingbird skins"—a stunning visual representation of the struggle for survival between the strong Osages and the weaker tribes they regularly raided. Other symbolic associations included the ancient raised-cross-in-circle motif on Indian petroglyphs and pictographs in eastern Missouri. Early iron trade axes made in France were stamped with that symbol, which represented the four sacred directions in aboriginal America long before it signified the Christian cross

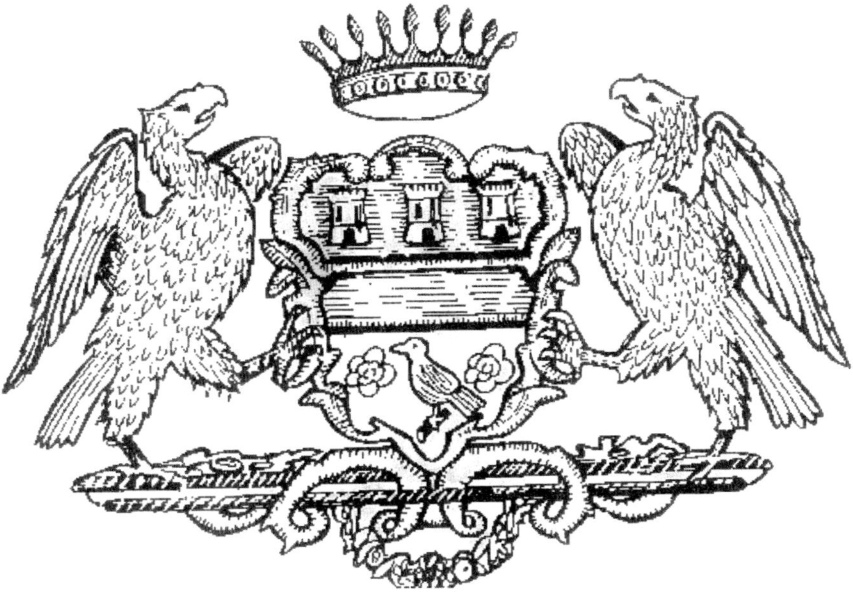

Laclède family coat of arms, redrawn from a 1909 print and used by the Pierre Laclede Honors College. *Courtesy University of Missouri–St. Louis.*

among Europeans. Moreover, the uniquely stylized "weeping heart" cutout on the large iron blades of "Missouri war axes," which became a trademark of French St. Louis, resembled the intertwined necks of male and female trumpeter swans found in Osage marshlands, a species that fought to the death to protect its young.[152]

Even more recognizable as a reinforcing symbol of cultural connectedness was the physical layout of St. Louis, which resembled Osage design elements as much as French colonial ones. The Osages imparted a sacred component in the planning of their towns. All longhouses faced east, and villagers pursued their daily activities believing that the sun's progress across the sky corresponded to the life cycle of humans, from sunrise (the bright light of new birth) in the east to sunset (the darkness of death) in the west. In addition, Grand Osage towns had a long east–west path that divided the lodges of the "Sky and Peace People" (*Tsi-Zhu*) clans on the north side from the "Earth and War People" (*Hon-Ga*) clans located south of that central lane. The *Ga-hi-ge* of War and the *Ga-hi-ge* of Peace "erected their lodges in the middle of the village, with the *Hon-ga* lodge on the south and the *Tsi-zhu* lodge on the north." Similarly, the principal long streets in early St. Louis were divided into northern and southern sections by the most prominent cross street, La Rue Bonhomme/La Rue de la Place (later Market Street), the only pathway to the Mississippi waterfront. Laclède's original, east-facing house was on the south, or *Hon-Ga* side, of "Good Man Street," which, for the Osages, gave symbolic significance to the residence of the French "chief." According to anthropologist Alice Beck Kehoe, *Hon-Ga* in the Osage language means a "venerated object," something "sacred or holy," and was associated with "ancient, or first, people—those who led." The *Hon-Ga* clans of Earth and War also identified with the power of fierce carnivorous birds.[153]

Laclède's large limestone house and company headquarters, measuring twenty-three by sixty feet, was the first residence that Chouteau's crew constructed in St. Louis. In addition to its priority and special placement, that structure symbolized the meeting of European and Indian worlds, since it was the only known St. Louis house built with the assistance of native people. Visiting Missouria women and children dug the cellar in the summer of 1764 using traditional methods—"carry[ing] the soil in wooden platters and baskets, which they bore upon their heads"—in exchange for imported European products. Laclède leased that sizable structure with a large center room to Spanish officials after their arrival in 1770, and it became the "Government Hall," where hundreds of Indian diplomatic delegations parleyed over the years. Chouteau's later renovations of the house he originally built for Laclède transformed it into the grandest mansion in the early West, as well as the international headquarters of the House of Chouteau—resonating with the commercial diplomacy of the frontier Indian trade and the class-consciousness of a Béarnais stone château.[154]

Visiting Indians would have noticed other characteristics that made early St. Louis seem familiar and welcoming. Except for a small group of the wealthiest businessmen born in France, the young town had an almost classless society, and as late as 1778, the population was "so mixed up that one cannot tell who is a farmer and who is a merchant." Initially, most whites and some blacks lived on free land distributed with an undocumented handshake on a first come, first served basis, often without considerations of birth, wealth, social status or occupation. In addition, St. Louis's population was no larger, and often much smaller, than many Indian towns, with the three hundred or so residents in 1766 barely growing to one thousand by 1803. Like Indian communities, St. Louis depended on kinship connections, family friends and neighborhood networks for common defense, construction projects and the care of sick or needy residents. St. Louisans also shared the Osages' emphasis on commerce over agriculture, and French, Indian and métis women tended the crops when their husbands, like Indian warriors, were absent for months at a time.[155]

Despite respectable harvests that belied their reputed "laziness," St. Louisans embraced the misleading *pain court* (short of bread) nickname for their town because it reflected their prudent, pragmatic decision to cultivate Indian hospitality rather than Indian homelands. As "tenants" who only "leased" Native Ground, St. Louisans ensured their security and prosperity by not allowing expansive agriculture to threaten animal habitats or tribal sensibilities. Such self-restraint avoided the Indian hostility generated by land-hungry Anglo-Americans, creating an alternative frontier population that did not fear "savages" or seek to eradicate "wilderness." By working with the former to derive wealth from the latter, French St. Louisans merged the best attributes of European humanitarianism and capitalism in "Indian Country," benefiting from "the delights and beauties of bountiful nature" while "enjoying free intercourse with all the commercial world."[156]

Like the Osages, early St. Louisans were gently governed by noncoercive, consensual means. Most of the Grand Osages' key policy decisions at the national level were made by the "Little Old Men," a council of wise, veteran warriors whose familiarity with the tragic costs of combat made them advocates of nonviolence. A similar "civil and military" council of six St. Louisans, led by a frontier warrior and Indian diplomat of "respectable old age"—Captain Saint Ange—governed the town between October 1765 and May 1770. Coming from an army family with 130 years of combined service on American frontiers, Saint Ange was already a highly respected symbol of a uniformed French "father" who had nurtured his Indian "children" in the ways of peace for decades. That Canadian had been stationed at Bourgmont's Fort d'Orleans as a young soldier and governed Vincennes (which was nicknamed "St. Ange") for a quarter century before becoming the last French commander of Fort de Chartres in 1764. His father had commanded that garrison three decades earlier, and his older brother, Pierre, who married a local métisse, died along with other Illinois troops in the Palm Sunday battle with the Chickasaws in 1736.[157]

The Osages knew Saint Ange because he had prevented one of their chiefs from tomahawking a British officer at a parley in 1765. But as supporters of Pontiac, the Osages would have appreciated even more the affectionate, trusting friendship between that famous chief and Saint Ange, even though the commandant had kept some Indiana tribes from joining his war against the British. Pontiac visited Saint Ange in St. Louis, and according to local lore, the commandant retrieved the chief's body after his murder at Cahokia on April 20, 1769, and had him buried in St. Louis wearing a French officer's coat. In 1901, the St. Louis chapter of the Daughters of the American Revolution honored Pontiac with a commemorative plaque placed near the intersection of Broadway and Walnut Streets, the reputed site of his grave. Whether or not his bones are there, it is significant that so many generations of St. Louisans have embraced that story as a symbol of the city's respect for Indians and resentment of the British.[158]

Next to Laclède, Saint Ange was the most valuable early resident of St. Louis. He was an "angel," indeed, because his incomparable experience and close ties with Governor Aubry in New Orleans made the new settlement a governmental capital less than two years after its birth, creating a tangible, as well as a symbolic, link with friendly French hospitality enjoyed by Indians at old Fort de Chartres. As an aging bachelor, Saint Ange lived with the Laclède-Chouteau family until his death on the day after Christmas 1774, and Indians would have noted the shared residence and close friendship of St. Louis's chief military official and its leading merchant, who combined their talents in diplomatic relations with native nations.

LACLÈDE'S PARLEY WITH THE MISSOURIAS

Sixteen months before Saint Ange's arrival in St. Louis, Laclède conducted important diplomacy that determined the town's Indian policies for years to come. In June 1764, the entire Missouria nation of about 150 warriors and some 450 dependents suddenly showed up to scare the hell out of Chouteau and his construction crew. They arrived in something of a panic, since "three hundred" Osage warriors had recently raided their village some two hundred miles up the Missouri River and threatened future attacks. As Chiwere Siouans related to the Otos, Ioways and Winnebagos, the Missourias had been a principal trading tribe at Fort d'Orleans in the 1720s but had since declined in population and prominence due to European diseases and the devastating raids of northern Algonquians. Now that the Grand Osages had made a recent trade alliance with Laclède, they sought to drive out weaker rivals. The Missourias came to the town that had ruined their lives in the hope that they could preserve their lives by living in that town. Although Chouteau emphasized that the Missourias had no "evil intentions," he sent an urgent message for Laclède to return from Illinois to meet with them.[159]

In a three-day parley with the Missourias, who stayed for two weeks, Laclède demonstrated his developing talents as an Indian diplomat. The Missouria chiefs stated that they were like wandering, hungry ducks and geese that were "worthy of pity" (i.e., deserved presents) and wished to build a permanent "nest" in St. Louis for protection from hostile birds of prey. Employing the traditional cadence and metaphors of Indian parleys as he addressed the Missouria women, as well as the men, Laclède refused to allow them to settle there, where they would literally be "sitting ducks," with too few Frenchmen to save them from vicious eagles and vultures in human form. Laclède had to protect his settlers from intertribal warfare and could not afford to alienate the Grand Osages by sheltering the targets of their raids. Moreover, the Missourias were getting in the way of the workers; Chouteau observed that they "did not allow us to be firmly in charge." Being a kindly "father," however, Laclède gave the Missourias gifts of awls and ammunition, vermilion and verdigris, as well as French-grown maize from Cahokia, before sending them on their way. Because generosity tempered his firm denial, the Missourias traded with the town for another quarter century.[160]

In that successful parley, Laclède demonstrated his independent decision-making. Henceforth, St. Louis would offer open hospitality to all friendly Indians, while allowing none to reside permanently within the town. His first principle contradicted a cardinal rule of Governor-General Kerlérec, who mandated that all major Indian parleys be held at Mobile, rather than in New Orleans, because "it is not advisable that people who might someday become hostile to us be familiar with the capital and its environs." Laclède's second principle diverged from the traditional French Illinois practice of dual settlements with "domiciled Indians." Because of Kerlérec's direct involvement with the Natchez massacre of over two hundred French colonists in 1729, Laclède appreciated the fatal consequences of crowding Indian lands and threatening their cultures. He also would have known that in 1743 French Cahokians had urged their Indian neighbors to move to the area of ancient Cahokia "so as to avoid the quarrels that the close proximity of the French and Indian villages frequently occasioned." When those Illini resisted relocation, Catholic priests plowed fresh fields for them at the new site and gave them presents before they would move. Laclède believed that permanent proximity bred contempt among culturally diverse populations, as it still does even among blood relatives, and he did not want personal tensions to erupt into social crises. Maintaining physical distance for most of the year would make the annual official visits of all tribal delegations truly special occasions for conferences and camaraderie.[161]

To complement those residential restrictions, Laclède organized the St. Louis fur trade on the *en dérouine* system already familiar to local Indians long accustomed to being visited in their villages by Canadian coureurs de bois. Laclède wanted tribes to remain in their distant homelands, harvesting and processing animals according to the Osage hunting calendar, until he dispatched his French or métis *engagés* and voyageurs each spring to buy furs in Indian towns. That encouraged "transient connexions" of intercultural sex to help solidify business transactions with blood ties, while resolving problems of transportation in an expansive trading territory. Even though all of the major hunting tribes in the region lived along rivers, their warriors were not proficient in navigating treacherous waters in unfamiliar bateaux or rafts loaded with heavy cargoes. Experienced boatmen, not Indians, transported huge mammal harvests to St. Louis. Missouri's Indians saw that "pick-up" system as a convenient courtesy, much preferable to the laborious process of carrying furs to distant forts and risking the raids of rivals along the way. The British, after 1763, alienated thousands of Indian hunters from the Great Lakes to the Mississippi Valley by establishing such isolated outposts staffed by intimidating soldiers. Laclède took advantage of that to increase his market share, but his larger strategic purpose was to focus annual Indian visits to St. Louis on diplomacy and hospitality rather than buying and selling. Thus, he reaffirmed the traditional distinction between presents and purchases, eliminated haggling in public and minimized intertribal jealousy by preventing trade competitors from knowing the volume and value of one another's harvests. Such prudent sensitivity to native sensibilities contributed to the special "spirit of St. Louis," which extended warm welcomes to all friendly Indians, whether or not they traded with the town.[162]

Making Money from Dead Mammals

Obviously, St. Louis would have developed far differently if Laclède and Chouteau had not been French pioneers in the western fur trade. After almost 275 years of European coercion, conquest and conversion had left a sad legacy of devastating microbes, massacres and missions across North America, St. Louis reaffirmed French Canadian views that the most positive and meaningful relationships with Indians were commercial. Fur trading was the only activity on colonial frontiers with the capacity to unite rather than divide alien populations, requiring Europeans and Indians to adjust their attitudes for greater compatibility without dramatically altering the special traditions and unique contributions that made each group supreme in the separate roles they played in a mutually beneficial business. Indians were indispensable partners because, in the classic French fur trade, they did all the animal harvesting and processing in their jealously guarded homelands. French merchants were responsible for importing the desirable products that Indians never had—trade goods of metal, cloth and glass from European forges, looms and furnaces—and exporting the "soft gold" of fur harvests to worldwide consumers.

Although Laclède named his town to honor a Christian warrior-king who attacked Muslim "infidels" in the Holy Land, the merchants of St. Louis could only make a killing in the fur trade if they protected, rather than destroyed, the local "heathens." Secular capitalists created a truly blessed land without the violence regularly perpetrated by religious fanatics in every age. The fur trade made peace and prosperity contingent on each other, as white entrepreneurs maintained close contacts with Indians, earned their trust, valued their contributions, supplied their needs and protected their lands, liberties and lifeways. By constantly crossing cultural borders and ethnic boundaries, fur traders developed an enlightened empathy with "noble savages" that European philosophers could barely grasp. They gained a precious, extensive knowledge of different peoples and new places through their frequent contacts with Indian wisdom-givers. As multilingual culture brokers, fur traders were the other colonists' eyes and ears on the frontier, and the best of them became sensitive, savvy diplomats with tolerant attitudes about Indian sovereignty and liberal views of sex with native peoples.

The close contacts between white traders and native trappers deep in the hinterland produced creative amalgamations of European-Indian customs and the procreative blending and bonding of bloodlines. "The French," wrote an Englishman in 1763, "gain the affection of Indians" by "their superior dexterity in address,...civility of usage" and "*matrimonial ties.*" Métis ethnogenesis—the creation of a new North American people of mixed heritages and hybrid cultures—represented the physical embodiment of such relationships. For a time, French royal policy supported such liaisons, and Jean-Baptiste Colbert, Louis XIV's chief minister, was perhaps the only European official in the seventeenth century who "favored intermarriage between the Indians and the French to produce one people." Several historians have argued recently that there was a European backlash against such sexual encounters in an effort to preserve French racial and cultural "purity." But what happened on frontiers stayed on frontiers, with actual backcountry behavior often conflicting with the idealistic expectations of elite officials in capital cities on both sides of the

Atlantic. Bonds of sex reflected the rare equality of leverage represented by codependent populations. Indians realized that only Europeans could provide sophisticated manufactured products from across the sea, while white traders knew that only God could make fur-bearing animals, with Indians controlling access to the last of the most desirable species on the planet. Both groups were grateful to, and for, each other, since each thought it was getting the better deal in the process of exchange. Physical intimacy has often resulted from far less compelling circumstances.[163]

Everyone involved in fur trading was seeking stability, order and uninterrupted access to products that could only be obtained safely, consistently and conveniently in an atmosphere of mutual trust. The personal integrity of Indian hunters and European merchants was essential for successful, sustainable commerce. Two modern concepts—*conspicuous consumption* and *planned obsolescence*—perpetuated fur trading over many centuries. Because muskets broke, ammunition ran out, beads got lost and cloth shirts rotted, Indians needed constant resupplies of imported trade goods, replacing the same consumer items season after season, while European merchants invested their profits in other areas. The scales were always tipped in favor of the white importers, even if wise native nations became merely reliant, rather than utterly dependent, on merchandise made abroad. The supply of animals might run out, but iron never did. The one safeguard against desperate Indians stealing an entire season's worth of merchandise was their need for—and the merchants' promise of—regular, reliable and *long-term* supplies of consumer items destined to wear out.

Founded just after the Jesuits were expelled from America and six years before Spain established permanent governance, St. Louis avoided the meddling by either church or state that had plagued, and sometimes paralyzed, the fur trade in Canada. Fur traders had always longed for, but rarely found, such a compatible commercial paradise so free of control, conflict, competition and the cross purposes of priests. Religion would play no role in the colonial St. Louis fur trade. While French Catholics and English Protestants sought separation based on intense biases, despite worshipping the same savior, secular merchants pursued self-interested commerce with "heathen savages" who often hated all Christians. If the common belief in Catholicism was the spiritual glue that bound French St. Louisans together, the lucrative Indian trade was the nondenominational economic engine that transformed a tiny traditional village into a cosmopolitan city with global connections. A shared cultural heritage was a centripetal force that created community cohesion as solid as the limestone ledge upon which the town was built. But since that rock represented the stability of a comforting home base, it encouraged centrifugal forces that allowed capitalists to reach geographically distant and culturally alien native nations, where compatible *behavior* counted more than inherited beliefs and the common desire for mutual profits superseded conflicting worldviews. Only the willingness of not-so-hostile "savages" with the knowledge and talents to transform stinking skins into gold made St. Louis *the* "center of manners, urbanity, and elegance" in Upper Louisiana less than a decade after its birth on a "wilderness frontier."[164]

A Great Flood—of People

The profitable cooperation of the Grand Osages was essential to the economic prosperity of St. Louis, but French families *made* the town, both literally and figuratively. Despite its founding in a period and a place that were technically Spanish, St. Louis would always be French at heart in terms of culture and commerce, purpose and personnel, as decisions in New Orleans and diasporas from Illinois preserved French traditions in the land of the Osages. Thanks to impeccable planning, location and timing, St. Louis profited from the fastest land rush of any French settlement in the eighteenth century. An influx of accomplished, acculturated and acclimated Illinois colonists ensured the viability of the boomtown only six months after the construction crew first arrived, and the greatest problem for Laclède and Chouteau was accommodating that throng in an orderly and efficient manner.

Laclède's recruiting efforts at Nouvelle Chartres worked all too well, and new arrivals claimed town lots so quickly that those property allocations were not even recorded in *Livres Terriens* (land books) for the first two years. Another eighty-one town lots that were recorded between 1766 and 1770 solidified the dominance of French people, property and culture before the arrival of the first Spanish lieutenant governor. St. Louis accomplished what Versailles had not by relying on *families*, not forts, to provide permanence in record time. If "a thousand families instead of a thousand soldiers had been sent here," wrote the Illinois commandant in 1752, "the stock of population would maintain itself and could only grow, whereas a thousand soldiers can only decrease." St. Louis validated the projections of Kerlérec and Maxent by demonstrating how an empty prairie could be "populated without expense to the kingdom," thanks to eager, grateful squatters who attended to the "defense of their homes" without the need for a large garrison of regular troops.[165]

Choice, not chance, lay behind Laclède's most significant achievement—transforming a mere trading license into an actual town. He demonstrated the utmost ingenuity in convincing the Illinois French to share his vision of a settlement both new and novel in the No Man's Land across the river. In 1814, Brackenridge observed that "it is indeed strange, how men can be induced voluntarily to tear themselves from the bosom of a refined and civilized society, to retire to a wilderness and become the neighbours of savages." But it was not so "strange" for the Illinois French, who came from a hybrid heritage of behavioral amalgamation, and sometimes genetically mixed ancestry as well, to blend birth traditions with innovative lessons learned through a lifetime of experience with cultural diversity. Laclède had to have those tolerant people used to living compatibly among Indians, sometimes in the same house. His colonists would be conservative in their desire to retain the stability and sanctity of old Catholic, kin-based communities but daring enough to be the first Europeans ever to inhabit a potentially dangerous site, without a priest to comfort them or troops to protect them. Those conflicting objectives were easier to reconcile because the move was a short one, and most of the early settlers made it with family and friends.[166]

For the past century, historians have engaged in rather silly criticisms of Laclède for founding a town, recruiting residents and distributing free land without having "even the semblance of [legal] authority as governor or commandant" to do so. Instead of suggesting that St. Louis should not have existed based on the formalistic technicalities of what constituted "normal colonization," we should praise Laclède's audacity and recognize, as he did, that the town was built on a *legal bluff* even more gigantic than its limestone ledge. Laclède acted appropriately for a "rogue" colonizer, especially considering the chaotic conditions in New Orleans, where French officials still governed more than six years after Louis XV had ceded it to Spain. St. Louis arose by individual initiative on land that France no longer owned or Spain yet controlled in a precious period of salutary neglect, when no supreme royal authority in Europe was paying attention. Even Louis Houck, one of the critics who harped on "illegality," credited Laclède's "forceful and dominant character" for "delivering" a healthy infant settlement, despite dubious parentage that made it a "bastard."[167]

Laclède's good judgment, great tenacity and powers of persuasion were essential for recruiting residents, since moving to St. Louis was not the only option for the Illinois French. They could choose to stay put, go to New Orleans or relocate to the older, more stable town of Ste. Genevieve on the west bank. That would have been the safer choice, and many Kaskaskia residents joined relatives there. But Ste. Genevieve could not accommodate all the Illinois émigrés, and new arrivals without kin in that town may have been treated as second-class citizens in a preexisting social hierarchy. The predisposition to farm or trade was also a consideration, with St. Louis proving more attractive to those who wanted to be merchants or hired hands in the fur trade. The lure of free land, which Laclède offered, should not discount or diminish the courage of the earliest St. Louisans. They were the ultimate risk-takers among the Illinois French, people who took a chance on a purely speculative venture that may have proved disastrous. But they were experienced squatters, willing to "invest" their very lives in a new venture in order to be on the ground floor as participants in an enterprise as novel as the original colonization of Illinois—and potentially more rewarding.

At least four "waves" of charter colonists populated St. Louis between February 1764 and March 1766, and Nouvelle Chartres was clearly the indispensable "mother" settlement of Laclède's infant town. The FIRST WAVE consisted of Chouteau's initial construction crew of skilled craftsmen and militia members from that town who were, or would be, married with sizable families. The SECOND WAVE of settlers came from the Fort de Chartres area, as well, just before or soon after June 15, 1764, the day that Commandant Neyon de Villiers formally evacuated most of his garrison. He headed to New Orleans in twenty-one bateaux and seven large pirogues loaded with six officers and sixty-three marines from the fort, plus eighty local civilians and a large amount of their possessions. Contrary to Chouteau's erroneous and slanderous allegations about the commandant's motives in his "Narrative," Neyon de Villiers had been "very Active in Enticing the Inhabitants of this [Illinois] Side, to go over to the other," if they did not wish to relocate to New Orleans. Almost everyone in Prairie du Rocher stayed put, but both Cahokia and Ste. Genevieve received new residents, with merchants and voyageurs generally choosing the former to continue in the Illinois River trade, while farmers more often selected the latter site.[168]

The remaining residents in or near Nouvelle Chartres would have had to make a critical decision about their future after the commandant's departure. British troops would not arrive for sixteen months, and it was more perilous to stay in a lonely, near-empty town than to follow friends to St. Louis. An early nineteenth-century American noted that the French "cannot bear the idea of separation," since for them to "live in a country without a neighbour in less than half a mile is worse than death." According to Victor Collot, "wherever we [French] go, we wish to plant ourselves…[with] our own tastes, manners, customs, and language….The French unite, and form themselves into towns and villages, whilst others disperse and melt into the mass of people" from other nations and cultures. Like sand in an hourglass, once a critical mass of people had abandoned Illinois, life was not as congenial in the old villages. With too few Nouvelle Chartres residents left to support it, the Church of Ste. Anne closed, and only a single priest remained to transfer the precious silver communion vessels to Prairie du Rocher, where they remain to this day (see color insert). A sudden shortage of farmers, craftsmen and consumers diminished both agriculture and commerce, but there were more immediate and serious "push" factors in June 1764. Ignoring Laclède's advice at their parley with him, the Missouria tribe did not head for home but went to Illinois instead. A few of the earliest St. Louis residents had fled when the Missourias arrived there, but they now returned to the west bank when those Indians passed through Cahokia on their way to Nouvelle Chartres. The returning colonists were grateful to be back on the high limestone ledge because a recent flood had devastated the American Bottom—validating Laclède's wise site selection in a very dramatic fashion. Saint Ange reported that the flood was an "inundation…so great" that it caused "the harvest [to be]…very bad" and began to "undermine the banks, especially below the fort, so that the village [Nouvelle Chartres] runs much risk."[169]

At least forty new *families* established permanent residency in St. Louis during the summer of 1764. Almost all were from the Fort de Chartres area, fleeing from "a state of anarchy and confusion" in political and economic affairs. Another flood the next year left Nouvelle Chartres "quite depopulated, the River having run away with half of it, and…will carry away the Fort next Spring [1766]." By 1765, there were only "three or four poor families" left near the old fortress. Chouteau described most poignantly how pragmatic colonists "pulled down" their houses and scavenged "the boards, the window and door frames, and everything else they could transport" to reuse across the river. Those activities were so frequent and extensive that an eyewitness declared that St. Louis was "formed out of the ruins of St. Philippe and Fort de Chartres." Although their lives and living quarters had been ripped apart, the undaunted émigrés from that garrison town would reconstruct both as part of the total inheritance—material as well as cultural—that the French East bequeathed to the French West.[170]

A third wave of settlers came to St. Louis in the fall of 1764, coinciding with the arrival of Madame Chouteau and her four youngest children in September. Director-General d'Abbadie gave her family preferential treatment (a clear indication that he knew of Laclède's liaison), since they were the only passengers in a "royal convoy" of three bateaux commanded by Antoine Berrard and Louis Chauvet Dubrueil—both natives of La Rochelle and high-ranking members of Laclède's clique of merchants born in France. In the same season, some farmers harvested their last crops in Illinois before moving to St. Louis, and thanks to Madame Chouteau's example, mothers of infants were reassured that the new town was safe. Also arriving that autumn were René Buet, a trader from Cahokia; Jean Baptiste Cardinal, a notable Illinois trader and farmer; Gabriel DeCarry, an interpreter of Indian languages from Fort de Chartres; Louis Deshetres, a miller from Cahokia; Louis Tesson Honoré, a Canadian-born trader from Kaskaskia; Jean Baptiste Provenchere, a wheelwright and farmer originally from Canada; and Alexander Langlois, one of three Quebec brothers who traded in St. Louis, Cahokia and Canada.[171]

The FOURTH WAVE headed for St. Louis shortly after October 10, 1765, the day when Captain Saint Ange, the last French commander in Illinois, surrendered Fort de Chartres to Captain Thomas Stirling's one-hundred-man contingent of Great Britain's Forty-second Regiment of Foot, the "Royal Highlanders" or "Black Watch." Only seventy-six men from the original twelve hundred troops in that unit would live to see Scotland again, and the tattered appearance of those soldiers from Fort Pitt provided "great encouragement" for French residents to move across the river with Saint Ange's soldiers—"most of whom did." On October 23, 1765, Saint Ange brought to St. Louis the last twenty French marines who served at Fort de Chartres, and these men, all born in France, represented a new corps of talent for years to come:

Dr. Andre Auguste Condé, post surgeon, son of a Bordeaux merchant
Jean Baptiste Hervieux, royal armorer and gunsmith
Lieutenant Eugene Pourré, *dit* Beausoleil, a noted St. Louis militia officer for decades
Lieutenant Pierre Francois de Volsey, a highly decorated officer who was married to a niece of Saint Ange
Lieutenant Pierre Picote de Belestre, son of the Detroit commandant, who married another niece of Saint Ange
Sergeant Pierre Montardy, who would become a St. Louis merchant
Sergeant Philibert Gaignon, who took up farming
Private Claude Tinon, who married a woman from Kaskaskia
Private Jean Comparios, who became a farmer
Private Nicholas Royer, who took up fur trading.[172]

The arrival of Saint Ange was one of the most significant events in early St. Louis history, but why did he relocate there instead of to Ste. Genevieve, the more mature town located far closer to Fort de Chartres? Only knowledge of Kerlérec's alliance of merchants and military officers can provide an adequate answer. Acting Governor Aubry reported to the Ministry of Marine on January 27, 1766, that "St. Ange...*following my orders*, passed to the other bank with his garrison," but "*he* has chosen" St. Louis "as the most convenient" site. Saint Ange, of course, wanted to join other members of the Maxent alliance, and his troops followed because Laclède's town was the one place that most needed their professional military skills and could best provide an income when their army pay ended. St. Ange's move was planned in advance, since six weeks *before* Aubry sent his letter to France, the leading British officer in Illinois reported that "French Emissarys" from St. Louis were encouraging "Inhabitants to leave us" by spreading the rumor "that all the French Officers are to be Continued by the Spaniards, and the Government of the other side [is] to be entirely French." Although Fort de Chartres marines could not legally kill redcoats anymore, at least they could wage a trade war with the British. Aubry believed that the St. Louis fur trade "is going to take a fall on the arrival of the English in the Illinois country, if one does not seek to increase it by carrying the commerce into the northwest of Louisiana and the northern part of the Mississippi River," which corresponded to the boundaries of Maxent's monopoly. "The Missouri" was "one of the greatest rivers in the universe," Aubry wrote, and the rewards of exploring that mostly unknown waterway will be "very beautiful and rare peltries" and perhaps "the discovery of the western sea"—allurements of adventure that probably appealed to frontier soldiers.[173]

When Commandant Saint Ange arrived with his authority intact, the "First City in the New West" also became the capital of Upper Louisiana, which more than compensated French residents for the loss of Old Illinois. An Englishman in Nouvelle Chartres reported that "the French have many Agents here," who are inducing the French "to leave their Settlements and go over to the other side of the river....The great attention they give to this new Colony appears very Extraordinary." Aubry served St. Louis well, since he convinced the first Spanish governor, Antonio de Ulloa, after his arrival in New Orleans on March 5, 1766, that Saint Ange should remain as commandant because of his incomparable skills in Indian diplomacy. Saint Ange may or may not have been commissioned in the Spanish infantry, but he continued as commandant until May 20, 1770—and, as the rumors reported, his administration was entirely French. He was ably assisted in governing St. Louis by royal officials from Fort de Chartres: Joseph Labuscière, notary, attorney and secretary, who produced 194 legal documents in the new town over four years, and Joseph Lefebvre (d'Inglebert des Bruisseau), former fort paymaster and experienced civil judge, who had held the fur trade monopoly at Fort de Cavagnal between 1744 and 1750. Saint Ange also bolstered the military capabilities of St. Louis by bringing from Fort de Chartres fourteen grenadier guns, fifteen hundred gunflints, eleven cannonballs, a half ton of bar lead for making musket balls and a large quantity of replacement parts for firearms, plus merchandise desired by both French and Indians: sixteen axes, twenty-seven tomahawks, 616 scalping knives, a gross of butcher knives and seventy-four trade blankets.[174]

The FIFTH AND FINAL WAVE of charter colonists went to St. Louis soon after the British completed their occupation of Fort de Chartres (renamed Fort Cavendish). In early December 1765, Major Thomas Farmar and Great Britain's Thirty-fourth Regiment of Foot arrived to relieve the Black Watch after a grueling five-month river voyage from New Orleans. They almost starved to death during their first winter at the fort because the "few remaining French inhabitants were antagonistic, and the Indians were insolent." That hostility forced British officials to postpone the administration of the required oath of fidelity to Great Britain until March 1, 1766. Although the French were allowed to practice their Catholic religion, they were "commanded" to declare their loyalty to King George III if they wished to remain in Illinois. Officials "forcibly" admonished them to "act in concert with His Majesty's officers," in order to spare that monarch "the necessity" of using troops to bring "the scourge of bloody war…into their country." That threatening, offensive language confirmed the worst rumors about an authoritarian "English yoke," and Illinois residents resented so many redcoats, who were nonetheless ineffective in protecting them from roving foreign Indians. British officals found it impossible to conduct a census, and while they waited for formal declarations from residents about whether they intended to stay or leave, many of them disappeared to the "French side" of the river. Some "drove off their Cattle in the night and carried off their Effects and grain," using the ferries at Cahokia or Kaskaskia, which British troops were unable or unwilling to prevent. As an officer lamented, "if the gentlest methods are not used with those that Stay…we shall lose them too."[175]

A Complex Community of Some Size

Historian Colin Calloway recently stated that in the transition to British rule in Illinois, "Kaskaskia, Cahokia, and Chartres became depopulated as some 2,000 people crossed the Mississippi and took up residence in the new towns at St. Louis and Ste. Genevieve." That figure is much too high even for a broad generalization with vague dating. The earliest known militia roster for St. Louis, dated July 27, 1766, listed the names of 128 males, aged sixteen to fifty, who were serving under old Captain Martigny, which would suggest a total white population of 300 or more. In 1771, Thomas Hutchins, an expert cartographer who had visited St. Louis, reported that the town contained "800 inhabitants, chiefly French," living in "120 houses, mostly built of stone," as well as "about 150 negroes." That is highly inflated, as well. In the 1773 Spanish census, St. Louis had 46 percent of the population in Upper Louisiana, with more white residents of all ages than Ste. Genevieve—444 to 400—but the latter's larger numbers of black slaves kept it in the lead, with a total population of 676 to 637. The misnamed "Bicentennial 1776 (Reconstructed) Census of St. Louis," compiled by Robert Parkin, listed 1,287 men, women and children of all races as living a dozen years after the founding of the town, with another 115 already buried in the Catholic cemetery. The former figure is, again, too high, since some people on his list arrived many years after 1776.[176]

Head counts alone tell us very little about a frontier society, and other sources are more revealing about how residents lived their lives. Of the 218 St. Louis militiamen, aged fourteen to fifty, on the infantry (167 men) and cavalry (51) rosters in late 1779, 67 percent—22 merchants, 17 traders, 84 boatmen and 24 hunters—were employed in the fur trade, compared with only 46 farmers, 22 craftsmen and 3 others (a courier, constable and musician). The skilled craftsmen included 4 blacksmiths, 4 carpenters, 4 masons and a sawyer, who built houses; 2 coopers, who made barrels and kegs needed in the fur trade; and 2 bakers and a butcher. In addition, residents were served by 2 cobblers, a tailor and a silversmith, who may have made Indian trade jewelry.[177]

As might be expected, an overwhelming number of those white male residents in 1779 originated in French fur trading regions—137 (63 percent) were born in Canada and 46 (21 percent) in "Illinois" (including St. Louis), but only 4 (2 percent) originated in New Orleans. Another 29 militiamen (13 percent) were born in France, which confirms the growing reputation of St. Louis as "a refuge of all the French"—a commercial magnet with a congenial culture and familiar language that appealed to immigrants near and far. But the town also symbolized cultural diversity, since many later arrivals originated in Spain, England, Ireland, Italy, Germany, Mexico, the Caribbean and "Indian Country"—making the term "Creole Corridor" inaccurate for reflecting such different backgrounds.[178]

St. Louis was racially diverse, as well. Among the earliest St. Louisans was a free black woman, Jeanette Fourchet, who owned a house and farm lot; she married two free black men, one of whom, Valentin, was a gunsmith and trader to the Osages in the 1780s. Joseph Neptune lived as a free African American, and the city census of 1796 revealed that there were forty-one other free blacks in town. "Spanish law was even more favorable to the slaves than was the old French Black Code," since Spain "had no problem about races mixing and encouraged slaves to purchase their freedom." The local use of the term *griffe*—meaning a child of an Indian and an African—confirmed that racial diversity included sexual relations between two nonwhite groups.[179]

While blacks could enjoy freedom, a large percentage of the Indians who lived in St. Louis were slaves: 15 percent of the town's population in 1766. Fur trading made St. Louis the regional capital of Indian slavery, a secondary "skin trade" that had always been a traditional component of frontier commerce. The Grand Osages did not keep slaves themselves, but they were the major suppliers of enemy captives to St. Louis merchants. Indian slaves from at least twenty different tribes lived in St. Louis, but none of them was Osage. Because the Spanish tried to ban the enslavement of Indians, those captives "disappeared" from censuses after 1770, while continuing to inhabit the town for many more decades. The research of Sharon E. Person recently revealed that *after* the 1769 Spanish prohibition, church records confirmed that 54 St. Louisans still owned Indian slaves. In 1770 alone, 37 residents owned 68 Indians (40 females and 28 males of all ages), and by 1803, 70 different residents had owned at least one. In the 1770s, 103 Indians were baptized in St. Louis, and half of them were slaves, while twenty years later, 48 Indians were baptized, but only 8 were slaves.[180]

The presence of urban Indians was to be expected in a fur-trading town, but so, too, was gender imbalance, due to the large numbers of young white males who worked in that industry. In 1773, St. Louis's male-to-female ratio among whites aged fourteen to fifty was 188 to 71, but reducing the severity of that sexual disparity was the greater availability of Indian women as lovers and spouses. This sampling of residents from Parkin's "Reconstructed Census" reflects the intimate roles that Indians played in making St. Louis society much more progressive with regard to interracial and multicultural relations than its Anglo-American contemporaries:

Alexis Alarie, an Illinois-born trader married to a métis wife, Marie
Louis Beor, a Canadian hunter living with Marie, a freed Indian slave
Louis Blanchette (founder of St. Charles), a Quebec hunter with an Osage wife and three children
Jean Bodoin, a trader from Ireland with an Indian wife
Jean Baptiste Brot, a voyageur with an Indian wife
The Cardinal family, with eight females born in "Indian Country"
The large Mongrain clan of Chouteau interpreters and traders of mixed, mostly Osage, ancestry
Michel Charleau, a middle-aged Mohawk
Charlot, a nine-year-old Mesquaki
Lafortune, a female Huron
Marie Josephe Duval, Pados Fournier and five more listed as Indians
Ciga and Elizabeth Lachapelle, both described as Osage wives
Jean Baptiste Dequirigoust, *coureur de bois*, living with Marie, a "sauvagesse"
Louis and René Dupré, brothers who lived with Charlotte, an Omaha
Jacque l'Arrivee, a Canada-born trader with a Sioux wife and three children
Louis Lirette, a Canada-born boatman, who fathered two children with an Indian "slave"
Louis Mahas, an Indian trader who was himself an Omaha Indian
Veronique Prunet Marcheteau, probably a Pawnee with a métis son
Francois Martin, a Canadian voyageur with an Osage wife
Joseph Pineau, a Kaskaskia-born farmer with a free Sioux wife, Angelique
Joseph Thibault, a hunter with a Pawnee wife and three children
Jean Tomaso Uvaldy, an Italian tanner with a Sioux wife and one child.[181]

Nous Ne Sommes Pas Tout des Sauvages ("We Are *Not* All Savages")

Nous sommes touts Sauvages ("We are all savages") was the ominous message that several French deserters from LaSalle's Fort Crevecoeur carved on a piece of wood in 1680 before fleeing into the forest. The defiant declaration by desperate individuals who abandoned familiar countrymen and resisted traditional subordination was a warning that close and frequent contact with Indians could make Europeans "wild," unleashing cultural contradictions they could neither comprehend nor control.[182]

Ninety years later, the French established an even more ambitious and long-term multicultural society at St. Louis that confronted the same issues: how many alien beliefs and behaviors could Europeans accommodate and/or adopt without becoming people they did not recognize or respect? Anarchy and tyranny were equal threats to social survival in a new settlement without a permanent priest to instill the moral teachings of the church or a strong royal governor to enforce the secular laws of the state. But neither resulted because the Illinois French were already comfortable with a community of negotiable conformity that indulged the freedom of individual behavior within established boundaries. St. Louis was perhaps the only place on the planet administered so congenially by resident and well-known French officials *who lacked the French king's authority*. In a consensual society, deference paid to the heroic old commandant and respect for the notary's knowledge of customary law sufficed to maintain social order while avoiding authoritarianism. "Civilized" behavior thrived in the "wilderness" because the émigrés from Illinois had long experience with a deferential society composed of masses and marines, patriarchal parenting and nosy neighbors, and they moderated their individualism in order to preserve community harmony. French St. Louisans were already well aware of what constituted crime and sin, and their greatest fear was being ostracized from the affection and protection of traditional village life, especially in a potentially threatening territory. They proved that contact with Indians did not promote savagery or stamp out the culture of one's upbringing, since hunters in deep forests, traders at distant villages and voyageurs on long expeditions yearned to return to congenial homes of reassuring familiarity.

As a mirror image of French Illinois culture, St. Louis experienced almost seven years of *good* luck in having new colonists create the society they wanted without outside interference or official coercion. Residents were free to experiment with social organization, but most found it hard to improve on the traditional Illinois system of local village governance and individual compromise derived from "the secret of real politeness—self denial." And who could be discontented "in a country where one can kill more…than can be consumed, and…everything is produced in plenty because the climate is favorable and the soil virgin"? If their new town was not an actual "State of Nature," St. Louisans could still tell Rousseau and other French philosophers something about a frontier utopia, "where every Man is allowed to do what he will with his own Person and Property, consistent with other

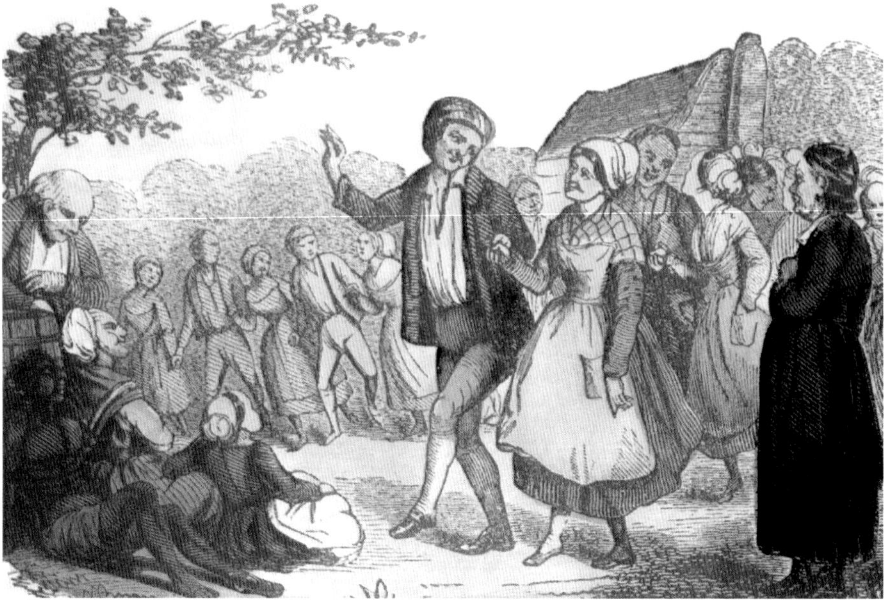

"Festivities" of the Illinois French, among the cultural celebrations transferred to St. Louis. *From author's copy of* Henry Howe, Historical Collections of the Great West *(1856)*.

Men's"—living "like Indians…much better than Men under Tyranny and arbitrary Government." Laclède's recruits lived safely, comfortably and compatibly in the heart of Indian Country with no fortifications to keep anyone out or anyone in. They enjoyed individual liberty, free enterprise, self-governance and other so-called "frontier virtues" that allegedly only "Americans" possessed, but the French did not need lawyers or jury trials, ballot boxes or legislatures, police or prisons in their pursuit of happiness. Such symbols of contentiousness and coercion "were of little use" in a small kinship community where "nearly all are connected by the ties of affinity and consanguinity" and "everyone knew how far to confide in his neighbor."[183]

St. Louis should have been called "a city on a hill" for marketing purposes because that new French settlement created a freer society than Puritan New England—avoiding harsh corporal punishments, witch hunts, pulpit harangues and Indian massacres. St. Louisans did not need a written "Mayflower Compact" to inhibit individual misbehavior for the good of society because they had a clearly understood "Osage Contract" that produced obvious rewards for adhering to the local laws of the Native

Ground. "The French took their civilization with them" when they moved to the West, and that included a respect for, and a dependence on, Indians. Dressing alike in moccasins, trade blanket capotes and buckskins, natives and newcomers "have been bred up together like Children in that Country," an eyewitness observed in 1765, "and the French have always adopted the Indians' customs & manners, treated them civilly & supplied their wants generously, by which means they gained the hearts of the Indians." Such exceptional traits of toleration and even affection far exceeded those of most frontier Anglo-Americans, who were known to attack even Indian *allies*—"cut[ting] and hack[ing] them to pieces." In 1766, Benjamin Franklin wrote that "it grieves me to hear that our Frontier People are yet greater Barbarians than the Indians, and continue to murder them in time of Peace." St. Louisans were neither victimizers nor victims when it came to violence, as they applied their live-and-let-live attitude to Indians as well as their own countrymen. Brackenridge observed that French residents in Upper Louisiana were "remarkable for their tame and peaceable dispositions."[184]

St. Louisans expressed their satisfaction with a congenial community of safety and ample subsistence with *joie de vivre*, but their hearty pursuit of earthly pleasures has upset "self-righteous puritans" in every generation. They "danced on Sunday after mass…played billiards at all hours" and reveled in "religious rituals and pagan ceremonies" on twenty-seven Catholic holy days each year. St. Louis lacked a church building for its first six years and a permanent priest for eight, but that did not prevent residents from celebrating Christmas, *La Guignolée* on New Year's Eve, Mardi Gras/Carnival or the Feast of Corpus Christi. They regarded "rum, sugar, and coffee…[as] the world, the flesh and the devil" and consumed prodigious amounts of alcohol. But drinking and dancing, gambling and gamboling, did not make St. Louis a Sodom and Gomorrah. Even a recent critic of such "destructive" behavior had to admit that it was "integral to the sustenance, growth, and survival" of early St. Louis. Residents "adapted religious, racial, sexual, and legal norms to suit their needs…that made it possible for the community to survive and thrive."[185]

The "conviviality of Catholics" played into British Protestant biases about the "lazy," racy and allegedly "hungry" French, so much so that *Pain Court* (or "Pencur") was the only name that many Englishmen used in referring to St. Louis. The French may have played hard, but they worked hard as well. In 1770, the first Spanish lieutenant governor praised "San Luis" as the most "modern settlement" in Upper Louisiana because of "the energy" that the residents had "hitherto exhibited." Those free French-Americans were also thoughtful. In 1771, a British officer put traditional anglocentric prejudices aside to commend St. Louisans, observing that "some of them have had a liberal education, are polite, and hospitable." As a minimal gauge of basic education, 43 percent of 70 adult white males were able to sign their names in 1769, and 45 percent of 78 adult white males did so in 1775. In 1770, 73 percent of a small subgroup of fifteen *leading* citizens produced a signature on an official document.[186]

LACLÈDE'S DILEMMA: TO BE A FUR TRADER OR TOWN BUILDER?

To his credit, the man from the Pyrenees developed into a more important frontiersman than almost any of the English-speaking, Indian-fighting "heroes" born in the American backwoods. Linking the boardrooms of the capital city to the beaver dams of frontier forests, he ensured socioeconomic stability, keeping the cycle of exchange in motion as the one person in the early years who converted Maxent's money into Osage mammals and back again. In November 1765, Sir William Johnson, the British superintendent for Indian affairs in the northern colonies and the unrivaled master of Iroquois diplomacy, paid a supreme compliment to Laclède: "The French…are erecting a Post near the Mouth of the Missouri, where a Frenchman is now Established who carries on a vast Extensive Trade, and is acquiring a great influence over all the Indian Nations." According to Acting Governor Aubry in New Orleans, "the commerce in peltry…[was] flourishing" at St. Louis between 1764 and 1766, when "a million" furs were exported to France. With such huge volumes, and profit margins that ranged from 100 to 300 percent, Laclède's business was booming. In October 1766, he boasted to his older brother, Jean, that his "net worth at that time…[was] more than 200,000 livres."[187]

When three British army engineers—Captain Harry Gordon, Lieutenant Philip Pittman and Ensign Thomas Hutchins—visited St. Louis in August 1766 at the invitation of Saint Ange, they validated Laclède's claims of "very great profits" as "the principal Indian Trader." Gordon reported that there were already fifty families living in as many houses in St. Louis, which "seems to flourish very quick." He also observed that the "sensible, Clever, and…well Educated" Laclède already dominated "the whole Trade of the Missouri…the Mississippi Northwards, and…along Lake Michigan." British officials estimated that the Upper Mississippi could yield 110,000 pounds of furs annually and the Lower Missouri about 100,000 pounds. Gordon warned his superiors that Laclède "will give us some trouble before we get the parts of this Trade that belong to us, out of his Hands." He noted that "our possession of the Illinois is only useful at present in one respect: it shows the Indian Nations our Superiority over the French." But that was wishful thinking based on military, not commercial, considerations, and Gordon had to admit that, "coop'd up at Fort Chartres…we make a foolish figure [and] hardly have the Dominion of the Country, or as much Credit with the Inhabitants as induce them to give us any Thing for Money, while our neighbours [at St. Louis] have Plenty on Trust." Such complaints confirmed that the French on both sides of the Mississippi were sticking together to squeeze out better-funded Anglo-American merchants from Philadelphia. "The French carry on the Trade all round us by Land and Water," Gordon lamented, "and even the small Quantity of Skins or Furs that the Kaskaskias and Peorias…get by hunting is carried under our Nose to…Pain Court [St. Louis]."[188]

In 1767, British general Thomas Gage observed "that of all the Systems of Indian Commerce…within my Knowledge, I found none equal to that adopted by the French, which a long Experience proved to be a good one." English officials could hardly believe that the French—so recently "reduced to the lowest state of distress, beaten in all quarters of the world, their Fleets destroyed, their trade and credit sunk, [and]…upon the very brink of national ruin"—had succeeded in "obtain[ing] *by the Improvement of Trade* that advantage and superiority which they could not by their *Martial* Efforts." The plans of Kerlérec and Maxent were working to perfection, as French merchants dominated the Indian trade on both banks of the Mississippi. Increasing numbers of French and Indian residents of Illinois followed wealth to the West, which forced the British to recruit Anglo-American settlers to revitalize agriculture and commerce in nearly empty Illinois villages. But by favoring land-speculators who controlled millions of acres, while forcing Indians to trade at distant forts, the British committed the two worst errors that doomed their frontier policies. Continuing that vicious cycle of miscalculations, the "Expectation of an Indian Rupture" would be countered by "English Power" to "root out" and "awe both the French & the Savages." British force was no match for French friendship, however, in making the fur trade profitable, and before 1770, English officials in London, Philadelphia and Kaskaskia had to admit that "there is no good Prospect that the Commerce of the Mississippi will prove of much advantage to Great Britain."[189]

Those developments and Laclède's early personal success encouraged him to think big, on an imperial scale, perhaps inspired by his twelve-volume set of Crevier's *Histoire des Empereurs Romains depuis Auguste jusqu'à Constantin.* More than anything, he wished to bequeath his financial empire to "Emperor Auguste of St. Louis." But the initial bonanza from a backlog of furs accumulated during the war years would not last long. As profits declined, Laclède was torn between priorities—should his primary focus and lasting legacy be the Indian trade or the French town he created? He tried to give equal attention and ample funding to both, purchasing Tayon's gristmill in 1767 to feed residents, while successfully defending French domination of the fur trade when Spanish officials proposed to run it. But the termination of Maxent's trade monopoly, about which Laclède may not have heard until 1766, was devastating, both financially and psychologically. Competitors swarmed into the area, and Laclède's market share plummeted, but he remained convinced that fur trading gave him the wealth and status to benefit the town. Laclède took a huge risk in May 1769 by buying out Maxent's 75 percent share of their company for a staggering sum of eighty thousand livres—in promissory notes, not cash. At that time, Laclède's warehouse contained twenty-two thousand livres worth of trade goods and stored furs valued at twenty-five thousand livres. His other property included twelve slaves (appraised at fourteen thousand livres), buildings (twelve thousand livres), livestock (five thousand livres) and furniture, household items, tools and farm implements (two thousand livres). In 1768, Laclède had the funds to purchase another homesite and to build a new fifty- by thirty-four-foot stone house on it. But by deeding the property to the faithful Auguste and the four "Chouteau" children he fathered, Laclède signaled his concerns about financial instability that would lead to a future foreclosure. He would be cash poor from then on, as interest accumulated on his debt to Maxent and the installment payments were repeatedly delayed.[190]

Facing greater expenses and growing competition, Laclède reduced the scope of his trade, concentrating on the thousand miles of the lower Missouri River and the Osage territory down to the Arkansas River. He was not able to sustain the Upper Mississippi River trade named in the original Maxent license, since its northern boundary near present-day St. Paul, Minnesota, was more than five hundred miles upstream. As Captain Gordon noted, British traders in Canada had easier access to those distant "Parts of this Trade," and they proved to be ruthless competitors. Laclède became more aggressive, however, in keeping illegal interlopers out of his reduced trading territory. In April 1765, he protected Maxent's monopoly by intercepting illegal trader Joseph Calvé, confiscating 6,485 livres worth of merchandise belonging to Jean Duchurrut and Louis Mirat of Ste. Genevieve. That resulted in a costly judgment in a New Orleans civil court. Seven years later, Spanish officials appointed Laclède to lead a twenty-man posse to intercept another interloper on *their* behalf. After a brief gun battle near the Missouria and Petit Osage villages, Laclède's men confiscated the contraband cargo of Canadian-born Jean Marie Ducharme, an Iroquois Indian and sixteen other crewmen. The posse divvied up a small portion of the captured merchandise, which included 150 bearskins, hundreds of deerskins, fifteen deer heads filled with bear oil, eight swan skins, sixty-two trade blankets, ten muskets, bearskin bales of dried squash and meat, a feather pillow and a trunk full of mirrors, needles, awls, scissors, thimbles, lockets, crosses and nose rings.[191]

After that 1772 incident, which yielded individual shares too paltry to risk one's life for, Laclède invested more of his time and money in improving St. Louis. He was getting older, and Madame Chouteau may have scolded him about what would happen to their large family if he got killed over nose rings. Laclède took his civic responsibilities seriously, even when he did not have to, because he was obviously proud of having founded such a flourishing settlement. Following the dissolution of the company, he could have returned to New Orleans or France at any time, but he did not. Laclède leased his original house to Spanish officials, made expensive improvements to his gristmill, which was still the only local source of flour, and in 1774, he built the town's first jail under a Spanish contract.[192]

But combining public responsibilities with private business did not work out well. Laclède earned lasting fame for nurturing St. Louis but at the cost of his fortune, as all of his other enterprises failed. Laclède's old financial obligations, coupled with his new town investments, finally caught up with him. In an amicable foreclosure in December 1777, Maxent claimed Laclède's buildings and lands in St. Louis but supplied his former partner with over twenty-one thousand livres worth of merchandise on credit for another trading season. Later that month, an embarrassed, sickly and despondent Laclède wrote a gloomy New Year's Eve letter to Chouteau while visiting Maxent in New Orleans:

> *Good-bye, my dear sir, I desire to see you again and to be able to manage these affairs myself, for it is hard and painful…to die in debt; one bequeaths only sorrow and embarrassment to friends when one dies poor. Such is my deplorable situation; one must die and not murmur. Adieu.*[193]

That was the last known communication between them, since Laclède died the following spring aboard his boat, called *Hope*, at the age of forty-eight. He was heading home to St. Louis and did not quite reach Arkansas Post, where his boat captain, Tropé Ricart, had him buried in the garrison's graveyard before reporting his death at St. Louis on July 19. Historians still debate whether Laclède died on May 27, or June 20, 1778, and there is support for both dates. However, Laclède's only biographer, Lucien Labarère, quoted a letter from Pierre to his brother Jean, dated *May 28*, while he was still in New Orleans. His friend Forstall attached a note before forwarding that letter to Pau, stating that he had accompanied Laclède on the first ten leagues of his voyage because he was "quite ill."[194]

Whatever the exact circumstances of Laclède's death, resolving his estate was even more confusing. Because of his well-known, but not legally recognized, "spousal" relationship with Madame Chouteau, there was "no relative nor heir to claim the right to his inheritance"—at least in America. For several years after 1778, Jean Laclède wrote letters to the French Ministry of Marine and the Spanish governor in New Orleans, claiming that he was the sole heir of his younger brother's estate. Citing Laclède's will of August 11, 1763, and his brother's letters to him, dated Christmas Day 1777 and May 28, 1778, Jean was convinced that Pierre was wealthy, had set aside a large fortune for him and intended to return to Bedous to bestow that inheritance in person. He was upset that his brother had lied to him about finances but was absolutely shocked to learn that Pierre had also kept his large American family a secret for decades.[195]

In addition to his "other life," Laclède was equally mysterious about bookkeeping, since he kept one set of accounts for Maxent and another ledger for the fur trading *pacotille* (private venture) he conducted with Auguste. In juggling so many responsibilities regarding trade and town, the city founder had great difficulty in keeping separate the government's official Indian gifts sent by Maxent, company imports for purchasing furs and the merchandise for his private transactions. Laclède insisted that he had "misappropriated nothing" and "diverted nothing" in confusing the ownership of an extensive inventory while wearing too many hats. In his New Year's Eve letter, Laclède apologized to Chouteau for the disorganized state of his complex, entangled finances. He owed money to merchants in St. Louis, La Rochelle (Monsieur Voye), Bayonne (Monsieur Cogombles) and, of course, to Maxent in New Orleans. But he held nearly twenty-eight thousand livres in IOUs (mainly uncollectible) from local residents.[196]

Acting as a town financier in much the same way that Indian chiefs were esteemed for their generosity, Laclède deserved great credit for sharing, rather than hoarding, whatever wealth he had. The final inventory of his property revealed that at least he would have looked the part of St. Louis's leading capitalist, carrying his silver-handled Toulouse sword and wearing a white linen shirt, white satin vest, blue silk trousers with silver braid, silk stockings, silver-buckled shoes and a brown morning coat with gold buttons. That inventory also showed that Laclède was not too proud to wear eyeglasses but was vain enough to use a curling iron. The Chouteaus kept his memory alive, with Auguste buying the water mill and pond at auction for 2,000 livres, plus some of his stepfather's two-hundred-volume library, while his mother paid 750 livres to keep the Grand Prairie farm in the family. Auguste's success in the trade he learned from Laclède allowed him to pay Maxent nearly 42,000 livres in January 1779 and over 41,000 livres the following summer (including 28,000 livres worth of IOUs).[197]

Laclède's Living Legacy

It is sadly ironic that although Laclède fathered four children with Marie Thérèse Bourgeois Chouteau, none of them bore his surname—which died out in America with his passing. That couple valued family, fortune and fame, but giving priority to family ensured personal satisfaction as well as professional success and proved far more valuable over time in providing stability to their beloved St. Louis.

While prominent Chouteau males are honored as heroes in the West, many Chouteau women should be credited with perpetuating a dynamic frontier dynasty of unusual stability despite a family business filled with debts, doubts and dangers. Marie Thérèse was as daring in defying social conventions as Laclède was in dealing with Indians, and the co-creator of their "royal family in the wilderness" was publicly acknowledged as the "Queen Mother" and "Matriarch of St. Louis" for half a century. After Laclède's death, Widow Chouteau lived independently in an imposing mansion between those of her two sons, made wise investments as a wealthy businesswoman and revealed her bourgeois mindset by suing a son-in-law for property damages in the death of a slave. When the matriarch died on August 14, 1814, at the age of eighty-one, she was survived by all but one of her five children, in addition to fifty-two grandchildren and sixty-nine great-grandchildren. Following her example, Chouteau wives, sisters, daughters, nieces and granddaughters extended and enhanced the family bloodline as "pelt princesses," even marrying first cousins in the ancient tradition of European royalty or Virginia gentry. The resilience of that ever-expanding dynasty over many generations was no accident, since marriage alliances were calculated with an accountant's eye for detail, as family pedigrees, special talents and business success were scrutinized for their potential to strengthen the "peerage" of self-made entrepreneurs that began with Laclède.[198]

The Chouteaus cherished their French heritage and recruited new family members from throughout France's old empire in North America—Montreal, Quebec, New Orleans, Illinois and Saint-Domingue—in the search for fresh blood and new business opportunities. But they also integrated a wide variety of other ethnicities into their extended family over successive generations, consolidating power and property within the cohesive bonds of kinship. John Francis McDermott, a Chouteau descendant himself, summarized the global reach achieved by that frontier family as it allied with "Walshes and Watsons of Ireland, Crooks of Scotland, Masures of Belgium, Bertholds of Italy, Cabannés, Sarpys, de Menils, Gourds, Montholons, Peugnets, Perdreauvilles, Provencheres, and Cortamberts of France, [and] von Phuls of Bavaria," in addition to non-French residents of the United States—"Carrs and Maffits of Virginia, Kingsburys and Hempsteads of Connecticut, Knapps and Tracys of New York, Ewings of Indiana, Morrisons of Philadelphia, Washburns of Maine, [and] Priests of Boston."[199]

The headaches and heartaches caused by Laclède's crushing debts at the end of his abbreviated life made the Chouteaus extremely cautious in arranging blood transactions with business implications. Thus, the formal marriage contracts of Auguste and Pierre Chouteau read like corporate mergers, as patriarchs of two merchant families negotiated on behalf of the bride and groom in front of the Spanish lieutenant governor. Prenuptial contracts provided financial security for the wives to be, as was the practice in both Béarn and Illinois, and large donations of cash were exchanged as "reciprocal proofs of…mutual affection" in the creation of a new "community of acquired goods…to be merged in a single mass."[200]

The senior Chouteau brothers married into French Illinois families, and their wives were the critical first "cuttings" from across the river that grew into the flourishing branches of the family tree in Missouri. In September 1786, thirty-seven-year-old Auguste married Kaskaskia-born Marie Thérèse Cerré (1769–1842), a rich heiress who was twenty years younger and had the same name as his mother. Her father, Jean-Gabriel Cerré (1733–1805), was a Canadian-born merchant who spent his first twenty-two years in Montreal, the next twenty-six in Kaskaskia and the last twenty-four years of his life in St. Louis. Cerré fathered four daughters but no sons, and Auguste's union with Marie Thérèse gave him two influential brothers-in-law: Pierre

Louis Panet of Canada, who looked after their eldest son, Auguste Aristide Chouteau (1792–1833), when he attended a Montreal school; and Antoine Pierre Soulard (1766–1825), the talented, influential king's surveyor for Upper Louisiana from 1795 to 1803.[201]

Auguste and Marie Thérèse had seven children who reached adulthood and two who did not. Their second son, Gabriel Sylvestre ("Cerre") Chouteau, a fur trader who donated his father's "Narrative" to the St. Louis Mercantile Library, lived until 1887, dying unmarried at the age of ninety-three. Their daughters, however, all married well. The oldest to reach maturity, Marie Thérèse Eulalie Chouteau (1787–1835), wed René Paul (1783–1851), a Paris-educated Frenchman who served in Napoleon's army; his brother, Gabriel Paul (1777–1845), married the second Chouteau daughter, Marie Louise (1799–1832), while Emilie Antoinette Chouteau (1802–1843) brought the Virginia-born Thomas Floyd Smith, a captain in the U.S. Army, into the fold.[202]

Auguste Chouteau's younger half brother and Laclède's only son, (Jean) Pierre Chouteau Sr. (1758–1849), married twice, at the ages of twenty-four and thirty-five, fathering eight sons and one daughter with wives who had roots in the Fort de Chartres area. His first wife was sixteen-year-old Pelagie Kiersereau (1767–1793), who inherited some ten thousand livres when her father, Paul, a charter colonist on Chouteau's work crew, died in 1772. She was raised by her grandfather, Joseph Tayon, the miller who assisted Auguste in breaking ground at the new town site. Pelagie gave birth to a daughter with the same name and three noted sons in fur trade history—Auguste Pierre Chouteau (1786–1838), one of the first permanent white residents of Oklahoma; Pierre "Cadet" Chouteau Jr. (1789–1865), who married his cousin Emilie Anne Gratiot and became the millionaire successor to John Jacob Astor's western empire; and Paul Liguest Chouteau (1792–1851), an influential agent to the Osages who married Constance Dubreuil, from another famous French fur trading family.[203]

Within a year of Pelagie's death, Pierre married sixteen-year-old Brigitte Saucier (1778–1828), granddaughter of Governor Kerlérec's architect of Fort de Chartres. That union allowed Pierre to fortify his fortune with business ties to three powerful brothers-in-law—James and Jesse Morrison and Pierre Menard, all merchants from Kaskaskia. The five sons of Pierre and Brigitte (the gracious hostess complimented by Lewis and Clark) are considered the founders of Kansas City. In order of birth, they were: Francois Gessau Chouteau (1797–1838), who wed his first cousin, Bernice Thérèse Menard of Kaskaskia (1801–1888), an important chronicler of life in western Missouri; Cyprien Chouteau (1802–1879); Pharamond Chouteau (1806–1831); Charles B. Chouteau (1808–1884); and Frederick Chouteau (1809–1891). Pierre's only daughter, Pelagie (1790–1875), married an Italian, Bartholomew Berthold (Bartolemeo Bertolla, 1780–1831), whose brother in Venice supplied St. Louis with the famous glass trade beads made there. Pierre's other sons and grandsons established several Indian families, which are discussed in the next chapter.[204]

The sisters of Auguste and Pierre also married well. In 1783, Marie Pelagie Chouteau (1760–1812) wed Sylvestre Labbadie Sr. (1737–1794), the Pyrenees immigrant who accumulated a huge fortune of 480,000 livres as Laclède's post-Maxent partner. Marie Louise Chouteau (1762–1817) wed Joseph Marie Papin (1741–1811) of Canada in 1779. He became a business partner of Labbadie and the Chouteau brothers after Laclède's death, and his daughter Julia married Spanish fur trader Benito Vasquez (1738–1810). In 1781, Victoire Chouteau (1764–1825) married Charles Gratiot (1752–1817), a Swiss-born Huguenot who became a successful merchant at Cahokia and a friend of George Rogers Clark. His extensive connections in London and Montreal greatly enhanced the Chouteaus' reach and revenues.[205]

Creating a Congenial Indian Capital

A wise government ought to found the basis of all...proceedings on the interest or power of... [its] *neighbors.*
—Perrin du Lac

When Laclède and Chouteau were voyaging up the Mississippi River in August 1763, General Jeffery Amherst, commander-in-chief of British armies in North America, expressed venomous personal opinions that would soon become offficial policy: "I wish there was not an Indian Settlement within a thousand miles of our Country, for they are only fit to live with the [animal] Inhabitants of the Woods, being more allied to the brute than to Human creation." His actions matched his harsh words when he decided to "send the Small Pox among...Indians" as a means "to extirpate this execrable race." Unlike English commanders and colonists, the French did not seek to eliminate Indians as either their first priority or their ultimate goal. Integrating lives and cultures in shared territories was far preferable to the dispossession of traditional native homelands—and, as St. Louis demonstrated, more profitable as well. If the British lost the allegiance of Indians in the East by their harsh policies, French St. Louis gained the affection of Indians in the West by its hospitable practices. From the beginning, the town demonstrated the spongelike qualities of frontiers, soaking up the lessons and legacies of intercultural contacts from other areas and earlier eras. A Spanish official observed that St. Louis was "surrounded...by a great number of savage nations," as well as the English, and was "exposed to...the barbarousness of the one and the jealousy…of the others." In fact, St. Louisans relied on wise diplomacy with *Indian friends* to counter the "barbarousness" of *English-speaking enemies*, who were the greatest threat to the survival and success of the town throughout the colonial period.[206]

The economic interests of French merchants seeking to do well and the political priorities of Spanish military officials trying to do good converged to make St. Louis a popular Indian capital in the turbulent years of the late 1700s. St. Louis was unique in being both an *official capital of governance* and the *dominant capital of commerce*, whereas in Illinois, Fort de Chartres had been the administrative center for Indian diplomacy, while Kaskaskia was the metropole driving the economy. Fur trading made French merchants wealthy, but *all* St. Louisans depended on their expertise in Indian *diplomacy* to protect their lives and livelihoods. A peaceful frontier was far more important than mere market share, and the distribution of private and publicly funded presents for Indian allies attracted trading and nontrading tribes to St. Louis in good economic times or bad. Those gifts were always separate from the purchases of furs. The commandant's official diplomatic presents for politically affiliated tribes and the merchants' gifts to trading partners meant that Indians often received twice the attention and double the merchandise. The Grand Osages qualified for European imports in both of those categories, as well as payments for furs, so that French merchants had twice the materialistic clout with them as Spanish commandants. Many historians take for granted that people have friends, while nations have interests, but such a distinction was not so clear-cut in St. Louis's relations with the Grand Osages. Because neither people felt pressure from a strong nation, trust among leading individuals in those two small, kin-based societies created an admirable alternative model of frontier development based on reciprocal accommodation rather than aggression. Unlike the short-term, frequently reassigned Spanish military officials, French merchants were permanent residents of St. Louis, which stabilized alliances with the longevity of personal attention and the remembrance of promises made and kept.

The Fort de Chartres Inheritance

Nouvelle Chartres gave early St. Louis most of its population, while Fort de Chartres established the lasting principles of Indian diplomacy in that new capital. Ample examples of French affinity for, and diplomatic sensitivity toward, native nations range from Samuel de Champlain's humanism in early seventeenth-century Canada to Kerlèrec's late eighteenth-century parleys at Mobile. But the model of Indian relations that was closest in time and space to St. Louis occurred under the Illinois regimes of Neyon de Villiers and Saint Ange at Fort de Chartres. A British officer wrote that when the commandant "made presents to the Indians…he received peltry and furs in return. [Since] the presents he gave were to be considered as marks of his favour and love for them, so the returns they made were to be regarded as proofs of their attachment to him." Another British observer stated in 1766 that "the French Commandants have always been Sharers in the Profits of [fur trading]…and do every thing in their Power to promote their common Interests" with merchants. Neyon de Villiers had long "captivated all the [native] nations" and was still performing "marvels of diplomacy" until he departed for New Orleans in June 1764, so the Maxent Model of pursuing self-interest in public service seemed to work.[207]

Saint Ange was not as venal as his predecessor, but his "practical knowledge of the Indians" was even greater. He personally maintained the continuity of French-Indian diplomacy from Illinois to Missouri and smoothed the way for the transition to Spanish-Indian diplomacy, by "employ[ing] affability and gentle methods, accompanied by…presents made at the right time." He always tried to deal honestly and honorably with Indians who had been his brothers in war, since it was "most advantageous to have…their friendship" in case they needed to be "summoned for [the] defense" of St. Louis. Personal experience taught him that Indian warriors "alone, with their method of warfare, will be sufficient to make the English refrain from attempting any undertaking" west of the Mississippi. Saint Ange was careful never to give the "slightest affront" to Indians through "jest or mockery," since they could be the "cruelest of enemies," and a "discontented tribe drags in its wake various other tribes allied to it." In May 1769, he conducted parleys at St. Louis with twenty-five tribes from four major language families, establishing the precedents of native diplomacy that influenced St. Louis's development for decades to come (see Table B).[208]

After the British occupied Fort de Chartres in late 1765, St. Louis became a multicultural magnet attracting most of the Indians who traditionally had traveled to dispersed French diplomatic capitals in Canada, Illinois and Louisiana. For most of the colonial period, at least 32 different native nations regularly held parleys in St. Louis, coming from the present-day states of Missouri, Kansas, Iowa, Nebraska, Arkansas, Oklahoma, Indiana, Illinois, Ohio, Wisconsin, Minnesota, Michigan, Tennessee and Mississippi, and in 1781, a record 130 tribes arrived to receive presents and advice after the

TABLE B

Native Clients of the Indian Capital of St. Louis

Visiting Indian Delegations, Representative Years // *Major Trade Partners, 1799, 1803*

1769	1777	1785	1793	// 1799	1803	(Trade Goods = $180 K)
Grand Osage	*	*	*	*	*	$35K (London prices)
Petit Osage	*	*	*	*	*	8K
Ioway	*	*	*	*	*	12K
Kansa	*	*	*	*	*	8K
Oto	*	*		*	*	8K
Pawnee	*	*	*	*	*	5K
Missouria	*	*		*	*	4K
Ponca				*	*	2K
Omaha	*	*	*	*	*	10K
Other Pawnee	*			*	*	4K

Minnesota Sioux	*	*			*	4K
Sauk	*	*	*		*	40K
Fox/Mesquaki	*	*	*		*	20K
----------						
					*	15K Lakota
					*	3K Mandan
					*	2K Arikara

Kaskaskia	*	*				
Cahokia						
Peoria	*		*			
Mechigamea						

Ottawa	*		*			
Potawatomi	*		*			
Saulteur	*					
Miami			*			
Piankashaw						
Shawnee		*	*			
Kickapoo	*					
Mascouten	*					
Menominee	*	*				
Winnebago	*	*				

Delaware		*	*			
Iroquois		*				
Cherokee		*				
Chickasaw		*				
Choctaw		*				

The most frequent contacts and consistent commerce were with the Lower Missouri tribes (bracket 1) and the Prairie Sioux, Sauks and Mesquakies up the Mississippi (bracket 2), while Illinois Algonquians (bracket 4) faded quickly. The Mid-Missouri River Lakotas, Mandans and Arikaras (bracket 3) began trading with St. Louis near century's end. The Great Lakes tribes (bracket 5) visited sporadically. The last five tribes sent delegates to a one-time conference.

Sources: Louis Houck, ed., *Spanish Regime in Missouri*, 2 vols. (1909) for the early years and A.P. Nasatir, ed., *Before Lewis and Clark: Documents Illustrating the History of the Missouri, 1785–1804*, 2 vols. (1990), especially p. 759, for the later period.

unsettling United States victory in the American Revolution. The town was a centrally located, easily accessible meeting ground where Indians from the Siouan plains, Caddoan prairies and Algonquian lakes could temporarily suspend their suspicions to conduct conversations without confrontations. Even though traditional tribal enemies could barely tolerate one another, they all literally embraced the French merchants of St. Louis, who encouraged "white and red sons…[to] visit each other, carry on their trade, and take good care of their wives and children." In a region ripped apart by decades of warfare, Indians were grateful that there was one *French* place of peace and safety, similar to the native calumet quarries of Minnesota, where all "red men could walk the white road" in the "clean earth" of a neutral site not "dirtied" by bloodshed. [209]

In only forty years, four different countries claimed sovereignty over St. Louis—but never Great Britain, which made the town even more attractive to a virtual United Nations of Native America. As native delegations declared, the Frenchman was their "first and true father" until he was replaced by a Spaniard, a supposed "new father," although the latter's lack of paternal attention and affection made him seem more like an indifferent "neighbor." The "Englishman [was only] a borrowed father, seeing that he made no alliance with our first father, the Frenchman." Director-General d'Abbadie understood those Indian sentiments, denouncing the British as a "people intoxicated with their success, who regard themselves as the masters of the world!" But he also expected "as much opposition on the part of the Indians to the Spaniards as to the English." When a temporary Spanish official first showed up in 1767 and tried to meddle in Indian diplomacy, French St. Louisans forced him to "adopt French practices in the government of the Indians" if Spain expected to "maintain…the same good relations and accord that the French have been able to preserve" with them.[210]

Commerce Was King

Since 1492, all European colonizers throughout North America had asked the same questions: could native populations be useful for the protection and prosperity of colonists, and would white settlements be better off with or without Indians nearby? By the time Spain's first lieutenant governor belatedly arrived in May 1770, Laclède and other French merchants had had six years to demonstrate the indispensability of Indians for making the fur trade the "sole and universal" source of profits and multicultural goodwill in St. Louis. "Self-interest is the motive force of all men," but the French financiers of furs took materialistic pragmatism to new extremes, creating a larger and more successful multicultural commercial enterprise than either they or their Indian partners had ever experienced. The leading merchants on the St. Louis "board of trade" quantified the usefulness of native nations in precise monetary terms. In assigning annual trade licenses, they calculated "shares" for each tribe, estimating how many 108-pound "packs" of furs would be delivered for the value of trade goods. Spanish lieutenant governors almost always took the advice of the richest merchants in granting official authorization because they supplemented their salaries with a portion of the harvests from the best trading tribes. Such conflicting public and private interests precluded frequent or long-lasting trade embargoes as a means of disciplining Indians. Maxent's monopoly created the initial Grand Osage-Laclède family alliance, and that remained the dominant economic power in Upper Louisiana for forty years, consistently controlling 50 to 60 percent of fur volumes and values.[211]

As early as 1768, fur exporters in New Orleans applauded Mammon on the Missouri. A "Memorial of the Planters and Merchants of Louisiana" in that year stated:

> *This trade is a very advantageous outlet for the products of several manufactures, which will shortly spread by encouragement. It is an abundant mine* [that]*...promises treasures more valuable than those of Potosi....From this exhaustless source arises the advantage of the public and of the individual. The merchant finds there a profitable sale for his goods; the laborer, employed in these journeys and in this trade, gets there the means of subsisting and of amassing a competency. The affection of the natives is kept up by frequent intercourse with the French, securing to them the results that necessarily follow from familiar acquaintance. Public security,...from which this trade with the barbarous nations that surround us has arisen, is preserved by it.*[212]

Between 1772 and 1775, St. Louisans shipped 625,000 pounds of furs to New Orleans, including 215,000 pounds of shaved and brain-tanned (dressed) deer leather and over 133,000 pounds of raw deerskins, when prices for them soared in France but soured in England. La Rochelle developed a booming market for book-binding with deer leather, and many a gentleman's library in fashionable France featured the "works" of Osage women along the "savage" frontier of Missouri. Even earlier, "deerskins were, after indigo, the largest export product of Louisiana," and in 1766 an envious British officer reported that the "principal Staple" of New Orleans was now "the Trade for Furrs and Skins from the Illinois," just as Kerlérec and Maxent had predicted. The Osages were the "true bankers of this region," since they produced the largest quantity of the best-quality deer leather, and their chamois-like "bucks" served as the main currency in Upper Louisiana long before St. Louisans saw an American dollar. In the mid-1770s, the Osages provided 64 percent of all deerskins but also 88 percent of bearskins and 44 percent of beaver pelts. As late as 1800, a visiting Parisian observed that Indian "peltries are the bills placed in circulation, and their hunting provides security for the fictitious specie upon which the merchants base their business." That commerce, "advantageous to everyone," was preserved and expanded by "bows, arrows, gunpowder, lead [and] guns."[213]

Representatives of both Bourbon kingdoms agreed that commerce was the predominant influence in relations with Indians along the Missouri River frontier, and they accepted the alternative white lifestyles that resulted. "License, laxity of conduct, and vice" were the "characteristics" of the early colonists, and "religion is given scant respect, or…is totally neglected." French and Spanish leaders in St. Louis also made no effort to "civilize" or Christianize the natives of Upper Louisiana for fear of offending them or altering their much-desired traditional traits as hunters. Ironically, fur profits from "heathen savages" were taxed for a time to support the construction of St. Louis Cathedral in New Orleans! Like France, Spain had recently suppressed the Jesuit Order at home and in its colonies, and the Inquisition, religious missions and crusading conquistadors were regrettable memories. Spanish officials in Louisiana tried to make amends for their country's genocidal "Black Legend," and in implementing the crown's progressive Enlightenment reforms, they were less rigidly Catholic and more catholic in their views of cultural pluralism. Their top priority was "preserving friendship with the Indians *at any cost.*" Governor-General Esteban Rodriguez Miró, who served in New Orleans from 1782 to 1791, was humane to a fault, employing "mildness and equity" to minimize violence. "Although the perfidy of the Osages is well known," he wrote to a subordinate, "it behooves us to observe always… international law in order to go on teaching them…[so] that the cultivated nations can never truly say that we have been imprudent or cruel." Even if the Osages make "a butchery of your post, killing as many people as they can,…you must listen to them without…mistreating them."[214]

Capitalizing on Diplomacy

Although "San Luis" had "no law, no faith, no king" (*sin ley, sin fe, sin rey*), it already deserved to be Spain's northernmost regional capital in the Western Hemisphere because of its success in merging valuable Indian diplomacy with profitable fur trading. In 1770, diplomatic expenses for the twelve principal native nations in the St. Louis District represented 56 percent of the total for all Louisiana's Indians, an increase of 44 percent over 1762, when Kerlérec had struggled just to procure enough shirts. The cost of administering all of Louisiana in 1778–85 had escalated 350 percent over the previous decade, and maintaining "Friendship of the Indian Population" alone amounted to 8.2 million reales.[215]

The annual Indian councils that Laclède and Saint Ange had begun quickly grew larger and more elaborate. A large parley in July 1778 attracted a who's who of important chiefs who came to St. Louis to welcome the new lieutenant governor, Fernando de Leyba. They included: Clermont, the "big medal chief" of the Grand Osages; Balafre, "the Scar," bellicose head of the Petit Osages; Missouria principal chief, Kaige; "El Comy" of the Kaws of Kansas; Chief Blackbird of the Mahas (Omahas); Kakieguemec of the Sauks; several Kickapoo headmen; and "El Tander" of the Mascoutens from Lake Michigan. Leyba opened the meeting in accordance with precise Spanish protocol, giving a speech (*parole*) to each delegation (dutifully translated and recorded) that expressed how honored he was that the chiefs had "taken the trouble to come to see" him. The tribes that presented Leyba with a gift of scalps were thanked and paid "at the accustomed rate and in the accustomed manner." He was obligated, however, to return to relatives any scalps lifted from the heads of friendly allies. In trying to dissuade such behavior in the future, Leyba followed this script: "If any tribe should bring me scalps from your tribe, would you yourselves be glad if I should receive them? I do not believe so." That sensitivity underscored Spain's commitment to universal peace by resolving intertribal disputes before they erupted into wider wars.[216]

Since most tribal delegations came to St. Louis "*en village*, that is to say, with their wives and children," Leyba prayed for a sufficient harvest of wheat and corn to feed several hundred Indian guests, who usually stayed for "two weeks, eating us out of house and home." Hospitality got so expensive that in 1771 the Spanish governor at New Orleans established a limit of 1,072 Indian "rations" of bread per year, which Pain Court *annually exceeded* by three to four thousand units in the next decade. At the parley of 1787, French merchants and Spanish administrators gave visiting Indians fourteen hundred jugs of "brandy made from sugarcane," which many local tribes "prefer[ed]…to any other present." But that was a parting gift to take home and not to consume at the conference, since Indians were "reasonable when in their right mind, [but] when drunk, they are importunate beggars, insatiable and tiresome," a Spanish official observed. Even though Indians sometimes drank at parleys, Spanish officials reported that "not one of them committed the slightest act of license" and certainly no serious violence.[217]

Trade fairs often coincided with the great councils, and in 1770, "daily Indian canoes [arrived], laden with food…and other trifles, which they sell publicly at their just price…and the Indians buy afterwards…what they need in the shops and stores and go away well satisfied." That rare image of reputedly "wild" warriors on a shopping spree raises the question of how St. Louisans behaved when so many different Indians were visiting. Town ordinances in the 1780s provide interesting answers. Topping the list of prohibited behavior for St. Louis residents was selling or giving intoxicating beverages to any Indian. Intercultural socializing had been a problem in the past, since citizens, "reckless of public tranquility," were regularly seen "drinking with the savages." In addition, African American and Indian residents were prohibited from "dress[ing] themselves in barbarous fashion, adorning themselves with vermilion and many feathers, which render them unrecognizable"—because once they were "thus metamorphosed," they risked being shot as hostile Indians. Officials insisted that nonwhite residents "clothe themselves…according to our usage and custom" to avoid such dreadful accidents, and they specifically prohibited blacks from holding night meetings or large dances. Any malicious rumors or suspicious activities that made residents "uneasy, restless, and giddy" were considered serious crimes. White citizens were required to be well armed during parley weeks, and at the sound of a warning cannon or a "general alarm by the drums," militiamen followed emergency procedures—grabbing their muskets and rushing to designated rallying sites.[218]

One such startling alarm may have been sounded in the summer of 1772, when Petit Osage and Missouria warriors—two of the "most evil-intentioned of all the nations," as an angry official noted—ransacked the decaying Spanish fort near the mouth of the Missouri River, "knocking down the tiny guard of five soldiers, and stole all the munitions and provisions." No one was seriously injured, but to demonstrate even greater insolence, those warriors then raced through the streets of St. Louis, "terrorized the town, and planted a British flag" there. Thus alarmed, residents tore down that enemy banner and restrained, but did not punish, the culprits. Petit Osages and Missourias were particularly susceptible to English merchants illegally entering their territory from Illinois or Iowa, and by parading the Union Jack under the noses of the French, they signaled their displeasure with Laclède's recent confiscation of Ducharme's contraband cargo. While it suited the Spanish to treat that incident as an isolated prank, the Indians' insatiable demand for gifts and trade goods was a constant concern.[219]

The Presence of Presents

The "good union and friendship which reigns between us and the nations of the Mississippi" depended on giving Indian delegations increasingly lavish "presents, which for many years past they have been accustomed, and which the [foreign] neighbors offer to them in great abundance." The most "official" diplomatic presents were the so-called "peace medals," which were usually accompanied by *paroles de valeur* (awards-ceremony speeches). Varying in size to match the rank of the recipient, silver medals with the profile of the reigning Spanish king were given to principal and subordinate "medal chiefs" and were hung around their necks by beautiful red silk ribbons. (St. Louis required twenty-five feet of those ribbons to accommodate the large number of honorees in 1787.) A particularly influential chief might also receive a military uniform, a silver-trimmed hat, a fancy fusil, a Spanish flag (*pabellone*) or even a campaign tent. Minor, third-rank chiefs received metal gorgets after 1787, while *considerados* (other tribal leaders) had to make do with *patentes*, testaments of their loyalty printed on paper or inscribed on parchment.[220]

At the conclusion of every diplomatic conference in St. Louis, the lieutenant governor also distributed more practical gifts "proportional to the number of each tribe." In 1787, those presents included 4 Spanish flags, several chiefs' garments trimmed with lace, 2,700 musket balls, almost 1,400 pounds of gunpowder, 2,500 flints, 360 knives, 71 tomahawks, 79 white blankets, 100 shirts, 500 needles, 338 hawk's bells, 408 combs, 108 pounds of tobacco and 70 pounds of vermilion. Between 1770 and 1803, Spanish St. Louis spent $8,000 to $30,000 each year on such official presents, with $13,500 being the annual average. In 1781, Commandant Francisco Cruzat "befriended 130 tribes of the Mississippi and Ohio districts" at St. Louis. Such delegations often numbered "forty to fifty men, without counting the women, and at the head of each of them a great chief…always comes." Such generosity may have enticed unusually diverse delegations of distant Indians—Iroquois, Delawares, Cherokees, Chickasaws and Choctaws—to visit St. Louis in 1785, seeking to receive similar "proofs of our disposition to live in good friendship with them."[221]

St. Louis quickly achieved a favorable reputation as the most generous gift-giving town in mid-America because of its unusual "dual authority" in dealing with Indians. The commandant and leading merchants distributed excessive amounts of presents, as both "fathers," for different reasons, sought to impress native "children" with their affluence—the tangible symbol of affection and respect. While the French merchants would not have given presents to any tribes they did not trade with, they followed Maxent's maxim of supplying merchandise at exorbitant markups when shipments of "royal gifts" from New Orleans were delayed or deficient in quantity. Thanks to Maxent's money, Laclède's St. Louis warehouse in 1769 was bulging with nineteen thousand livres' worth of Indian presents and another twenty-two thousand livres' worth of merchandise to purchase furs. In 1778, Laclède's last shipment from his subsidiary warehouse at Arkansas Post contained over sixty tomahawks, fifty-five muskets, almost a ton of sugar, fifty-two cases of liquor, three hundred rolls of leaf tobacco and eighty-four mirrors.[222]

Generosity worked well for French merchants, but similar permissiveness in gift giving by Spanish governors was a symptom of perennial military weakness that promoted diplomatic meekness. In 1782, the St. Louis commandant spent over seventy thousand pesos on presents for Indian allies (the "ramparts" of defense)—more than double his budget for military expenditures but far cheaper than building forts or paying soldier salaries. Even though St. Louis was "the principal and most necessary post for the security of the province," its veteran military officers never had more than three dozen soldiers at their disposal. Most Indians valued the valor of European leaders more than their generosity, and if commandants lacked the power and personality to enforce their policies, gifts became mere bribes from intimidated weaklings, who were scorned by battle-scarred warriors. Pandering with presents diminished, rather than enhanced, Spain's reputation among increasingly arrogant Indians. One official admitted that all he could do to stop Indian violence was to "put on an angry face," renounce raiding warriors "as his true children" and deny them gifts. When that did not work, it was "customary to give them some gift greater than usual, as that is the only means which can compel them to go back." In fact, "medals are to be kept on hand to be given out if some good Indian has to be rewarded or some bad one cajoled." Another frustrated official wrote that "for the petty interest of acquiring a packet of powder, a knife, or some other trifle," Indians will "say that black is white."[223]

St. Louis became a true *Indian capital* when its European leaders realized that their ability to control affairs was an illusion unless the Osages consented to, and cooperated with, their policies. The French priority of trade and the Spanish paucity of troops created ideal conditions for those dominant warriors to bend all whites to their will, not vice versa. European territorial sovereignty was a delusional myth, since two extensive Indian empires actually determined the destiny of Louisiana. Far from "marveling at the power of the Spanish nation," the mobile warriors of the thirty thousand Comanches on the southern plains and ten thousand Osages in the central prairies were the real arbiters of power. Hostile to each other, those nations divided the rich Arkansas Valley between them, using that river as the north–south boundary that separated their domains. Compared to the vicious Comanches, who terrorized Mexico, Taos, Santa Fe and San Antonio by kidnapping whites, gang raping captives and torching towns, the Osages were much less threatening as they slew other Indians and only vandalized colonial settlements. Since Spain allocated most of its military resources to protect its largest settlements and lucrative mines in the southwest from the Comanches, the Osages benefited from the salutary neglect of embarrassed commandants without an army to command. The Comanches belittled the Osages for being "slaves of the Europeans," but the Osages always held the upper hand in Missouri, since their permissive "parents" in St. Louis gave them increasing quantities of guns to enhance their power, while having no way to limit it.[224]

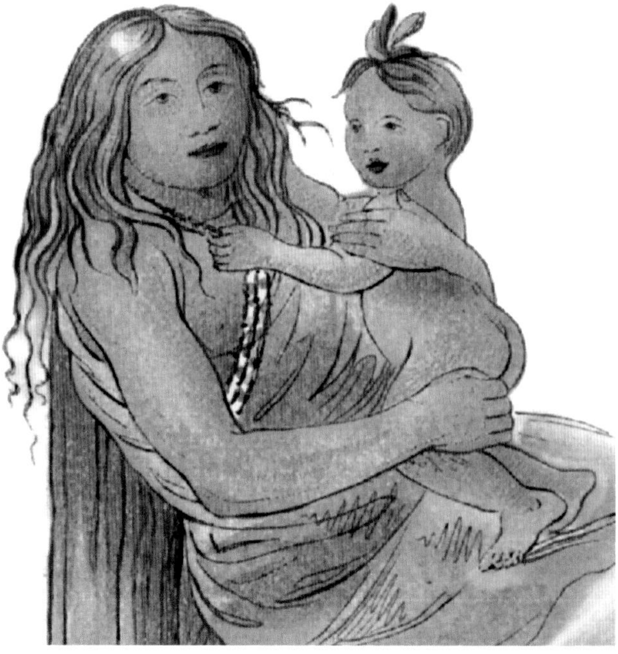

Osage mother and baby, representing a significant but neglected aspect of St. Louis heritage. *1866 George Catlin print in author's collection.*

Sexual Politics

The Grand Osages grew increasingly insolent as their white St. Louis "fathers" perpetually acknowledged their tribal strength and stature with excessive gift giving. In a three-tiered configuration of authority, the top Spanish military official depended on the leading French merchants to deal with their Osage business partners, but since those Indians monopolized the largest fur harvests, European traders were dependent on *their* goodwill, not the other way around. A few of the most respected Frenchmen, however, exerted increased personal influence through their sexual relations with Osage "country wives" of high status, using those important women to solidify business transactions with blood ties. And they kept it up for decades. By literally giving something of themselves to enhance the bonds of friendship, French St. Louisans gained a greater understanding of native cultures at the most intimate and meaningful level as they enjoyed the pleasures of sin for a season.

"Nothing is more flattering and agreeable to savages than to see themselves visited in their villages," a Spanish official observed but did not practice. There was one thing more flattering: having sexual intercourse to reinforce commercial intercourse on frequent visits to "Venus Country." Adhering to the *en dérouine* method of village trading adopted from French Canada, St. Louis voyageurs had regular access to Indian women and were beguiled by their "foul voluptuousness," in the critical view of a Spanish official. But that tradition took on new meaning and increased significance when *leading* Chouteau men spent many youthful years living among the Osages and fathering métis children. There was a fifteen- to seventeen-year age difference between many elite French merchants and the young Euro-American heiresses they eventually married, leaving ample opportunity for years of Indian liaisons. Auguste fathered four known métis with Osage women in their homeland and/or with Indian slaves living in St. Louis. But several of Pierre's sons founded entire Indian families over many decades. One of them, Paul Liguest Chouteau (1792–1851) married Indian women for his third and fourth wives. His son, Edward Liguest Chouteau (1800–1853) was a métis, and he married an Osage, Rosalie Capitain(e); their children were Louis Pharamond Chouteau (1838–1872), Marie Louise Chouteau (1839–1911) and Sophia Rose Chouteau (1842–1923). Pierre Mellicour Papin (1793–1849), son of Marie Louise Chouteau and Joseph Marie Papin, also fathered an Osage son. For generations, Indian Chouteaus have continued to live on the Osage Reservation in Oklahoma and throughout the United States. One of the most famous was Yvonne Chouteau, the prima ballerina of the

Ballet Russe de Monte Carlo in the 1940s and 1950s. The proliferation of mètis was yet another aspect of French-American culture that St. Louisans brought to the trans-Mississippi West.[225]

Such marriages (or liaisons) "in the fashion of the country" (*à la façon de pays*) represented "an extraordinary gesture on the part of an Osage family," according to tribal historian Louis F. Burns. Most sex involved "third daughter (*Ah sin ka*) marriages," but the status and personality of the white man could lead to unions with a second daughter (*We ha*), or even a first daughter (*Me nah*) in extraordinary cases. Although the children of those relationships were "accepted as Osages if they lived by Osage customs and laws," the implications for European family genealogies were significant. According to historian Tanis C. Thorne, by 1800 at least one adult in perhaps 80 percent of St. Louis households may have had one-eighth or more of Indian ancestry. That would confirm what a St. Louis resident reported: "Here the Spaniard, the Frenchman, and the American have in turn held rule, and their blood, with no slight sprinkling of aborigines, now commingles in the veins of inhabitants." In the 1825 (Second) Treaty of St. Louis, William Clark inserted a special provision that allocated 27,000 acres on the Osages' new Kansas reservation to forty-two "half breeds" with European surnames. Receiving 640 acres per person were three generations of Osages fathered by French traders and interpreters named Chouteau, Chardon, Larine, Mongrain, Reneau and St. Mitchelle, among others.[226]

St. Louisans practiced an even more novel "fashion of the country" when leading French families publicly acknowledged their Indian offspring or otherwise linked their surnames with métis in Roman Catholic baptisms. Sharon E. Person's recent book, *Standing Up for Indians*, analyzed all three hundred Indian baptisms recorded in the Old St. Louis Cathedral archives from 1766 to 1821. They reveal important genetic ties and/or cultural connections between eighty-seven French fathers or spouses and members of twenty-one different tribes. Osages were named in forty-seven baptisms of all types, some of which merely represented fictive, pseudo-kinship between intercultural business partners, not alliances of blood. By standing up for Indians, many of whom would never convert to Christianity, Chouteaus and other French godparents treated the ritual of baptism like a calumet pipe ceremony, creating useful ties with cultural others for mutual advantage. At a place and a time focused on the essential need for Indian cooperation, there were no limits to French appeasement and accommodation if a Catholic sacrament could be adapted to the secular world of Osage commerce. "What developed in St. Louis society was more than just a simple coexistence, or even sharing, of Creole and Indian cultures," Person observed. "It was a dynamic, syncretic culture, geographically close to Indian partners and simultaneously removed from the Spanish center of government in New Orleans."[227]

Laclède's Village Becomes Chouteau's Town

The great intangible in the long and successful Osage alliance with the Laclède-Chouteau family was the personality of leaders in both cultures—a combination of affability, integrity, patience and empathy capable of transforming a business partnership into true friendship and actual kinship. Continuing Osage confidence in that special family alliance was critical to the future of St. Louis when Laclède died suddenly in 1778. The Grand Osages supported the trade of twenty-eight-year-old Auguste, his twenty-two-year-old half brother, Pierre (who frequently resided with the Osages and became their favorite trader) and their new brother-in-law, Sylvestre Labbadie Sr. of Tarbes. Despite a severe shortage of trade goods immediately following Laclède's death, that new partnership shipped 161,227 livres' worth of furs to New Orleans in 1779 along with only seven other St. Louis merchants.[228]

Even more importantly, when Laclède's perilous pyramid of mounting debts came crashing down, Auguste prevented any panic among residents over the loss of the town founder. Laclède and Maxent had trained Chouteau well, and the young merchant was fully prepared to expand the Indian trade and to assume civic leadership without his dear comrade—achieving more wisdom about the West than either of his mentors had in their shorter life spans. In many ways, Maxent became a substitute stepfather to Auguste after Laclède died. His relationship with Chouteau was not that of a greedy tycoon or ruthless rogue, for he accepted payments far lower than what Laclède owed him and even spread them out over ten years without charging interest. Maxent took Chouteau under his wing as he had done with Laclède, and Auguste respected the senior merchant for having subsidized his stepfather's career and assisted in the founding of St. Louis.

After Laclède's death, the maturing Chouteau brothers and the aging Maxent enjoyed their greatest successes. Maxent maximized his political power and financial prowess even more during the Spanish regime than he had under the last French governors of Louisiana. Complementing his forty-five-year career as a private merchant, Maxent maneuvered himself into several public offices. He became Spain's commissioner of Indian affairs and trade for all of Louisiana in 1770, supplying massive quantities of imported gifts to forty native nations at a huge markup. In 1781, he was appointed "Lieutenant Governor and Captain-General in all matters relating to the respective Indian nations that inhabit the provinces of Louisiana and West Florida" due to his family connections with two Spanish royal governors. Maxent's daughter Marie Elizabeth (Isabel) wed Governor Luis Unzaga y Amezaga (in office, 1769–77), who was later appointed captain-general of Cuba, while daughter Marie Félicité became a Spanish countess by marrying Governor Bernardo de Gálvez y Madrid, count of Gálvez (served 1777–84), later viceroy of New Spain.[229]

In addition to his special ties with Maxent, Chouteau's New Orleans connections gave the rising merchant a key advantage over trading rivals. In 1780, Auguste was one of only two St. Louis merchants who was born in New Orleans (Pierre was the other one), and he served successive Spanish commandants as an official envoy to power brokers in the Crescent City. Officials in both capitals had complete faith in Chouteau, who gathered and shared intelligence with them as he delivered important dispatches during the American Revolution. His privileged conversations with royal appointees (including Maxent) dramatically enhanced Chouteau's stature as a community leader as well as a businessman. In 1778, a young merchant at Cahokia, the Swiss-born Charles Gratiot, suggested to his Montreal partner that they should move their headquarters to the "Spanish Side," where they could "do a brilliant and lucrative business" by working with "people who are not to be suspected of misconduct"—such as the Chouteau brothers, already well-regarded for their ties to "Mr. De Macksan [Maxent], Merchant in that City [of New Orleans] who alone has the Governor's permission to sell Indian goods."[230]

As with most other things dealing with the founding and development of St. Louis, Maxent was the master to emulate. The Chouteau brothers followed his lead by making strategic marriage alliances to revitalize bottom lines with bloodlines. By 1781, Gratiot was a brother-in-law, and the noted Kaskaskia merchant, Gabriel Cerré, was Auguste's father-in-law. That well-capitalized Chouteau-Chouteau-Labbadie-Cerré-Gratiot consortium became a rock of stability when the American Revolution stirred up waves of change throughout the Mississippi Valley. St. Louis became a key player and the near-equal partner with New Orleans in supporting the American cause against the hated British after both France and Spain became allies of the United States in 1778–9. While Maxent was the right-hand man to his fighting son-in-law, Governor Galvez, in successful military offensives against the English at Natchez, Manchac, Baton Rouge, Mobile and

Pensacola, the Chouteau clan helped maintain a "continental store" at St. Louis, which funneled supplies from New Orleans to George Rogers Clark's army of Virginians occupying Illinois after invading Kaskaskia, Cahokia and Vincennes.[231]

That assistance to allies would have ominious consequences for a small town with no fortifications, giving the British only the most recent reason to invade St. Louis. English merchants had long coveted its "benevolent" reputation among Indians as the "Big Town" of the fur trade, enriched by the "enchanting and altogether Elisian" lands of the Osages. The strategic location of Spain's capital of Upper Louisiana was a tempting target with potent political symbolism for Great Britain's war in the West. Unfortunately, St. Louis was within easy striking distance of commercial rivals from British Canada based at the Mississippi trading town of Prairie du Chien, only three hundred miles to the north.[232]

In early 1780, Lieutenant Governor Patrick Sinclair of Michilimackinac planned to capture that "rich furr Trade" and avenge the past "injuries done to the [British] Traders who formerly attempted to partake of it," and he promised Canadian merchants "the exclusive trade of the Missouri to those who would capture and hold the posts on the Spanish side of the Mississippi." He appointed Captain Emanuel Hesse, a Pennsylvania-German Loyalist and Prairie du Chien merchant, to assemble an invasion force. Although a contemporary reported that the attackers included "1200 Indians…with some 50 Canadians and 35 Englishmen, painted like Indians," there were probably only 750 of them, almost all "northern Indians" and a handful of multicultural commanders from Britain's Indian Department of frontier fighters, not legions of regular redcoats. The principal leaders included Chief Wabasha of the Mdewakanton Dakota (Sioux of the Minnesota prairies); Matchekewis, Pontiac's old Ojibway ally who had captured Fort Michilimackinac in 1763, now leading Ottawa warriors; Sergeant J.F. Phillips of Britain's Eighth Regiment of Foot; and two old competitors of St. Louis—Jean Marie Ducharme and Joseph Calvé—seeking to avenge Laclède's confiscation of their merchandise years before. Other attacking Indians included Sauks and Mesquakies from Rock River and assorted warriors of the Potawatomies, Winnebagoes, Green Bay Menominees, Kickapoos, Mascoutens and Ioways. The predominant use of Indian allies was a necessity given Britain's shortage of other troops, but those warriors were a key component of the invasion, since St. Louis's well-known open-door policy regarding Indian hospitality was expected to allow native attackers an "easy admission" into the town.[233]

Because it took so long to assemble and move those forces, the attackers lost the element of surprise. Everyone in Upper Louisiana, it seemed, knew that an invasion was coming. As early as February, Auguste Chouteau reported the rumors he had heard in New Orleans, while at Cahokia, Gratiot might have been even better informed, since his Canadian business partner was among the invaders. St. Louis's main advantage was having mobile fur traders serving as its eyes and ears along every major river and in many Indian villages, and a number of residents spotted familiar faces heading downriver in force. Some of the attacking Indians actually traded with St. Louis, and the temporary shortage of gifts for area tribes following Laclède's death, coupled with British generosity in bribing recruits, may have induced formerly friendly Indians to demonstrate their displeasure by trying to sack the town. Apparently, no St. Louisan gave intelligence to the enemy because the attackers were quite surprised to encounter the town's new trenches, stone tower, cannon emplacements and expanded ranks of well-armed defenders.[234]

Those hasty military preparations were the work of the much-defamed Lieutenant Governor Leyba. Although resented for the authoritarian way in which he "shook down" rich merchants to pay for town defense, Leyba mobilized residents to build an incomplete stone tower and to dig a mile of trenches around the perimeter of the town. He also called up the small Spanish garrison at Ste. Genevieve under Lieutenant Silvia Francisco Cartabona, as well as sixty militiamen under François Vallé. Virginia "Big Knives" under General Clark's subordinate officers guarded the eastern flank at Cahokia. Probably fewer than three hundred men—only twenty-nine of them uniformed Spanish soldiers—fought to defend St. Louis, and the city's militia, untested by combat, contained eighteen men over fifty and eleven teenagers.[235]

The Battle of St. Louis commenced at the north-side trenches about one o'clock in the afternoon on Friday, May 26, 1780. "The combat," as Leyba reported, was "furious and full of carnage," lasting some five hours. But the Indian warriors were disheartened long before then, enduring cannon blasts of solid shot and shrapnel while failing to entice defenders from the safety of their trenches. The British blamed the Sauks and Mesquakies, who were reluctant attackers but bold deserters, for abandoning the field. Almost all the casualties were civilians who were caught in the open when the signal cannon was fired. One day after celebrating the Feast of Corpus Christi, shocked survivors discovered the corpses of fourteen whites and seven blacks—"scalped, entrails opened, cranium[s] crushed, limbs mutilated, bathed in blood, and scattered here and there," according to Leyba. Seven St. Louisans suffered wounds, while another twenty-five residents (thirteen blacks and twelve whites) were "carried away" as captives. One of the dead slaves and five of those captured belonged to Madame Chouteau, while some of the first families of St. Louis—the Riviéres, Chancelliers and Roys—suffered a total of three men wounded and three taken prisoner (all would return). The toll of fifty-three casualties, representing about 7.5 percent of the total population, could have been far worse. The mutilated corpses revealed the ferocity of the attack, but the larger number of captives, mostly taken during the Indians' retreat, represented their frustration with the futility of the attack. Beyond the town's borders, Indians captured another forty-six people, including several boatmen at various locations, while Kaws reportedly seized and burned alive eight unidentified men farther up the Missouri River.[236]

Despite bitter recriminations against Leyba and near-disastrous blunders by inexperienced defenders, the Battle of St. Louis was a watershed event, forever memorialized as *L'Annee du Grand Coup*. The blow had not been so big, but surviving that assault in 1780 served as a rite of passage and a testament to the bravery, ingenuity and community spirit of the scrappy, defiant residents who repulsed the only attack on their town in the colonial period. Clark's forces successfully defended Cahokia with few casualties, but it is a myth that Anglo-Americans, with their "superior frontier skills," crossed the river to save "incompetent" French St. Louisans. The battle also offered an assessment of St. Louis's Indian diplomacy. The Sauks and Mesquakies, who had long traded in St. Louis, had joined the British invasion force (a negative), but they fled the field, ultimately dooming the attack (a positive). The scales were tipped in favor of continuing a relationship based on materialistic appeasement, however, when the Sauks turned over several British medals and flags, apologized for the attack, accepted new symbols of Spanish loyalty and resumed their trade with St. Louis—"remaining faithful to us…as a rampart against our enemies."[237]

And where were the Osage "ramparts" in St. Louis's time of need? They may have gone onto the plains for their annual summer bison hunt before the battle, but since the Osages were most formidable as charging cavalry in surprise raids, even their best warriors would have been slaughtered by so many crouching Indian musketmen. Although they had tacitly supported Pontiac's alliance without committing warriors, the Osages traditionally avoided involvement in Great Lakes Indian affairs, concentrating their fruitful warfare west and south of St. Louis. The Chouteau brothers probably wanted the Osages to stay away from the fray, for the deaths of invaluable hunters would have jeopardized their status as successful, and increasingly prominent, merchants.

Auguste Chouteau was the biggest individual "winner" in the Battle of St. Louis, as the growing, soon-to-be-fortified settlement transitioned from the infancy of "Laclède's Village" to the adolescence of "Chouteau's Town." Chouteau was well on his way to replacing Laclède as "First Citizen," as he made his main contributions in nonmercantile activities following the 1780 attack. He remained the official courier between St. Louis and New Orleans, as well as the envoy and official purveyor of presents to several tribes. When Lieutenant Governor Cruzat returned to St. Louis for a second term of office following the death of Leyba in late June, he commended Chouteau for his "honor, activity, and zeal," as well as "love for the royal service which he has shown on various occasions." Cruzat commissioned Chouteau as the ranking officer in the First Company of the St. Louis Militia and authorized him to design the first true fortifications for the town due to his "capacity" for the task. Although Chouteau thought of himself as an architect, a mere sketch map was probably his only contribution to that project.[238]

Chouteau's Capital of Capital

St. Louis survived its near-death experience to emerge stronger than ever as a maturing regional capital of increasing stature. When it celebrated its twenty-fifth anniversary in 1789, St. Louis became the oldest French town in Upper Louisiana, since the Great Flood of 1785 (*L'Annee des Grandes Eaux*) had "entirely submerged" Ste. Genevieve and forced a complete relocation of residents to a rebuilt town at a new site. Spared the natural disasters that would also ruin Kaskaskia and New Madrid, and avoiding a major epidemic until the smallpox outbreak in 1800, St. Louis was "the happiest [place] on earth and lacks nothing." A visitor in 1787 described it as "the handsomest & genteelist village I have seen on the Mississippi," whose "inhabitants…are more wealthy" than any others in the Illinois Country on either side of the river. It was "fast improving and will soon be a large place." By 1791, St. Louis had a total population of 1,188, compared to only 923 for Ste. Genevieve, with the capital city taking a commanding lead in the whites-only category, 837 to 580. "Better built than any Town on the Mississippi," St. Louis contained about "200 Houses, most of which are of Stone," and architecturally, it became older than New Orleans by 1795. The "Good Friday Fire" of 1788 consumed over 850 buildings in

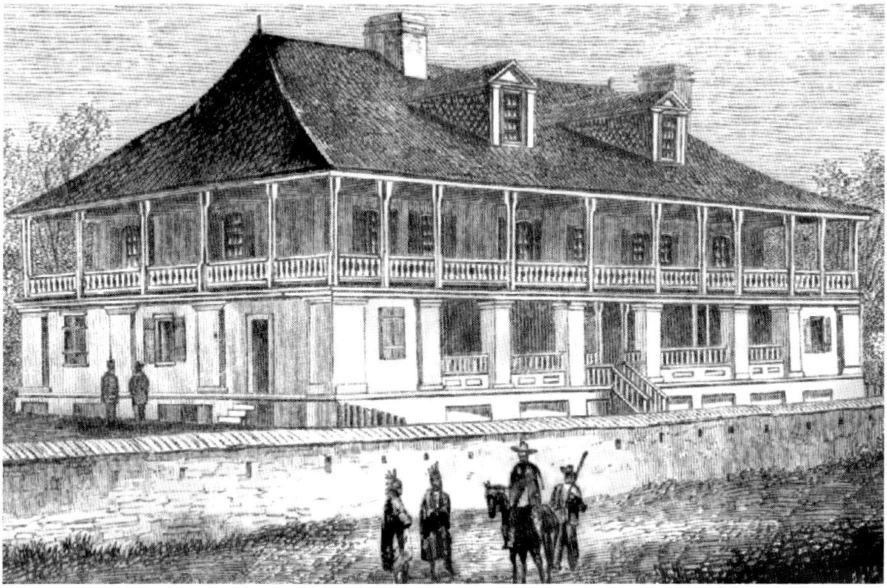

Chouteau's 1790s mansion, remodeled from Laclède's first residence, was the grandest home in the French West. *From* Shewey's Pictorial St. Louis, Past and Present *(1892).*

the Crescent City—some 80 percent of all structures, including key public buildings. A hurricane struck New Orleans in 1793, and two more in August 1794, and in between the city suffered an epidemic of yellow fever. Then, in the Christmas season of 1794, a second major fire destroyed another 200 structures, including "all remaining French buildings save the Ursulines' convent," which is today the "only extant building in New Orleans from the French period." The old wooden city was rebuilt in brick and stone, with tile roofs and metal balconies, reflecting Spanish architectural tastes and construction codes in today's misnamed "French Quarter."[239]

Ironically, the famous mansion that Auguste Chouteau built was a more authentic reflection of colonial French Louisiana architecture than any large contemporaneous home within the city boundaries of New Orleans. In 1789, Maxent sold Laclède's first house to Chouteau for $3,000, and he extensively remodeled his boyhood creation until it had the "appearance of a castle," attracting European nobility as frequent tourists. Chouteau built a full second story on walls that were two and a half feet thick, and all of the distinguishing features above ground level were new. Laclède's warehouse, stable and other outbuildings remained in the backyard, and Chouteau encircled everything with a ten-foot-high stone wall two feet thick, which included gun ports every ten feet. The new home and company headquarters of the House of Chouteau occupied an entire block in the prime town center, and it long remained a community showplace. Chouteau's "hospitality center" featured a dining room with three large tables, forty-six chairs, forty tablecloths and forty-two pounds of sterling silver eating utensils; floors of shiny black walnut; a crystal chandelier; eleven landscape paintings and several framed engravings (many of them portraits of Napoleon). He also had ten beds; a fancy clock with a bust of Voltaire on top; and a large personal library, including sixty books by Voltaire alone.[240]

Chouteau probably modeled his home after Maxent's Marigny House, which he had visited. Located beyond the French Gate in the region now known as Fauxbourg Marigny, that beautifully proportioned and well-designed residence bore a striking resemblance to Chouteau's later mansion. Built of stone, it was two stories high, with thick, square lower columns supporting more delicate ones above to form airy, wraparound galleries on both levels. The steep hipped roof featured two prominent dormers and two large chimneys, and a high stone wall surrounded the property. Chouteau designed his home to advertise the House of Chouteau, the dominant business in Upper Louisiana, just as Maxent's properties signaled his success in Louisiana's capital.[241]

Maxent died in August 1794, near the time that Chouteau finished his renovations, and the master merchant's estate included multiple mansions and four large plantations encircling New Orleans, with one alone totaling thirty-three thousand acres. He also owned 209 slaves; a sawmill, lumberyard and rum distillery; a wine cellar with three thousand bottles; watercraft and warehouses of every size and description; four carriages; and several hundred head of livestock. Chouteau's extravagant furnishings for entertaining were certainly inspired by his familiarity with Maxent's even more magnificent possessions, which supported lavish hospitality, including twelve hundred pieces of beautiful crystal, exquisite Parisian silverware, 960 napkins, a mahogany billiard table, a clavichord, gold-framed mirrors, twenty-two oil paintings, a library of forty-seven hundred books, two London-made globes and a gilded copper clock shaped like a birdcage, with a mechanical bird that sang an aria on the hour. Although Chouteau tried to match Maxent's affluent lifestyle, the old charter member of the "devil's empire" had an insurmountable advantage by living in a seaport city, having two governors as sons-in-law, enjoying enormous profits from transatlantic smuggling and practicing the ethics of a seafaring pirate.[242]

Honoring the Legacy of Maxent and Laclède

The decade of the 1790s opened with the Grand Osages still the most powerful commercial and military force in Upper Louisiana, exploiting the presence and presents of St. Louis to pursue their own objectives. They remained more culturally dominant than European-dependent, and it was the whites who had to adapt to Osage ways and wishes rather than the other way around. Despite a steady stream of imported products that had entered their world, the Osages were selective in adopting "the comforts of the civilized, without losing the virtues of the savage state"—finding in the "absence of artificial wants…the great secret of personal freedom." Unlike the Creeks and other deerskin-trading tribes in the English southeast, the Grand Osages preserved their most vital traditions and did not abandon essential craft skills. Warriors numbered 1,200 well into the American period, and they continued to make their famous orangewood bows (*bois d'arc*), which remained their preferred hunting weapon for feeding their families, while still intimidating enemies.[243]

The Grand Osages were too shrewd to succumb to widespread alcohol addiction, which was the scourge of Indians in the colonial East and later West. Unlike other tribes, the Osages never traded land for liquor, and whites in different eras recognized them as some of the "soberest" Indians. The Chouteaus were not about to poison their close friends and blood relatives with alcohol. Their Osage alliance resembled a stable, monogamous "marriage," whereas the later free trade era under the United States produced the greatest alcohol abuse, as unscrupulous traders treated Indians more like one-time "prostitutes" than lifelong "spouses."[244]

Trade monopolies worked in Upper Louisiana. By favoring "only a very few" conscientious, licensed traders with exclusive access to tribes they knew and cared about, the Spanish government sought to preserve positive relations and sustainable fur profits for "coming generations." The Grand Osages were similarly pragmatic about their business affairs, being careful not to overhunt their territories, which never ran out of animals. They refused to deplete the "principal" of their mammal empire by cashing in too much "interest" in annual harvests, and they even created a new position—Protector of the Land (*Moh shon Ah ke ta*)—to help preserve vital natural resources.[245]

But the pandering policies of St. Louis made the Osages believe too much in their own superiority. Given Osage strength and Spanish weakness, most St. Louis commandants found it "necessary to temporize with them to some extent, and handle them as tactfully as possible in order to restrain their excesses, as the few forces in the country do not permit anything else." The official rationale was that even if the Osages "never do any good," they were always capable of doing worse—"a great deal of harm." If they ever launched an all-out war on the whites in Missouri, the Osages would "tire [themselves] out…kill[ing] the poor inhabitants," and any survivors would "be obliged to emigrate." Spanish commandants continued to overlook occasional Osage attacks on outlying settlements as long as they respected and protected the capital. St. Louisans were content to be the "most favored" trading town of the best fur producers in the region, even at the expense of other colonists, who rarely enjoyed similar success or safety. A Spanish official in 1788 actually admitted that he allowed a war chief to raid, kill and enslave Indian neighbors because "he shows us much affection" and "has never done any harm to *our* district." Two years later, the St. Louis commandant declared that the Osages were "tranquil," ignoring allegations that some of their warriors had murdered a settler near Ste. Genevieve. Such selective reporting and casual concern for other colonists obscured the reality of deteriorating conditions because lieutenant governors rarely ventured out of secure St. Louis, which enjoyed immunity from violence through the generosity of its gifts.[246]

It was quite clear that the Europeans in St. Louis needed the Osages more than the Osages needed them, and if those warriors intimidated the Bourbon populations in the West, they had the same impact on the British in the East. The Spanish put up with isolated acts of Osage violence because their reputation as the most warlike tribe helped keep the British bogeymen at bay—a much higher priority. In 1767, the Grand Osages were the only area Indians who refused to attend a major British conference of native nations at Fort de Chartres, and decades later, they remained hostile to intrusions by, or alliance with, English-speaking populations. The Osages could have profited more as predatory enemies of St. Louis than its allies, and all white residents knew it.[247]

That was little comfort for Ste. Genevieve, however, which was repeatedly victimized by Osage thefts because the merchants there did not have the intimate leverage of the Chouteaus, and the town's livestock was too tempting to ignore. The Osages remained notorious horse thieves because it was easier to steal than to breed the female war ponies they rarely allowed to get pregnant. That was a practical and timesaving solution for a people who found large herds of horses difficult to move, feed and protect. Osage war parties forded the Mississippi near Ste. Genevieve, along an ancient buffalo trace that was part of the extensive "Warrior's Path" running across the continent. Returning from raiding, they often stole fresh mounts from that town to get them back home, while stopping to barbecue stolen French cattle. Officials at Arkansas Post also complained that the Osages regularly raided the nearby Quapaws and killed white hunters with impunity. Similarly, the Spanish at Natchitoches protested when the local Caddos were forced to move their village to avoid Osage attacks, and they feared that local cattle ranches would be future targets. Commandants as far away as Texas condemned St. Louis's permissive policies toward the Osages and complained even more about the preferential treatment that the town and its closest Indian allies received from senior officials in New Orleans.[248]

With regard to deadly violence against whites, the Osages compared favorably to other large native nations from the Appalachians to the Rockies, and considering what widespread atrocities their "imperious and insolent" warriors could have committed, the Osages were generally good neighbors. Most of their "depredations" involved property crimes, and rare killings usually involved persistent poachers and/or whites who fired first. No historian has evaluated how many raids on white settlements by distant tribes the Osages may have averted by their constant warfare with multitribal invaders of *their* Native Ground. According to Osage author Burns, his nation killed "over a thousand" poachers in the late eighteenth century, as ancient tribal enemies became new commercial competitors. From St. Louis to New Orleans, Spanish officials became increasingly concerned, however, since the entire region "rarely enjoyed peace among the numerous tribes." A report in 1793 claimed that "there are no nations in these territories who are not at war with the Osages."[249]

But "instead of dreading their many enemies, the Osages were almost flattered by the hostile world that surrounded them." The proliferation of firearms increased the ferocity and "insolence" of a new generation of young warriors, who needed battle honors to advance their personal reputations, elevate their statuses in the nation and marry choice wives. To address the growing strength of their adversaries, the Osages developed new war strategies. The peace-oriented Little Old Men suffered an erosion of control, and "the power of the band chiefs grew in proportion," leading to more small-scale revenge raids not authorized by first-rank chiefs. That was probably a reaction to the influx of Anglo-American settlers and "foreign" Indians in the 1790s, and traditional St. Louis diplomacy was unable to prevent increasing violence because French and Spanish leaders had less control over those immigrant populations.[250]

The Osages employed *selective* acts of terrorism, using the "voice" of violence to attract attention and to get their way. Such "vexations" were traditional in intertribal warfare, since the Osages regularly decapitated Indian enemies and even played kickball with their heads. The shock value of an occasional gruesome slaying was a purposeful, tactical substitute for widespread warfare, which should have been comforting to white populations. Instead, they became increasingly paranoid about the unpredictability of such unspeakable horrors—focusing disproportionately on the mutilation of corpses rather than the murders themselves as "new proofs" of Osage "perfidy." In 1788, Pierre la Buche, a fifteen-year-old mulatto, "found…just the head of his father, scalped down to the eyes," at their hunting camp near Ste. Genevieve. Two years later, Osages allegedly "cut to pieces and scalped" Baptiste Le Duc near Natchitoches, while another victim was "shot through the body" with bullets on Osage lands. Most killers were never caught, and the Grand Osages were often accused of crimes actually committed by other Indians.[251]

Spanish indulgence of the Osages had always been based on their fear of them, and no atrocity was so shocking as to result in the execution of a single Osage in colonial Upper Louisiana. The tribal enemies of the Osages that were treated more harshly by Spanish officials became violent vigilantes to rectify that judicial prejudice. Chief Pacanné of the Miamis criticized the double standard that privileged the Osages, who "get nothing but caresses, and are supplied with everything," even "when they steal, pillage and kill." As early as 1772, Potawatomies and Saulteaux had killed the two leading chiefs of the Petit Osages and chopped an arm off one of their warriors. In the last two decades of the eighteenth century, the Osages lost two hundred to three hundred warriors as their enemies began to fight back. The five "most redoubtable" Texas tribes of the Wichita alliance were ready to attack the Osages in 1790. The following year, a diverse collection of Cherokees, Chickasaws, Sauks, Shawnees, Mascoutens and Delawares held a multitribal "congress" to organize a massive offensive against their common Osage foes.[252]

The cocky, imperious Osages had overplayed their hand, and even the most timid officials throughout Louisiana began to doubt the benefits of appeasement upon hearing the 1788 rumor that the Osages "say that in order to have [goods], it will be necessary to kill [some] of the French." Emboldened or intimidated by the Indian enemies of the Osages, New Orleans officials imposed a trade embargo, finally realizing that "one crime unpunished always encourages the commission of a second." The dilemma faced by Lieutenant Governor Manuel Perez in St. Louis was that the Grand Osages and Petit Osages were "the worst two tribes…and at the same time the strongest"—but traders always "returned [from their villages] well content[ed], having done a very good business." But orders were orders, and in early November 1791, Perez met with an Osage delegation to inform them that the embargo would continue unless they handed over a high-ranking hostage to guarantee good behavior. Discontented with Perez's disrespect of their commercial productivity and cultural pride, the Osages retaliated by blockading the Missouri River and confiscating cargoes. The defiant warriors stated that although Perez was "master in his town, so they were masters here"—meaning everywhere else in Upper Louisiana. Pierre Chouteau facilitated the Osages' defiance by ignoring the commandant's trade embargo and smuggling new muskets and blankets to them. In March 1792, they gave him twenty-five thousand acres of land along the Lamine River in central Missouri, because he had "fed our wives and our children" and "always assisted us with…advice." Furthermore, the Grand Osages promised to defend him "if some nation disturbs thee."[253]

The aggressive actions of the Osages even turned gentle Governor Miró against them, and by the spring of 1792, his successor was seeking a genocidal solution to the "Osage problem." That new governor was Francois-Louis Hector, baron de Carondelet et Noyelles, a Burgundian nobleman and former commander of the French king's elite Walloon Guards. He conferred with post commandants about an all-out war, and Perez in St. Louis reported that "reduc[ing] the Osages by force" was possible but not physically or financially feasible. He estimated that it would cost over twenty-one thousand pesos to field a mere seven hundred Indian mercenaries for even a short campaign against twice that number of Osage warriors, who, like "ancient Scythians"—or speedy "vipers"—could strike suddenly and then retreat into "impenetrable places" to ambush any pursuers.[254]

Hearing rumors about the need to "annihilate" the Grand Osages, the Chouteau brothers advised officials to "stop irritating" them because it only made their warriors "fiercer." With blood kin and business interests on both sides of the frontier, the Chouteaus intervened as trusted culture brokers, seeking to prevent a war that would ruin a quarter century of harmonious Indian relations and destroy St. Louis's lucrative fur trade. According to historian James Neal Primm, the "Osages trusted and respected the brothers" largely because those talented Creoles "could think as they thought, speak as they spoke, and live as they lived," even "sitting in council with other elders and chiefs."[255]

In May 1794, Auguste Chouteau and a delegation of six Osage leaders met with Governor Carondelet in New Orleans. He had been an outspoken advocate for war and against trade monopolies, but his abrupt about-face on those issues suggests that, for one last time and in the final months of his life, Maxent may have intervened to convince yet another royal governor to support the proven commercial diplomacy of the Chouteaus. Before his death in August, Spanish officials were planning to promote Maxent to brigadier general of the Louisiana militia. Private profits and public policy again converged in a monopoly scheme reminiscent of Maxent's original "St. Louis Project," as the Chouteau brothers sought a lucrative alternative to bloodshed. They proposed *increasing* trade with the Osages far away from white settlements, which would curtail their raiding while keeping them out of the clutches of rival British merchants who were emboldened by the embargo. The Chouteaus would build, furnish, provision and partially staff a trade fort near the Grand Osage villages at Marais des Cygnes in exchange for an exclusive six-year monopoly (later extended to eight years) on their fur harvests. That would give the Osages the respectful treatment they expected and all the merchandise they needed, provided by private, not public, funds, so that they would be less inclined to pillage colonial settlements.[256]

Governor Carondelet approved the plan, but as the Osage leaders headed home, a Chickasaw ambush killed three of the most prominent members of the delegation—Jean Lafond, a *Ga-hi-ge* of the Grand Osages; La Vent, a Petit Osage *Ga-hi-ge*; and Le Soldat du Chene, a respected warrior. Their deaths did not kill the fort project, but internal tribal disputes over choosing Lafond's successor split the Grand Osages, from which they never recovered. The Chouteaus went too far in promoting the compliant Pawhiuskah as the principal leader of the Grand Osages, in violation of both hereditary qualifications and the principle of dual chieftainship. In protest, the rightful claimant, the young Gratomohse or Clermont II (Iron Hawk), led a large group of supporters south to the Verdigris River near present-day Claremore, Oklahoma, joining other Osages who had long preferred to live in the Arkansas River Valley because of its abundant game. Additional Osages, especially wild young warriors from the leading Bear and Panther war clans, also moved south, where they would be insulated from northern enemies and isolated from the machinations of the Chouteaus and Spanish officials.[257]

Only Pawhiuskah's pro-Chouteau Grand Osages and some Petit Osages would benefit directly from Fort Carondelet, which was built at Halley's Bluff in southwestern Missouri. Following Laclède's example, his heirs used materialistic means to cater to the pride of those loyal Indians, who needed flattery more than ever after the rancor of tribal division. Merchandise had symbolic, and even spiritual, value, and the Grand Osages felt that their exclusive trading post made them more "distinguished" and gave them "preponderance" over other Indians, including kinsmen now living elsewhere. The Chouteaus dispatched white colonists to live and work there, and Pawhiuskah's people found it most gratifying and respectful that Pierre and his wife and young children resided among them. Pierre was greatly loved by the Grand Osages, while Auguste was much feared, and together, the brothers exercised "an authority there that no other whites could have" due to their "good counsels" and "accredited ascendancy" among those Indians. Playing "good cop" and "bad cop" created "a contrast which did no harm in restraining" the Grand Osages, according to Spanish officials, who praised the brothers for "diverting and dissuading" their violence through an "arduous" and daring enterprise. It was no surprise that the formerly "intractable" Osages suddenly became "tranquil," because the Chouteaus were dealing with the most devoted, and now warrior-depleted, subgroup of that nation. Nevertheless, "depredations" declined, and a major war was averted by providing abundant supplies of desirable trade goods to Indians whom St. Louis still needed as allies.[258]

The savvy Chouteaus also profited, of course. In demonstrating once again that even much-feared Indians would support European settlers on frontiers of reciprocal respect and mutual rewards, the Chouteaus made a lot of money for their "honor, activity, and zeal" as conciliatory diplomats in "the royal service." Their monopoly gave them nearly 60 percent of the St. Louis fur market and "approximately 42 percent of the entire Upper Louisiana Indian trade" for most of eight years. Their estimated profits were 33 percent on an annual average of 96,000 pounds of pelts, but in one two-year period, the Fort Carondelet Osages harvested 236,000 pounds of furs. The Chouteaus' huge profits prompted jealous St. Louis rivals to lobby for an end to monopolies and to form the "Company of Discoverers and Explorers of the Missouri River," which dispatched three trading expeditions as far as the Mandans in failed efforts to develop distant fur markets not controlled by the powerful brothers. A more serious threat came from Manuel Lisa, a Spanish trader on the rise, who succeeded in ending the Chouteau monopoly on June 12, 1802. But he did not make a profit at Fort Carondelet, and when it was abandoned, the Osages added four swivel cannons to their arsenal as a final reward.[259]

Fort Carondelet ranked second only to the founding of St. Louis as a significant symbol of how French commercial diplomacy achieved private profits and public protection in league with the still-dominant Grand Osages. The widespread Indian-Indian and white-white factionalism confirmed the high stakes involved in preventing cross-cultural atrocities throughout Upper Louisiana. Fort Carondelet was a successful Chouteau colony of Laclède's colony of Kerlérec's colony, with Maxent's legacy apparent in all of them.

The founding of St. Louis as a corporate colony provided the model for Fort Carondelet, which was also called "the fort of the Osages," while that Chouteau outpost may have inspired the U.S. government's later fur factory at a different Fort Osage with a far more sinister purpose.

Indians of Consuming Interest

The Chouteau brothers supplied the Grand Osages of Fort Carondelet with the greatest variety of quality products by expanding their trade in two different fur markets three thousand miles apart. Great Britain was the new center of international fur commerce after the French Revolution all but destroyed France's role, and England's industrial revolution mass produced the most desirable merchandise for the Indian trade. British shoe manufacturers in the 1790s were purchasing more deerskins than hat makers bought beaver, so the Chouteaus enjoyed higher profits on their regular shipments of premium Osage deer leather to New Orleans. But British Canada was becoming a more attractive market, too, in the decade after 1793, when 70 percent of Montreal fur exports to Europe were "other than beaver." About $400,000 worth of furs from areas south of the Great Lakes were being shipped to Canada each year in the 1790s, and the Chouteau brothers accounted for at least 10 percent of that total, thanks to the popularity of Missouri peltries of feline, canine and weasel species. Those fancy, delicate furs could not tolerate the heat and humidity of a voyage to New Orleans, and it was more difficult to ship heavy merchandise from that city up the treacherous Mississippi than down from Canada. [260]

The Chouteaus procured the London exports desired by Osage and French customers alike by sending their all-French voyageurs from St. Louis to Michilimackinac, the "Gibraltar of the North"—a tiny, turtle-shaped island in the beautiful "inland sea" created by the confluence of Lake Michigan and Lake Huron. In defiance of the 1783 Treaty of Paris, the British flag still flew above that island haven for contraband traders until 1796, and the United States did not begin regulating the Mackinac trade until 1804. The Chouteau brothers dealt with the Montreal-based merchants of the North West Company (NWC), the main rivals of the older Hudson's Bay Company until those firms merged in 1821. Most prominent in the trade with St. Louis were Todd, McGill & Company; Grant, Campion & Company; Myer Michaels; Isidore Lacroix; Claude Laframboise; George Gillespie; Joseph Bleakley; and Richard Pattinson. The Chouteaus established their

Montreal-Michilimackinac connection at a most propitious time, since the NWC invested £40,000 sterling in the fur trade in 1788 and tripled that amount just five years later. Those Canadian capitalists welcomed furs from Spanish St. Louis because it was outside United States control.[261]

According to the esteemed fur trade historian Paul Chrisler Phillips, "Auguste Chouteau appears as the only St. Louis merchant with the credit and standing to deal on a large scale with Montreal" in the 1790s, and he likely "handled most of the export of furs from St. Louis to Canada." But that obscures a more important point about the expanding House of Chouteau. Auguste partnered with Pierre, and both of them depended on the special personal relationships that brother-in-law Gratiot and Auguste's father-in-law Cerré had in London as well as Montreal. Those "most prominent of the St. Louis fur merchants" constituted a *family* enterprise of undaunted commerce thanks to Gratiot's business associate, John Henry Schneider of London.[262]

In a single shipment, Schneider became the major transatlantic provisioner of Fort Carondelet and St. Louis. His eight-page invoice for March 27, 1794, listed over £1,166 worth of merchandise that he bought in Great Britain with a year's advance notice, shipped to Montreal on the vessel *Le Levant* and then had Todd and McGill's engagés transport to Michilimackinac by canoes to await the arrival of the Chouteau convoy. Schneider's cargo included trade goods for the Osages at Fort Carondelet—10,000 European-knapped gunflints, 50 powder horns, 2,160 knives, 2,160 awls, 4,300 rings, 224 pounds of blue and white glass beads, 670 virgin wool "point" blankets and 200 pounds of vermilion red body pigment. But Schneider also provided French St. Louisans with the wealth of the world, including 108 pairs of Nathan Phillips–brand Moroccan leather shoes; silk stockings, formal gloves and fancy hats; cloth from England, Ireland, Russia, Holland and India, including linen and lace, silk and muslin and cotton and canvas; thirty pounds of Hyson tea from China; and the best patent medicines rarely found on the frontier. Pierre Chouteau received a custom-made saddle that Schneider procured from Sam Beazley of London, with tacking, stirrups and his initials all in sterling silver.[263]

To supplement Schneider's shipment, Todd, McGill & Company of Montreal and Andrew Todd of Mackinac in 1794–5 alone sold the Chouteaus fifty thousand white and black porcelain beads; two thousand pounds of Canadian maple sugar; fifty pounds of Caribbean sugar; thirty gallons of rum; twenty-seven gallons of Madeira wine; fifty pounds of chocolate; metalware and pottery of all varieties; one thousand pounds of gunpowder; and two Algonquian-made birchbark canoes "with gum and sails," worth 250 livres apiece. The merchandise for St. Louis was baled with heavy canvas and marked with a stylized "AC" above an "I," indicating the Illinois Country as the destination of those valuable commodities. (See the color illustration of the Chouteau bale marked "AC" over "M," indicating Mackinac as the *destination* of furs.)[264]

The Chouteaus' heyday as successful contraband traders with Montreal and Michilimackinac between 1794 and 1803 gave St. Louis a significant share of the transatlantic fur market, while Spain failed to profit from the animal harvests in its own territory. Auguste and Pierre were daring internationalists willing to violate the laws of three nations to conduct their illicit business with the best partners. They employed a London agent with a German surname to procure products from Europe and Asia; shipped them to Scottish, Irish, Jewish, English, French and U.S. merchants at Montreal, Michilimackinac and Detroit; paid for cargoes with a complex variety of national currencies (British pounds sterling, Nova Scotia pounds, Montreal pounds, French livres and American dollars); transported London products via Canada to St. Louis by Indian canoes; and hired French, Creole, Canadian, Spanish, Celtic, mulatto and métis voyageurs to deliver merchandise to Siouan, Caddoan and Algonquian tribes throughout their trading territory. The Chouteaus' versatility, ingenuity and tenacity in exploiting the most profitable markets for their furs provided a model of laissez faire economics across international borders that presaged our modern era of globalization. Indifferent to the flags that flew above St. Louis or the Straits of Mackinac, they prospered by their broad vision and multicultural contacts. Their recognition of Michilimackinac's commercial significance and future potential was affirmed when John Jacob Astor, who had proposed a partnership with the House of Chouteau in 1800, established his original headquarters of the American Fur Company there in 1810.[265]

THE INFLUENCE OF AFFLUENCE

The international trade stimulated by the Fort Carondelet monopoly was a fitting climax to three decades of Chouteau-Osage relations, as the 1790s represented the high-water mark of French St. Louis's sophisticated consumer society in the colonial era. Flush with rare European imports that everyone desired in Upper Louisiana, that city of global trading "flourished and became the parent of a number of little villages on the Mississippi and Missouri." St. Louis resembled the hub of a great wheel, with "spokes" connecting it to

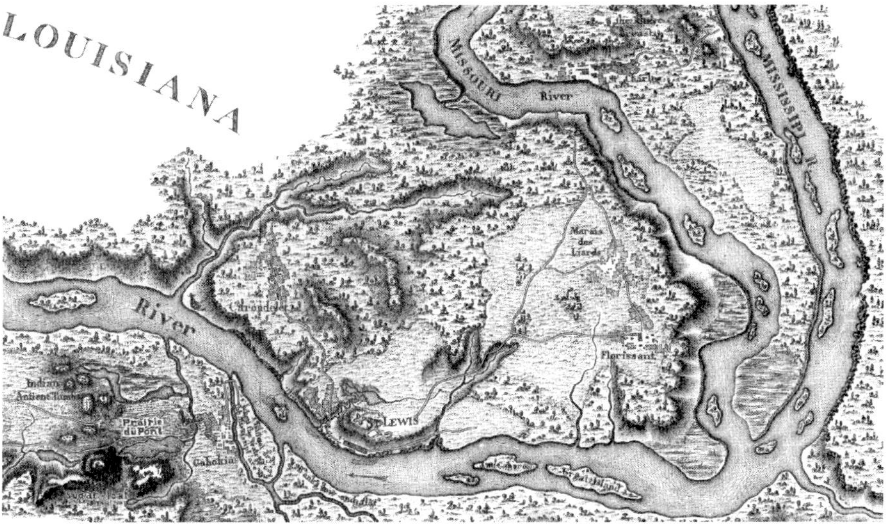

St. Louis and nearby satellite settlements it enriched, 1796. *From Clarence Alvord,* Collections of the Illinois State Historical Library, II *(1907), based on Collot's map.*

satellite settlements stimulated by its economic success. Its zone of commercial influence included the Missouri River villages of St. Charles (founded in 1769), Marais des Liards, now Bridgeton (1786), Portage des Sioux (1799) and Florissant/St. Ferdinand (1780), a suburb founded by some of Laclède's charter colonists who relocated to farm some of the richest topsoil in North America. South of St. Louis were Carondelet (1767), New Ste. Genevieve (1790), New Bourbon (1797), New Madrid (1789) and small communities of lead miners and salt producers. About thirty-three hundred people lived in those areas by 1796, when they harvested 75,000 bushels of maize, 35,000 bushels of wheat and 25,000 pounds of tobacco; extracted 219,000 pounds of lead and 6,000 bushels of salt; and pastured nearly 4,000 cattle and 600 horses. St. Louis was hardly *pain court*, contributing almost 6,000 bushels of wheat and 5,000 bushels of maize, 2,000 pounds of tobacco, 250 horses and at least 1,200 cattle to those totals. In his 1804 "Narrative," Chouteau recognized Laclède's foresight in selecting the site of St. Louis with "its central position *for forming settlements*." It was one more legacy of the French founders, which is today recalled in the modern motto of the Regional Chamber and Growth Association: "St. Louis, Perfectly Centered. Remarkably Connected."[266]

By 1800, St. Louis's seven hundred white residents enjoyed a high standard of living comparable to seaport cities and defied the frontier stereotypes of crude cabins, deficient diets and scarce schooling. The influence of affluent consumerism in that urbane capital of "refinement and fashion" attracted a disproportionate number of wealthy European-born citizens with excellent educations, expensive tastes and enormous talent. "St. Louis was always remarkable…for a degree of gentility among the better sort of its inhabitants," and those who followed in the footsteps of the intellectual Laclède included: Dr. Antoine Francois Saugrain, an army surgeon who knew Jefferson in his native Paris; Louis Chauvet Dubreuil, son of a La Rochelle avocat; Claude Mercier, a physician and surgeon from France; Father Pierre Joseph Didier, former procurator of the Abbey Church of St. Denis in Paris; Benito Vasquez, an army adjutant and merchant from Galicia, Spain; Jacques Ceran de St. Vrain, a merchant whose brother was St. Louis's last Spanish lieutenant governor; Charles Sanguinet, son of a Quebec notary; and Antoine Soulard of Rochefort, a French navy veteran who was the king's surveyor for Upper Louisiana. Those well-read residents, plus another sixty equally prominent individuals, owned as many as three thousand volumes in the capital city of the "wilderness." Their minds were as open as the Missouri frontier, and freethinkers like Chouteau had several books that were banned by the Catholic Church.[267]

TABLE C

Average Annual Fur Varieties, Volumes and Values Traded at St. Louis, 1790–1804

SELECTED MAMMALS {NOT COMPREHENSIVE}*	POUNDS	PRICE/POUND	WHOLESALE ("ILLINOIS") VALUE#
Brain-tanned Deer Leather	97,000	$.40	$38,770
Deerskins (*chevreuil*) "in the hair"	6,381	.50	3,190
Raccoon (*chat*)	4,248	.25	1,062
Fox (*renard*)	802	.50	401
Beaver (*castor*)	12,281	1.20	14,737
"Cow skins" (probably female bison)	189	1.50	283
(Black) Bear (*ours*)	2,541	2.00	5,082
Buffalo (*boeuf*) Hides & Robes	1,714	3.00	5,142
Otter (*loutre*)	1,267	4.00	5,068
Subtotals (rounded off):	126,400		$73,800
+Tallow/Animal Fat (in pounds)	8,313	.20	1,662
+Bear Grease (in gallons)	2,340	1.20/gal	2,572
Total Gross Value (rounded off)			$78,000
Minus Estimated Value of Trade Goods (rounded off) (includes all shipping costs and other expenses)			$61,000
Leaving an Estimated Net Profit of approximately 27 percent:			$17,000

*Omitted species were: martens, fishers, muskrats, squirrels, bobcats (*pichou*), lynxes/wildcats, skunks and ermines regularly harvested in the Missouri River Valley.

#Retail prices in London would have been approximately twice this amount.

Auguste Chouteau claimed that he compiled this statistical summary in 1805, but it was not printed until 1811 in Zadok Cramer's *Ohio Navigator* (p. 268). The version here was part of the "Missouri Produce" section of "Descriptive Observations on certain parts of the Country in Louisiana," by Anthony Soulard, surveyor general of Upper Louisiana, in a letter to J.A. Chevallié of Richmond (translated into English by a Dr. Mitchill). It appeared in Zadok Cramer, *The Navigator: Containing Directions for Navigating the Monongahela, Allegheny, Ohio and Mississippi Rivers*, 8th ed. (Pittsburgh, PA: Cramer, Spear and Eichbaum, 1814), 342–43.

The thriving and diversified regional economy built on "the skin of the deer that runs in the woods" disproved Jefferson's belief that hunting societies were invariably "primitive" and devoid of civility. While he refused to distinguish between subsistence hunting of Appalachian Americans for individual consumption and commercial mammal harvesting by talented Indians for worldwide markets, the residents of Upper Louisiana recognized that the "true basis [of their]…prosperity" was the "abundant fur trade." Although profits are difficult to determine, most historians agree with Amos Stoddard's estimate that "the average annual value of furs and peltries in Upper Louisiana during the last fifteen years of Spanish rule…[was about] $203,750," with yearly profits averaging $55,000. That latter figure seems too low, even though it was still a considerable sum. Chouteau's 1805 report on the average value of furs traded in St. Louis between 1790 and 1804 (see Table C) was so incomplete as to seem intentionally deceptive in downplaying the profitability of his town. Those figures may reflect only *his* trade with the Osages, although he probably omitted the Fort Carondelet monopoly and surely did not wish to advertise his contraband commerce. Due to cultural, economic and governmental factors, French St. Louisans made substantial profits "off the books" in the Michilimackinac trade and other markets, with Spain's feeble enforcement and negligent collection of duties being major factors. As early as 1776, a Spanish official reported that the "annual commerce of the colony [of Louisiana] was about 600,000 pesos, of which only about 15,000 pesos passed through legitimate channels."[268]

What no statistics could measure was the increasing pressure on only three to four thousand Missouri Osages to keep their lands, animals and market share from succumbing to strong rivals as they traveled farther, hunted longer and worked harder to maintain their trade dominance after the Arkansas schism. But Fort Carondelet was a model of stability compared to the chaos that engulfed the rest of the region, as British traders, Anglo-American settlers, immigrant tribes from Ohio, northern Algonquians and breakaway Osages made Upper Louisiana bellicose and bloody. In March 1800, near the mouth of the Meramec River, an American named Adam House was found with his "head cut off and laid at his side, scalp taken and body full of wounds from musket shots." Nearby was his eight-year-old son, Jacob, who was also decapitated but neither scalped nor otherwise mutilated. His "face [was] smeared with blood," and he had "a small piece of maple sugar in his mouth." Another son, aged fourteen, had a musket wound but was found alive in a ransacked house with dead cattle in the yard (one decapitated).[269]

Those grisly murders outraged St. Louis's new lieutenant governor, Charles de Hault Delassus, a French nobleman born in Flanders and, like Governor Carondelet, a former officer in the Royal Walloon Guards. He ordered Osage chiefs to come to St. Louis for a reckoning, or he would hold Commandant Pierre Chouteau of Fort Carondelet responsible for their "barbarous actions" and send him to "the hot country" (New Orleans, not hell). Delassus did not know who had committed those crimes, so he called in every Osage leader he could reach. When two hundred Missouri and Arkansas Osages arrived in St. Louis on August 28, they were surprised to find Delassus calm and conciliatory. Chief Pawhiuskah of the Grand Osages of Missouri and "La Cheniere" of the Arkansas defectors were "lodge[d]…and entertain[ed]" in the mansions of the Chouteau brothers for an entire week, which "cost them a great sum." In addition, Delassus hosted a dinner party for four of the principal delegates, which left them "very well satisfied." A single Arkansas Osage admitted to committing the murders and was locked up, while, as a gesture of goodwill, the chiefs made peace with Shawnees, Miamis, Delawares and Kickapoos who were also in town. Seeking to preserve the "greatest harmony" with old Indian allies when white enemies were more threatening, the lieutenant governor was less interested in punishing ruthless warriors than in putting them to work. Because the Osages were contrite, polite and surprisingly cooperative, Delassus decided to keep them warlike *in his service* by giving presents appropriate to that goal. Included in his "tokens of good friendship" in "the name of this Government" were parting gifts of 100 muskets, 100 pounds of gunpowder, 300 pounds of bullets, 300 gunflints, 288 large knives and 50 hatchets, all provided by Auguste Chouteau.[270]

That was hardly a reprimand for violence, but French merchants and Spanish diplomats in St. Louis thought it perfectly normal to arm Indian allies with guns and "scalping knives" so that they could defend a wilderness homeland that made everyone in the area much richer and wiser. If Osage warriors were increasingly irascible in defending their hunting grounds, senior chiefs knew when to show a milder, most congenial and highly rational side of the Osages' complex personality, long known to the Chouteau brothers. Residents in eastern cities would marvel at the "civilized" Osages, wearing Canadian silver jewelry and Chinese silk neckerchiefs, who did not flinch when huge naval cannons boomed salutes. The French who were privileged to know the admirable traits of "hostile savages" could not conceive of living in the United States, where the genocidal conquest of Indians was "normal" national policy. The Shawnees and Delawares who had relocated to Upper

Louisiana to escape slaughter by U.S. troops in Ohio did not appear to be the "animals of prey" that President Washington called them in eradicating their "Savage Fury."[271]

St. Louisans were increasingly concerned that Americans who demanded such atrocities to procure property would ruin the traditional harmony with local Indians. French residents, therefore, were ecstatic to learn, in late 1802, that Emperor Napoleon had reclaimed Louisiana from the Spanish. At long last, a more powerful and glorious France would nurture its distant colonial countrymen, whom King Louis XV had abandoned. No one was happier than Chouteau, who admired Napoleon for intimidating the hated British, owned over a dozen books about the emperor and displayed several printed portraits of him in his mansion. He and the other "orphaned" Creoles anticipated a golden age under the protection of a powerful new imperial administration. But Napoleon's ambitious plans for Louisiana and the Caribbean ended with the defeat of his soldiers in the Haitian Revolution, and French-Americans had to endure a further insult by another fickle ruler. After he signed them over to the United States, Napoleon had the nerve to declare his "regret" in "separat[ing] ourselves from" those who "*have been* Frenchmen….Let them retain for us sentiments of affection, and may their common origin, descent, language, and customs perpetuate the friendship."[272]

The same old problems with French colonization—too little concern at home for too few people here—now left St. Louisans once again abandoned and at the mercy of a powerful and pompous United States, the only nation to own, govern and coordinate comprehensive policies for both sides of the Mississippi in Upper Louisiana. When Delassus learned of the Louisiana Purchase in August 1803, he realized that St. Louis's peaceful and prosperous relations with Indians would soon be a memory. In forecasting fur profits for 1804, that depressed and disgusted official wrote only, "The Devil may take all!"[273]

As that special world of multicultural tolerance in Upper Louisiana was about to be lost, visiting Frenchmen left vivid and complimentary accounts. Perrin du Lac described St. Louis as the "most important town" at a "beautiful and salubrious situation, surrounded by a country of exuberant fertility." Its "inhabitants, employed in trade and the fine arts," would have made that an even more "considerable town under any other government than Spain"—which had treated the region "like a gangrenous growth [isolated] from the body of the state." Louis Vilemont imagined himself in an "aërostatic chariot," looking down on the "horn of abundance which nature seems to have bestowed upon this beautiful region." Nicolas de Finiels also saw a utopia—but a societal one viewed at ground level, which had been created by people, not nature. He praised "the Affection" that the French "effortlessly generated in the hearts of all the Indian nations," while the "English, Anglo-Americans, and Spanish nations have succeeded only in inspiring fear and alienation." The "proximity of the Indians," he claimed, had "altered the native traits of the colony's first settlers," imparting a distinctive character to them. The result was "a rather interesting mix—basically something that a philosopher might see as the point at which the human species should have stopped, in order to have the best chance of obtaining happiness."[274]

Epilogue

Finding and "Fixing" St. Louis

The time is not far distant...when the uncultivated wilds of the interior part of the continent, which is now only inhabited by the tawny sons of the forest and howling beasts of prey, will be exchanged for the votaries of agriculture, who will turn those sterile wildernesses into rich, cultivated and verdant fields.
—William Fisher

Time could not stand still, and the human species would not stop—especially the relentless march of Anglo-Americans across the continent. At the dawning of a strange new era, St. Louis was in a precarious position—a victim of its own success on a prosperous frontier that increasingly attracted the unwelcome attention of intruders. For French residents and their Osage allies, the period of "Louisiana's adolescence was the most felicitous time that the region has experienced thus far," while the American takeover was a traumatic, transformative event that revolutionized the futures of both peoples. The town was located where the east–west Anglo-American Corridor of Indian Conquest (employing the peace of wars in a settler empire that cultivated Indian lands to harvest food) intersected the north–south French Corridor of Indian Commerce (employing the wares of peace in a sutler empire that cultivated Indian labor to harvest furs). Those converging paths of diametrically opposed frontier cultures were like the crosshairs of a gunsight, and St. Louis was right in the middle, bracing for a blast.[275]

When Meriwether Lewis and William Clark arrived in St. Louis in December 1803, they made one of their greatest discoveries—a multicultural

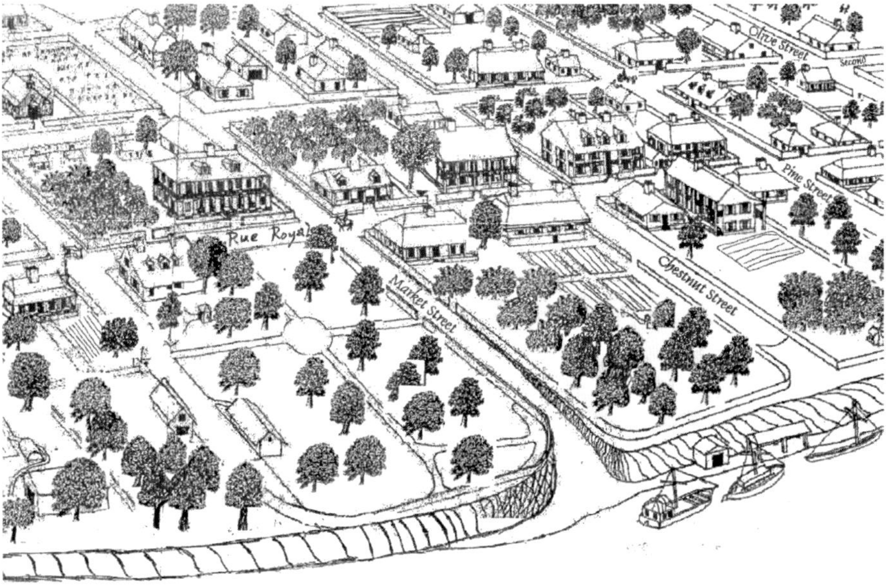

St. Louis as an affluent capital when Lewis and Clark arrived. *Courtesy Dr. Robert Moore Jr. and the National Park Service, Jefferson National Expansion Memorial.*

commercial city of affluent French civility situated in a lucrative "wilderness," where they could get a hot bath, splendid food and indispensable information, including already prepared maps of the Missouri River. When Captain Amos Stoddard, the first U.S. commandant, reached St. Louis in February 1804, he, too, was impressed. "The town," he wrote, "contains about 200 houses, mostly very large and built of stone; it is elevated and healthy, and the people are rich and hospitable; they live in a style equal to those in the large seaport towns, and I find no want of education among them." A month later, when the stars and stripes were raised above St. Louis to more tears than cheers, Stoddard proclaimed that "Upper Louisiana, from its climate, population, soil and productions…will, in all human probability, soon become a *star* of no inconsiderable magnitude in the American constellation."[276]

For forty years, St. Louis had been the thriving "emporium of trade" and a "center of…elegance" as the capital of a growing district that now contained twelve thousand people by Stoddard's count. Nonetheless, the new U.S. "sovereigns of the country" were determined to "*fix*"—irrevocably change—St. Louis because the success of the French alternative to frontier development violated American sensibilities and policies. Ideological prejudice is a dangerous thing, often preventing people from accepting the obvious if that reality runs counter to their beliefs of what *should* be. Stoddard denigrated the "compact villages" of the French, finding that the more "*extensive* settlements" in Upper Louisiana were "made by *English Americans*," who were "industrious" farmers, not Indian traders. Refusing to credit the equally "industrious" Osage hunters, whose loyalty and labors had stimulated a robust regional economy that benefited thousands of white residents, Stoddard stated that the fur trade "at best only afforded a precarious subsistence." Another Anglo-American in St. Louis, who would later govern it, agreed:

> *As long as we are* Indian Traders *and* Hunters, *our settlements can never flourish, and…I care not how soon the savage is left to traverse in solitude his own Deserts, until the approach of cultivation obliges him to retreat into more gloomy recesses.*[277]

Alien Invaders from Another World

That anti-Indian bias was shared by all the American military officers that St. Louisans had to deal with earliest and longest, especially Lewis, Clark and Governor William Henry Harrison of the Indiana Territory, who initially administered Upper Louisiana. All were Virginia-born, slave-owning plantation gentry who had served in President Washington's army that conquered the Ohio Indians in the 1790s. Native peoples called Washington "Town Destroyer," as they had his great-grandfather in the 1670s, since Mount Vernon and Washington, D.C., were both built on the bones of their ancesters. Virginians had been conquering Indians since the early days of Jamestown, and as tobacco inevitably destroyed the land that determined social status, generations of Virginia "Long Knives" (*Noyatunga* in Osage) had created "terror-tories" by invading successive western frontiers. Indian hunters, fur traders and wild animals all had to be removed to provide precious "civilized" lands required in a rapidly expanding farming culture. "English America" had mushroomed from 250,000 to 5.5 million people in the eighteenth century, and in 1803, Virginia was the largest state in both area (an estimated 117,000 square miles) and population, with over 514,000 whites and 346,000 black slaves. Indians in the East referred to all land-hungry Anglo-Americans as "Virginians"—aggressive, greedy enemies whose outrageous "Virginia lies" resulted in the loss of tribal homelands as a notorious "habit of empire."[278]

Virginia was the "new Rome" and "mistress of the Union," with a "dynasty" that controlled the presidency for thirty-two of the first thirty-six years of the United States. No son of the Old Dominion was more expansionistic than President Jefferson. His father was a surveyor, land speculator and famous cartographer who, like most planters, cast covetous eyes on the fertile lands beyond the Appalachians. Young Jefferson's guardian, Dr. Thomas Walker—"the Cardinal Richelieu of southern land speculation"—discovered the Cumberland Gap route to Kentucky in the 1750s and was planning to explore the Missouri River a decade before Laclède and Chouteau got there. John Mitchell's famous 1755 map of North America already depicted Virginia's western border, based on sea-to-sea royal charters from the early 1600s, extending into present-day Kansas, with the future states of Virginia, Kentucky and Missouri sharing a common southern border. "Osages" was written on that map, sandwiched between Virginia's ancient boundaries, and many Virginians regarded that territory as theirs for the taking. When he was governor of Virginia, Jefferson supported George Rogers Clark's invasion of the Illinois Country, which brought the old Creole towns into Virginia's expanding empire, with "Fort Jefferson" built along the Ohio River and Randolph County—Illinois's first—named for the family of Jefferson's mother. By 1774, "Louisiana" was being called "the Western Parts of Virginia."[279]

The Louisiana Purchase was not the work of just any Americans; it was specifically and largely accomplished by Virginians. "For Jefferson, Virginia's future and America's were inextricable, even indistinguishable," and he doubled the size of the United States using other Virginians—his secretary of state, a special envoy in Paris and the two famous explorers who would forge the "future path of civilization" to "receive…the overflowing tide of *our own* population." The "vast and restless" Virginians were described as "a plague of locusts" destined to "gain all the vast continent occupied by the Indians"—and the Indian capital of St. Louis was a prime target, ripe for reform. Anglo-Americans had been warring with the French for control of the continent since 1689, and St. Louis's close physical, cultural and historical connections with Fort de Chartres were ominous, indeed, considering the raids that its marines and allied warriors had conducted during the French and Indian War. Virginians in Jefferson's Blue Ridge Mountains could never forget or forgive the "barbarities and depredations [that] a mongrel race of Indian savages and French papists have perpetrated upon our frontiers"—searing memories that Jefferson immortalized in the Declaration of Independence with his hate speech condemning the "merciless Indian savages, whose known rule of warfare is an undistinguished destruction of all ages, sexes, and conditions." In 1754, Washington himself had almost been killed by a kinsman of Saint Ange—Captain Louis Coulon de Villiers—who sought revenge for Washington's admitted "assassination" of his younger brother, Ensign Joseph Coulon de Villiers, sieur de Jumonville.[280]

The Louisiana Purchase was equivalent to another military defeat for the French, and their old cultural enemies regarded the St. Louisans as decadent, deplorable and dangerous people of loose morals and lost empires, with a strange language, superstitious rituals and a habit of sleeping with "savages." A kinsman of the Clark clan wrote that French-Americans were "an idle, lazy people, a parcel of renegadoes from Canada," who were "much worse than the Indians." Thus "tainted by the wilderness," they depended "chiefly on the savages for their subsistence," and "they scarcely raise as much as will supply their wants, in imitation of the Indians, whose manners and customs they have entirely adopted." The Virginia "sovereigns" who occupied St. Louis served a president who believed that the rural "cultivators of the earth are the most valuable citizens," while "cities…[were] pestilential to the morals, the health and the liberties of man." In 1800, Jefferson even took satisfaction from recent outbreaks of "yellow fever [that] will discourage the growth of great cities in our nation." He also denounced Catholicism as "the lowest grade of ignorance," writing that "history…furnishes no example of a priest-ridden people maintaining a free civil government." Knowing that many U.S. Protestants linked his religion with the rapacity of Indian warriors, the first Catholic bishop in the United States, the Reverend John Carroll of Baltimore, went out of his way to denounce the "cruelties practiced by the savage Indians" and to applaud their eradication by "just and necessary warfare." Bishop Carroll was the spiritual administrator of St. Louis, and the literal "Indian-lovers" in that French Catholic city were truly isolated when the universality of the Roman Church was compromised by regional cultural ideology, since Carroll's family was the richest of all Chesapeake plantation owners.[281]

A Sinister Season

The Virginians who carried Jefferson's "Empire of Liberty" into Missouri believed that French St. Louis fur traders had made "bad Indians" even worse, corrupting them with rum and rifles. Most threatening to Americans was the Chouteau-Osage alliance, and it became the first target of militant administrators. Because President Jefferson regarded the Grand Osages as the greatest native nation in Upper Louisiana, he invited them to be the first trans-Mississippi Indians he parleyed with, meeting their delegations for three successive years, beginning in 1804. He knew that the United States "must stand well" with the Osages, "because in their quarter we are miserably weak." The president lacked military resources of sufficient strength to engage the Osages in battle, but he was determined that there would only be one supreme power in the *American* West. Initially, as the professed "father and friend" of the Osages, Jefferson promised them continued commerce and no loss of their traditional territory. But that was a "Virginia lie," since he secretly informed his military officers that "commerce is the great engine by which we are to *coerce them* & and not war." Jefferson wrote to Governor Harrison in February 1803 about his plan to have "good and influential" Indians "run into debt" with white traders, for then "they become willing to lop them off by a cession of lands." He would tolerate fur trading only as a temporary, expedient means to placate the Indians and preserve the peace until the United States mustered enough military strength to enforce even harsher policies. Then, as he boasted to Harrison, "we [will] have only to shut our hand to crush them." He ended his message ominously: "I must repeat that this letter is to be considered as private" and never divulged to "the Indians. For their interests and tranquility, it is best they should see only the present age of their history."[282]

The Louisiana Purchase could not have come at a worse time for the Grand Osages with "French hearts," since they were warring with all area Indians. Recently reduced in population by smallpox and influenza, as well as the division of their nation, the Osages endured a series of military defeats after 1797, as enemies from the Comanches to the Kickapoos launched devastating raids. The attack with the most far-reaching consequences occurred in October 1805, when Potawatomies under Main Poc (Withered Hand) raided a Petit Osage village, slaughtering thirty-four women and children and capturing sixty others. Jefferson tested the Osages' obedience by ordering them not to retaliate. In August 1806, U.S. Army captain Zebulon Montgomery Pike ransomed forty-six of those Osage captives and took them home. Pike judged it a "miracle of extraordinary forbearance" that proud Osage warriors had not avenged that horrific raid in the traditional manner. "They have become a nation of Quakers," he observed with amazement, "in obedience to the injunctions of their great father" Jefferson. That event made it clear that U.S. military officials would be directing Indian affairs in Missouri from then on.[283]

According to the leading Jefferson scholar, Peter S. Onuf, "the history of Jeffersonian statecraft was one of ruthlessly exploiting regional power imbalances," based on "the convenient self-delusion that republicans operated on a higher moral plane than their corrupt European counterparts." The president grew increasingly aggressive with visiting Osage delegations, and after the Pike episode in 1806, he was downright dictatorial to the Indian "Quakers" he no longer feared—and thus ceased to respect. Acting on his belief that "weakness provokes insult & injury, while a condition to punish often prevents it," Jefferson told the chiefs that U.S. citizens needed their lands and that they should begin to "clothe & provide for their families as we do" by farming rather than hunting. The president was coercing them to alter centuries-old traditions of gender relations, requiring men to become farmers rather than warriors and hunters, and women to become housewives instead of farmers and leather manufacturers. In 1806, Jefferson offered a sinister warning to any Osages who might resist his dictates: Americans "are strong, we are numerous as the stars in the heavens, & we are all gun-men," who "do not fear any nation."[284]

Friendly French merchants and solicitous Spanish commandants had made the Grand Osages vulnerable to such unexpected aggression by convincing them that all whites would forgive their transgressions as long as their furs made Europeans wealthy. Osage harvests were still valued at $63,000 per year, but their fur trade lost whatever leverage it had when the Lewis and Clark Expedition discovered the first huge supply of premium beavers on U.S. lands. Locating in the high altitudes of the Rockies what had never existed in the nation's southern latitudes, those Virginians lost no time in transforming the St. Louis fur trade from a multicultural partnership in the harvesting of deer into a system of whites-only beaver trapping with no Indians to pay or placate. By 1808, Osage hunters were expendable, and their lands were now considered much more valuable than the mammals on them—just in time to provide farms for the thousands of U.S. citizens thronging into Missouri. Lewis and Clark praised the Osage homeland as "an extent of country nearly equal to the State of Virginia, and much more fertile," because its rich, virgin soil had never felt a plow. The United States could get deerskins elsewhere, but not such "immense tracts of fine Country" with "four salines…unequalled by any known in North America."[285]

Only three months into Governor Lewis's administration, he moved swiftly to "demean" and cripple the Grand Osages. He suspended trade at the height of the hunting season and declared that they were "no longer under the protection of the United States." He authorized Shawnees, Delawares,

Kickapoos, Ioways and Sioux to attack the Missouri Osages—but only if their warriors used "sufficient force to destroy or drive them from our neighborhood." Confused by the sudden negativity in their relations with American officials, and not wishing to add "gun-men" of the United States to their growing list of enemies, some of the more compliant Osage chiefs obeyed Lewis's command and dutifully reported to the new U.S. fur factory and military garrison being built at Fort Clark (soon to be Fort Osage) near present-day Independence. There, General Clark coerced them to sign a shocking treaty of dispossession as punishment for their alleged "lawless depredations" against American settlers. Under duress, they ceded 52,480,000 acres (half of Arkansas and almost all of Missouri) to the United States, receiving "less than one-sixth of a cent per acre," in order to have the government protect them "from the insults and injuries of other tribes." That followed Jefferson's advice in 1803 of "abruptly proposing" land cessions when Indians assembled to discuss other matters. Clark also required the Osages to live and trade only

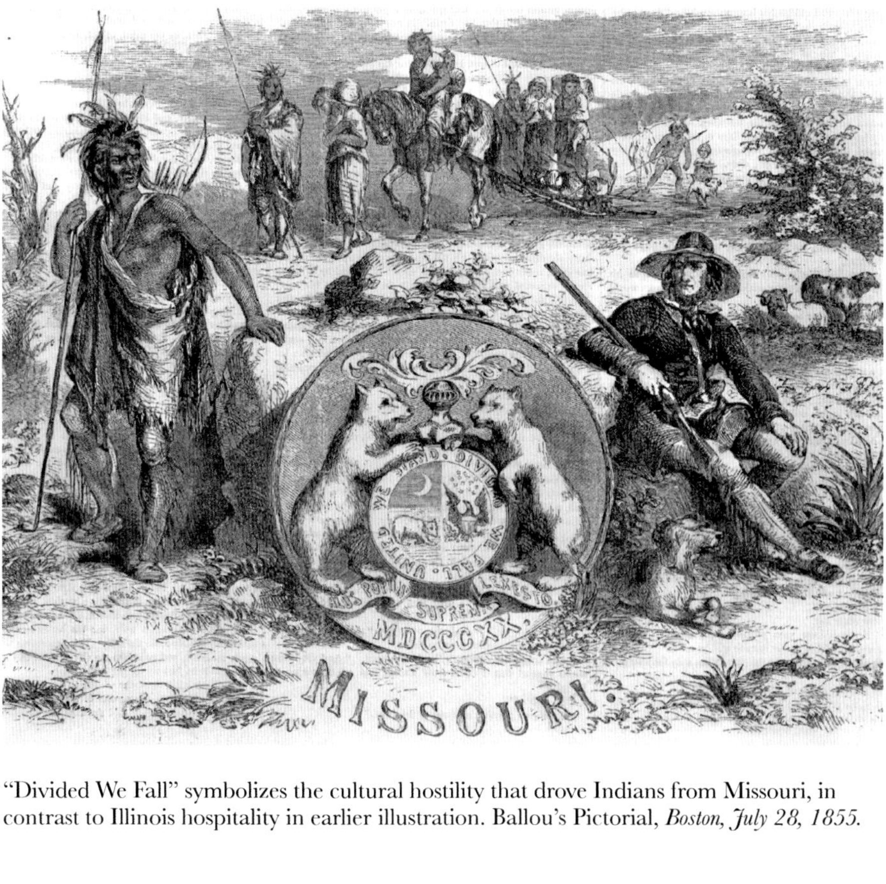

"Divided We Fall" symbolizes the cultural hostility that drove Indians from Missouri, in contrast to Illinois hospitality in earlier illustration. Ballou's Pictorial, *Boston, July 28, 1855.*

at Fort Osage under the scrutiny of U.S. soldiers and to respect a new fixed "boundary line between our nations." Clark's apartheid policy was a product of Virginia frontier racism, reflecting the "necessity of preventing a white and Indian population from remaining in immediate contact with each other" to "prevent the two parties from intermixing."[286]

Leaving the Grand Osages with a mere sliver of far western Missouri, the 1808 Treaty of Fort Osage was a naked land grab that violated Jefferson's promise to respect "Indian rights of occupancy." The Osages were the first native nation located entirely west of the Mississippi to be victimized by his dispossession obsession, and that treaty—which cost them an empire and an industry, their independence and traditional way of life—represented a greater betrayal than the Cherokees' Trail of Tears. The Grand Osages had never warred against the United States, and they had been very helpful and hospitable to Lewis and Clark. But Pawhiuskah's people had become too civilized, too accommodating and too hemmed-in by hostile Anglo-Americans before they realized that politeness, obedience and proximity bred contempt from domineering U.S. officials. Clark declared it "the hardest treaty on the Indians that he ever made, and that if he was damned hereafter it would be for making that treaty." He had reason to fear a tenure in hell because he wrongly accused the Osages of attacking whites but took their lands anyway. In 1816, he admitted to Jefferson that those "torments of this frontier" had been committed by "tribes East of the Mississippi & high up that River," but he was "compelled to vary from principle" and punish the Missouri Osage victims of enemy raiders rather than the perpetrators. But gaining land was the real goal, since the far more predatory Arkansas Osages did not forfeit territory in 1808 because whites did not need it—yet. Despite his regrets, Clark dispossessed all Osages of their remaining fifty thousand square miles in 1825, and his report to Congress a year later falsely claimed that "most of their lands [had] *fallen* into our hands." Forced to leave the state they had helped create, the fragmented factions of the Osage nation came together on a reservation in eastern Kansas, having realized the futility of goodwill and the viciousness of "Virginia lies."[287]

The Chouteau Dilemma

And where were the Osage-loving Chouteau brothers when all of that was happening? Initially, in 1803 and 1804, both Chouteaus tried to mediate on behalf of the Osages when they thought that the United States wanted to get along with Indians in a society of inclusion rather than moving them along into an exile of exclusion. The two brothers entertained the American "sovereigns" in their grand mansions, trying to make good impressions as helpful advisors to the powerful strangers. Auguste Chouteau was at a disadvantage because no other St. Louisan so personified French "deficiencies" than the fifty-four-year-old patriarch of a Catholic, Creole, commercially focused city of non-English-speaking Indian lovers. He was an isolated alien in his own land, especially suspect as the leading merchant to the Osages, a master of native diplomacy and an actual "Indian father"—the very characteristics that American leaders found particularly objectionable and potentially treasonous. How could either Chouteau brother claim credit for pacifying the Osages at Fort Carondelet when U.S. military officers distrusted even an Indian *peacemaker* as a "dangerous personage [who] controls the Savages as if they were Machines and can make them Commit the greatest excesses…[by] making presents"? By wanting Indians to *like* them, the French incurred the wrath of many Anglo-Americans, who regarded such cross-cultural influences with suspicion because of their own failed attempts to make Indians like *them*.[288]

But the novice "sovereigns" in a strange land were so desperate for information that they took their time to see if the Chouteaus would be "useful or dangerous." Lewis and Clark asked so many questions about the region and its resources that Auguste Chouteau drafted his famous "Narrative of the Settlement of St. Louis" over the winter of 1803–04 for their benefit. Only a fourteen-page fragment of that document survives, so we cannot know everything that Chouteau wrote. But in the short beginning portion, he described how St. Louis was founded and praised Laclède and Saint Ange for their leadership in avoiding Indian wars—while *never mentioning the Osages* and making only slight, vague references to fur trading. The Americans could only conclude that the *city of St. Louis* mattered most to Laclède's heirs as his and their greatest legacy. The Virginians became convinced that the Chouteau brothers would be useful as advisors, multilingual diplomats and treaty negotiators, but especially as supportive liaisons with other French St. Louisans. President Jefferson might well overlook their unsavorty pasts if the Chouteaus would act more like *city* fathers than Indian fathers, abandoning their Osage kin to cooperate in making St. Louis the first commercial and diplomatic capital of the U.S. West.[289]

Chouteau's "Narrative" confirmed that he expected all people—friends or foes, of whatever race or culture—to act and react on the basis of self-interest, with almost all relationships and issues being negotiable for practicality and survival. As pragmatic capitalists, the Chouteau brothers accepted the reality that numerical superiority, military supremacy and commercial indispensability had shifted from the cooperative Grand Osages to coercive Virginians representing the considerably greater power of the United States. Neither rational nor emotional arguments could deter or alter the Indian removal policies of Jefferson, which were already in full swing on both sides of the Mississippi. All French St. Louisans faced dispossession, too—of 1.4 million acres in suspect Spanish land grants—that legions of American lawyers would litigate into the 1830s. The Chouteau brothers alone had "about 198,000 acres" at risk, and like other "foreign" French Catholics, they were concerned about their futures in a new territory at the mercy of outsiders. The Louisiana Purchase Treaty promised U.S. citizenship to the French, but there were unsettling delays and disturbing developments before that happened. Jefferson compounded the confusion with an intimidating statement in his second inaugural address of 1805: "Is it not better that the opposite bank of the Mississippi should be settled by our own brethren and children than by strangers of another family?"[290]

Equally troubling to the Chouteaus was a slippage of power and social prestige among other French St. Louisans. Brackenridge observed that "the principal inhabitants" who had "bask[ed] in the sunshine of favor" under the Spanish suffered the most "anxiety," having "lost much of that influence which they formerly possessed, and are superseded in trade and in lucrative occupations by strangers." The lower classes in Upper Louisiana, Brackenridge declared, "were formerly under a kind of dependence, or rather vassalage, to the great men of villages, to whom they looked up for their support and protection." But the local economy flourished under the Americans, as "specie became more abundant, and merchandise cheaper [while] landed property was greatly enhanced in value." A growing middle class was now challenging the old grandees. "They feel and speak like freemen, and are not slow in declaring that formerly the field of enterprise was occupied by the monopolies of a few, and it is now open to every industrious citizen."[291]

The Chouteaus had many "sticks" hanging over them, so they chose to take the "carrot" offered by U.S. officials in order to retain their social status and financial dominance among residents old and new. Long the masters of adaptive transitions in perpetuating their transactions, the Chouteaus preferred to use governments than to be used by them. In 1804 alone they built the boats that transported the last Spanish officials to New Orleans (demanding cash instead of credit vouchers), supplied the Lewis and Clark Expedition with experienced French voyageurs and proper gifts for western tribes and assisted

Governor Harrison in dispossessing the Sauks and Mesquakies of fifteen million acres (while claiming tens of thousands of acres for themselves). A grateful Harrison thanked the Chouteaus by lobbying for St. Louis to remain a regional capital when the separate territories of "Louisiana" and "Orleans" were created in 1805. What most solidified intercultural trust, however, was Pierre Chouteau's negotiation of the Osage dispossession treaty of November 1808. That betrayal must have been painful for both Chouteaus, who had spent so much of their lives around campfires with Osage kin. But loyalty was variable in turbulent times, and serving American interests was the only option left to leaders who wished to remain pertinent and prominent in the "family city." By using the Chouteaus in taking Osage lands, U.S. officials were testing their loyalty and value, since only by voluntarily dissolving their oldest Indian blood alliance could those Frenchmen prove that they were very useful and not a bit dangerous.[292]

As businessmen, the Chouteaus were always on the lookout for sweetheart deals, and they were delighted to discover that Lewis and Clark were as obsessed with getting rich as they were. When the United States canceled the heavily subsidized Spanish trade monopolies, while remaining interested in fur profits from new areas, Pierre Chouteau and his oldest son (but not Auguste) joined Clark, Lewis's brother and other merchants in creating the St. Louis Missouri Fur Company in 1809. Thanks to a generous government subsidy procured by Governor Lewis, that company sent trappers, as well as traders, into the distant beaver country, ending the deer dominance of the Osages forever. But it was a key first step in securing prosperous mercantile careers for future Chouteaus in the Far West. Over time, profitable business relationships minimized the cultural differences between the western French and eastern Anglo-Americans, and the Chouteaus were integrated into Jefferson's "Empire of Liberty" even though they could not speak English. Those "French founders are still celebrated today," Jay Gitlin wrote, because they literally "earned a place in the city they had created," allowing St. Louis to avoid "the marginalization that was the fate of other non-Anglo communities" taken over by the United States. The fact that it was easier for the French to ally with the Virginians in *Le Pays des Caucasiens* because of a common race, European lineage and mutual appreciation of capitalism and private property enhances the accomplishment of the Laclède-Chouteau family in maintaining such a successful and long-lasting alliance with Indians who shared none of those compatible characteristics.[293]

The End of a French Beginning

After a commercial career of half a century, Auguste Chouteau retired as an active merchant in 1816, and until that year, "St. Louis had remained confined to the original three streets that Laclède had plotted." Advancing age and declining health were personal factors in that decision, but his timing coincided with increasing U.S. bureaucratic restrictions on fur trading. It was symbolically significant, given Auguste's French heritage, that Canadian fur exports declined from 302,427 pounds in 1816, the year he retired, to a mere 71,039 pounds in 1829, the year he died. The old patriarch was probably relieved to be free of day-to-day financial stresses, and he redirected his energies to a variety of endeavors in a retirement of "busy idleness." As French author Victor Collot observed, while "reputation diminishes the moment" a military hero retires, a merchant could find fulfillment "with glory and dignity [by] doing always something better than what he has done before." For the last dozen years of his life, Chouteau remained active as an investor but became increasingly prominent as a philanthropist, funding charities, schools, churches and other civic improvements—all of which enhanced the stature of the city that was first in his heart.[294]

But Chouteau maintained an involvement in the fur trade that Laclède had taught him, and ironically, that most French of professions earned him "accredited ascendancy" in the national capital named for Washington. "No man in America was better qualified to decide upon the best plan of conducting that [fur] trade than Colonel Chouteau," wrote a U.S. official, "who has pursued it in this country for forty years with such success as to have amassed an immense fortune by it." Chouteau wrote two reports on Indian affairs for the secretary of war and helped Clark and Governor Ninian Edwards of the Illinois Territory negotiate seventeen treaties with a multitude of tribes between 1815 and 1817. Chouteau's unrivaled expertise had given St. Louis a prominent position in relations with all of its many rulers, and his advice to cabinet officials represented the culmination of an acculturative transition from a French alien of doubtful loyalties to a trusted advisor on frontier issues.[295]

Chouteau continued to cultivate unlikely friendships with Clark and Harrison, the most aggressive dispossessors of Indian homelands before 1830, revealing his traditional savvy in working with powerful "chiefs" of any culture who could benefit his town and family. Harrison told Jefferson that Chouteau was "a gentleman who is justly Considered…the first Citizen of Upper Louisiana," due to the "Amiableness of his character" and "the superior information" he shared. As late as 1817, the hero of Tippecanoe and future president was still writing Chouteau "with great respect and regard" because of "the civilities I received from you." The Chouteaus "inducted" Clark into the family "Junto" of old French political lobbyists. A St. Louis contemporary credited the "personal and powerful influence of Col. Auguste Chouteau, John P. Cabanne, Gen. Bernard Pratte, Maj. Pierre Chouteau, Sylvester Labbadie, and Gregoire Sarpy—all Frenchmen, all men of wealth, of distinction, of great influence"—with securing a U.S. Senate seat for Thomas Hart Benton in 1821. They chose wisely, for Benton became a vocal prophet for the West in his thirty-year career, and in 1822, he helped abolish government-run fur factories, which had long competed with the Chouteaus, Astor and other private merchants.[296]

"Patriarch" Chouteau did more to develop St. Louis in the half century following Laclède's death than any other person, holding a multitude of offices and never abandoning the town he had helped create. When Missouri was admitted into the Union in 1821, thanks to the booming population of the St. Louis district, it became the first new state located entirely west of the Mississippi—and the only one there with a constitution written in French as well as English. When Chouteau died in 1829, St. Louis was an *official* city, with a fire department, police force and plans for its first public waterworks. St. Louis had a branch of the Bank of the United States, replacing the pioneering Bank of Missouri, which Chouteau had operated out of his basement years earlier. The new U.S. Army installation at Jefferson Barracks recognized the need for military defense that militia officer Chouteau had foreseen in 1780. By 1820, St. Louis had over three hundred homes—seventy-seven of stone and seventy-five of brick—which surely pleased its original "architect." Chouteau lived to see over 250 steamboats dock at St. Louis in a single year and just missed the recognition of his city as a "national port of entry for foreign goods," which he would have found ironic. His descendants became the first investors in the "steamboat boom" on the Missouri River, expanding commerce from Laclède's original waterfront "over a larger territory…than [almost] any other city in the Union."[297]

St. Louis was the crown jewel in America's western empire, but the French were denied the credit for the city's development in a population increasingly dominated by new immigrants. Missouri had been compromised by Virginians and their culture, as symbolized by the absence of Indians in the new state, the westward expansion of largescale slavery, the proliferation of plantations in several counties that are still called "Little Dixie" and the naming of the state capital "Jefferson City" in 1826, the year of Jefferson's death. Today, Missouri has more monuments, landmarks and sites named for Jefferson than any state outside Virginia, and the flagship campus of our land grant university even displays his original tombstone.

Jefferson died deeply in debt during a prolonged agricultural depression that sent mighty Virginia into an irreversible economic and political decline, while Auguste Chouteau died a very wealthy man in a city on the brink of a fur trade boom in the Far West. Chouteau's estate included almost 21,500 acres of land, in addition to much real estate in the city, plus another 39,000 acres of debatable legality. He left some $83,000 in IOUs, mortgages and promissory notes from eight hundred people; over $17,000 worth of appraised personal property, including his library of six hundred volumes; and fifty slaves, ranging in age from eight days to 102 years. But Chouteau had only $32 in cash, which reflected a fur trader's traditional reliance on credit. What could not be measured by accountants was his sterling legacy—"written in the hearts of his numerous circle of friends"—which would endure as long as the First City of the New West inspired all seekers of fortune to find fresh adventures beyond the distant horizon.[298]

Chouteau was the last survivor of Kerlérec's merchant and military alliance, and despite his frequent adaptations to new challenges, he remained largely a product of a hybrid eighteenth-century "frontier enlightenment," which made him wiser than European philosophers who had never met an Indian. The wisdom that Chouteau gained in his many western experiences made him particularly conscious of hypocrisy, and he must have fumed when Stoddard stated that the Jeffersonians wanted to "emancipate Indians from their chains of ignorance and barbarity," making them "no longer the enemy of other men." Chouteau had spent his adult life doing a far better job of accomplishing that goal than military officers from a nation of native conquerors. The Indians Chouteau knew personally were not "a faithless and ungrateful set of Barbarians" but already possessed the ideal qualities of U.S. citizens—"the highest notions of Liberty of any people on Earth," ever ready to fight "when they think their Liberty [is] likely to be invaded"—for "Nature has given [them] a soul which disdains the chains of tyranny." But Native Americans would have to wait nearly a century after Chouteau's death to become citizens in their own land.[299]

Chouteau's life challenged the pervasive prejudices that denied French-Americans and American Indians much-deserved recognition as equally important creators of our country. Living in the special Osage homeland that made St. Louis prosperous, he and his incomparable family embraced progressive attitudes about cultural diversity that cultivated peace over many decades. For perhaps the first time since that era, our America of many hues and multiple heritages can fully appreciate the enlightened perspectives of Laclède, Chouteau and their French and Indian friends. They are now relevant again. Their lives on the eighteenth-century Missouri frontier presaged the lessons of the late twentieth century, when people began to think globally and to appreciate a common humanity extending beyond the narrow boundaries of a single birth culture. The founders of St. Louis demonstrated little patriotism for any nation, which helped them accept and promote the radical but wonderful idea that history will judge societies by their victims more than their victories. In his last government report, Chouteau reminded American officials of the invaluable principle that had made the "spirit of St. Louis" so special. Finding success on a distant frontier of many cultures, he wrote, requires "a complete knowledge" of different "customs, characters, habits, [and] way of living—without which one will always err and fall from errors to errors."[300]

Notes

Introduction

1. Epigraph from Pierre Chouteau's letter to John F. Darby, February 16, 1847, in *Report of the Celebration of the Anniversary of the Founding of St. Louis on the Fifteenth Day of February, A.D. 1847* (St. Louis, MO: Chambers and Knapp, 1847), 25; obituary quote from the *Missouri Republican* newspaper for that date. The best short biography of Chouteau is in the *Dictionary of Missouri Biography*, ed. Lawrence O. Christensen, William E. Foley, Gary R. Kremer and Kenneth H. Winn (Columbia: University of Missouri Press, 1999), which will be the authoritative source for all famous St. Louisans.
2. The prediction quote is from Chouteau's "Narrative of the Settlement of St. Louis," in *Early Histories of St. Louis*, ed. John Francis McDermott (St. Louis, MO: St. Louis Historical Documents Foundation, 1952), 48. That prophecy was allegedly made by Laclède in December 1763, but Chouteau did not record it until 1804, which may have reflected more 20-20 hindsight than any foresight forty years earlier. A new edition of Chouteau's "Narrative," originally published as an English translation in 1858 and last reprinted in 1952, will appear in 2011, accurately dated and completely annotated for the first time: J. Frederick Fausz, ed., *Chouteau Decoded: The Famous Memoir on the Founding of St. Louis in a New Edition for Modern Readers* (forthcoming).
3. Joe Harl, "History and Archaeology of St. Ferdinand Church: Unearthing a French Colonial Complex in Florissant, Missouri," *Gateway: Magazine of the Missouri History Museum* 27, no. 1 (2007): 57; James D. Kornwolf, *Architecture and Town Planning in Colonial North America*, vol. 1: *Continental*

Powers and Peoples in North America, 1562–1867 (Baltimore, MD: Johns Hopkins University Press, 2002), 365.

4. Doug Moore, "Arch Grounds Renovation Sheds Little Light," *St. Louis Post-Dispatch*, December 11, 2010, A-1, A-4. Even though a new Mississippi River bridge connecting St. Louis with old French Illinois will open in the anniversary year of 2014, no one is considering naming it after Laclède and Chouteau.
5. Moore, "Déterminé L'Effacement: The French Creole Cultural Zone in the American Heartland," *Gateway: The Magazine of the Missouri History Museum* 30 (2010): 20; http://itsawonderfulcity.org/frenchstlouis.aspx (accessed May 27, 2008).
6. Jay Gitlin, *The Bourgeois Frontier: French Towns, French Traders, and American Expansion* (New Haven, CT: Yale University Press, 2010), 2–5, 9–10, 190 (quote).
7. Alvord, *The Illinois Country, 1673–1818* (Springfield: Illinois Centennial Comission, 1920), 365, 379; Patrick Griffin, *American Leviathan: Empire, Nation, and Revolutionary Frontier* (New York: Hill and Wang, 2007), 12; Philip Marchand, *Ghost Empire: How the French Almost Conquered North America* (Toronto, ON: McClelland & Stewart, 2005), 8, 120.
8. Wade, *Urban Frontier* (Chicago: University of Chicago Press, 1959), xviii, 1–3, 6–7, 20, 22, 59–60, 63.
9. Richard White, *The Middle Ground: Indians, Empires, and Republics in the Great Lakes Region, 1650–1815* (Cambridge, UK: Cambridge University Press, 1991); Kathleen DuVal, *The Native Ground: Indians and Colonists in the Heart of the Continent* (Philadelphia: University of Pennsylvania Press, 2006). On the intellectual heritage of French-Indian relations, see Gordon M. Sayre, *Les Sauvages Américains: Representations of Native Americans in French and English Colonial Literature* (Chapel Hill: University of North Carolina Press, 1997); Edward Watts, *In This Remote Country: French Colonial Culture in the Anglo-American Imagination, 1780–1860* (Chapel Hill: University of North Carolina Press, 2006); and Roger Hall Lloyd, *Osage County: A Tribe and American Culture, 1600–1934* (New York: iUniverse, 2008), esp. 64–71. What the eighteenth-century French considered their special cultural traits is summarized succinctly in David A. Bell, "The Unbearable Lightness of Being French: Law, Republicanism and National Identity at the End of the Old Regime," *American Historical Review* 106, no. 4 (2001): 1–41; see also David A. Bell, *The Cult of the Nation in France: Inventing Nationalism, 1680–1800* (Cambridge, MA: Harvard University Press, 2001).
10. Jay Gitlin, "Constructing the House of Chouteau: Saint Louis," *Common-Place*: "Early Cities of the Americas," 3, no. 4 (July 2003), http://www.

common-place.org/vol-03/no-04/st-louis (accessed June 10, 2006); Stephen Aron, *American Confluence: The Missouri River Frontier from Borderland to Border State* (Bloomington: Indiana University Press, 2006), intro; Robert Englebert, "Merchant Representatives and the French River World, 1763–1803," *Michigan Historical Review* 34, no. 1 (2008): 63–82; Special French Heritage Issue of *Gateway: Magazine of the Missouri History Museum* 30 (2010); Gilles Havard and Cécile Vidal, "Making New France New Again: French Historians Rediscover Their American Past," *Common-Place* 7, no. 4 (July 2007), http://www.common-place.org/vol-07/no-04/harvard (accessed November 26, 2008).

11. Patrick Huber's book review in the *Missouri Historical Review* 102, no. 2 (2008): 127; Henry Marie Brackenridge, *Views of Louisiana* (Chicago: Quadrangle Books, Inc., 1962 [orig. publ. 1814]), 126; Louis Houck, *History of Missouri* (Chicago: R.R. Donnelley & Sons, 1908), 1:355; Ste. Genevieve historical marker in Rita K. Coulter, *Discover the French Connection Between St. Louis and New Orleans* (Elmhurst, IL: Interhouse Publishing, 1977), 64.
12. Carl J. Ekberg, *Colonial Ste. Genevieve: An Adventure on the Mississippi River*, 2nd ed. (Tucson, AZ: Patrice Press, 1996), 11 (quote), 42, 157, 415, 417, 428, 432, 434 (map), chap. 13; Ekberg, *French Roots in the Illinois Country: The Mississippi River Frontier in Colonial Times* (Urbana: University of Illinois Press, 1998), 25–26; Ekberg, *François Vallé and His World: Upper Louisiana Before Lewis and Clark* (Columbia: University of Missouri Press, 2002), 45 (first), 90 (demise); Walter A. Schroeder, *Opening the Ozarks: A Historical Geography of Missouri's Ste. Genevieve District, 1760–1830* (Columbia: University of Missouri Press, 2002), 12, 63–66, 225, 232–40.
13. Morris S. Arnold, *Colonial Arkansas, 1686–1804: A Social and Cultural History* (Fayetteville: University of Arkansas Press, 1991), 5–6, 17. The only authenticated *permanent* European towns in the trans-Mississippi West that predate St. Louis are Santa Fe, New Mexico, founded in 1609 (the oldest of all), and Natchitoches ("Nackatish"), Louisiana, established in 1714 (the oldest within the Louisiana Purchase Territory).
14. Dena Lange and Merlin Ames, *St. Louis: Child of the River and Parent of the West* (St. Louis, MO: Webster Publishing, 1939); Schroeder, *Ozarks*, 78, 216, 225; Brackenridge, *Views of Louisiana*, 122; Charles Gayarré, *History of Louisiana: The French Domination*, 2nd ed. (New Orleans, LA: James A. Gresham, 1879 [orig. publ. 1854]), 1:359; R.G. Robertson, *Competitive Struggle: America's Western Fur Trading Posts, 1764–1865* (Boise, ID: Tamarack Books, 1999); James Haley White (1805–1882), "Recollections of St. Louis and Its Men Fifty Years Ago," typescript in the Missouri History Museum (MHM) Library and Research Center folder, "St. Louis Reminiscences," n.d., 10.

The "Creole Corridor" is "an important cultural zone stretching from Cahokia, Illinois, to Ste. Genevieve, Missouri, on both sides of the Mississippi River" (*Gateway* 30 [2010]: 2). Those boundaries omit St. Louis, which was the French-dominated administrative, economic and diplomatic capital of Upper Louisiana, and its global commerce spawned most of the area's satellite communities on the west bank. St. Louis should not be excluded because it outgrew the small, rural villages and left no colonial structures that attract tourists, since it made such significant contributions to the history of French America. *Les Amis' Self-Guided Tour* [of the] *Creole Corridor District: Mid-Mississippi River Valley* begins by "departing from St. Louis" without noting that significance.

15. Peter Charles Hoffer, *The Historians' Paradox: The Study of History in Our Time* (New York: New York University Press, 2008). The 1964 bicentennial publication, *Heritage of St. Louis* (St. Louis Public Schools, 1964) stated the wrong founding date (p. 2), revealed the myth on the Chouteau tombstone (p. 23) and provided a photo of the 1923 Knights of Columbus monument on the St. Louis riverfront showing *Linguest* as Laclède's middle name (p. 3). The history section of the City of St. Louis website begins badly by stating that Laclède received "a land grant from the King of France" and describes Auguste Chouteau as a "scout" (http://www.stlouis.missouri.org/about/history.html). Tim O'Neil did an excellent job of alerting the public to the "Date of St. Louis' Founding Disputed" in the *St. Louis Post-Dispatch*, Febuary 14, 2010, A-1, A-6. Stan Hoig, *The Chouteaus: First Family of the Fur Trade* (Albuquerque: University of New Mexico Press, 2008), 3–9, confused the kings and Chouteau's ages, among other egregious errors. See http://www.nps.gov/archive/jeff/LewisClark2/Circa1804/StLouis for the birthdate error and Carl J. Ekberg's *Stealing Indian Women: Native Slavery in the Illinois Country* (Urbana: University of Illinois Press, 2007), 82, 84, for Laclede's wrong death year. In his most recent book, *A French Aristocrat in the American West: The Shattered Dreams of De Lassus de Luzières* (Columbia: University of Missouri Press, 2010), 111, Ekberg correctly states Laclède's death date but then makes Liguest his middle name. McDermott spelled the name LaClède in his *Histories* volume of 1952 and *Private Libraries in Creole Saint Louis* (Baltimore, MD: Johns Hopkins Press, 1938) but Laclède in his edited volume, *The French in the Mississippi Valley* (Urbana: University of Illinois Press, 1965), and other works. The *St. Louis Magazine* error is found at http://www.stlmag.com/media/St-Louis-Magazine/February-2007/The-Garden-of-Good-and-Evil. Colin G. Calloway, *The Scratch of a Pen: 1763 and the Transformation of North America* (New York: Oxford University Press, 2006), 129, misstated Chouteau's relationship

with Laclède. Tanis C. Thorne, *The Many Hands of My Relations: French and Indians on the Lower Missouri* (Columbia: University of Missouri Press, 1996), 68, 289, spelled Liguest with a *q*; Shirley Christian, *Before Lewis and Clark: The Story of the Chouteaus, the French Dynasty that Ruled America's Frontier* (New York: Ferrar, Straus and Giroux, 2004), 26, claimed that it was a "second surname," while W. Raymond Wood, *Prologue to Lewis and Clark: The Mackay and Evans Expedition* (Norman: University of Oklahoma Press, 2003), 16, wrote "Pierre de Liguest Laclède." The numerous websites of local cultural institutions that guess at the correct name order are not nearly as creative as Walter P. Tracy's 1927 publication, *Men Who Make Saint Louis the City of Opportunity*, which displayed Liguest as both Laclède's middle name and surname on the same page (11).

The Pioneer from the Pyrenees

16. Part I epigraph is from William Vincent Byars, "The Dead of Old Time" poem, in Walter B. Stevens, *St. Louis: The Fourth City, 1764–1909* (St. Louis, MO: S.J. Clarke Publishing, 1909), 1132. The chapter epigraph is from Louisa Stuart Costello, *Béarn and the Pyrenees: A Legendary Tour to the Country of Henri Quartre* (London: Richard Bentley, 1844), 346, translating a stanza by the Béarn poet Cyprien Despourrins (1698–1759), who lived near Laclède. Throughout this chapter, I have relied on illustrations by Thomas Allom and descriptions of sites by the Reverend G.N. Wright in the rare *France Illustrated, Exhibiting Its Landscape Scenery, Antiquities…etc.* (London: Fisher, Son & Co., [1847]).
17. Pierre Tucoo-Chala, *Le Pays de Bearn* (Pau: M.C.T., 1984), frontispiece, 7, and passim; *Dordogne, Bordeaux & the Southwest Coast* (London: Dorling Kindersley Ltd., 2006), 8, 11, 14; *France* (London: Dorling Kindersley Ltd., 1994), 439–51; Émile Houth et al., *Visages de Gascogne et de Béarn* (Paris: Horizons de France, 1948). Also see Michel Grosclaude and Dominique Bidot-Germa, *Histoire De Béarn* (Orthez, 1986) and Peter Sahlins, *Boundaries: The Making of France and Spain in the Pyrenees* (Berkeley: University of California Press, 1989).
18. Timothy Jenkins, *The Life of Property: House, Family and Inheritance in Bearn, South-West France* (New York: Berghahn Books, 2010), 10–11, 28–30; *Dordogne*, 8, 38–39; Francis Miltoun, *Castles and Chateaux of Old Navarre* (Boston: L.C. Page & Co., 1907), chaps. 10, 15.
19. Lucien Labarère, *Pierre de Laclède Liguest (1729–1778): Le Fondateur de St. Louis (Missouri) 15 Février 1764* (Saint-Jean-de-Luz: Benjamin á Bandol, 1984),

1–2, 4; Bell, "Unbearable Lightness of Being French," 21; Pierre Bourdieu, *The Bachelors' Ball: The Crisis of Peasant Society in Béarn*, trans. Richard Nice (Chicago: University of Chicago Press, 2008), 74–75, 102; Vincent J. Pitts, *Henri IV of France: His Reign and Age* (Baltimore, MD: Johns Hopkins University Press, 2009), 6–8 and passim. In 1620, Henri's son, Louis XIII, "announced that the Huguenot territory of Bearn, in his ancestral ministate of Navarre immediately *southwest of France*, would have to permit Catholic worship"—upholding "the rights of Bearnais Catholics against the policy of exclusive Protestant worship laid down by his own grandmother, Queen Jeanne d'Albret of Navarre." It was Louis who "turned Louis IX's feast day into an annual religious celebration" and "made 'St. Louis' the password for entry past his guards" (A. Lloyd Moote, *Louis XIII, The Just* [Berkeley: University of California Press, 1989], 121–22).

20. Pitts, *Henri IV*, 2–8, 21–24, 39; Pierre Goubert, *The Course of French History* (London: Routledge, 1991), 101–06.

21. Jenkins, *Life of Property*, 7–9, 15–17, 32–37, 43–44.

22. Ibid., 9; Bourdieu, *Bachelors Ball*, 102–03, 161–62; Leslie Choquette, *Frenchmen into Peasants: Modernity and Tradition in the Peopling of French Canada* (Cambridge, MA: Harvard University Press, 1997), 35.

23. Labarere, *Laclède*, 1–4; Roger Gordon Molyneux, *Grammar and Vocabulary of the Language of Béarn* (Princi Negue, 2002), 34–35; *Dictionary of Missouri Biography*, s.v. "Laclède."

24. Costello, *Béarn and Pyrenees*, 5–6, 356–60; Sarah Stickney Ellis, *Summer and Winter in the Pyrenees*, 2nd ed. (London: Fisher, Son & Co., 1841), 133–35; Alfred Cadier, *La Vallée d'Aspe* (Pau: Mon Helios, 2002).

25. Costello, *Béarn and Pyrenees*, 342 (Despourrins quote), 359–60; Ellis, *Summer and Winter*, 122–25, 381; 383–85; Arthur Young quoted in Bourdieu, *Bachelor's Ball*, 103–04.

26. Ellis, *Summer and Winter*, 375–77, 387–88; Costello, *Béarn and Pyrenees*, 361.

27. Ellis, *Summer and Winter*, 131–32, 209–10, 215–19, 224, 386–87.

28. Goubert, *French History*, 83, 159; Ellis, *Summer and Winter*, 131, 137, 209, 226, 362; *France*, 390–91, 445; Colin Jones, *The Cambridge Illustrated History of France* (Cambridge, UK: Cambridge University Press, 1999), 170–71.

29. Labarere, *Laclède*, 7–8.

30. Ibid., 4–6, 125–26; Alfred Cadier, *Le Protestantisme en Bearn et au Pays Basque* (N.p.: Kessinger Publishing LLC, 2009 [orig. publ., 1895), 209.

31. Labarere, *Laclède*, 6–8.

32. Ibid., 6–11; Stevens, *Fourth City*, xiii–xiv. On Béarn vultures, see illustrations in *Dordogne*, 16–17, 55.

33. Labarere, *Laclède*, 4, 100, 125–26; Molyneux, *Grammar and Vocabulary*, 131, 158; *Dictionary of Missouri Biography*, s.v. "Laclède."
34. Labarere, *Laclède*, 3, 21–22.
35. Ibid., 23; Costello, *Bèarn and Pyrenees*, 25, 29; Lafitau information from the Dictionary of Canadian Biography Online. An excellent modern map of eighteenth-century Pau is in Tucoo-Chala, *Le Pays de Bearn*, frontispiece.
36. Costello, *Béarn and Pyrenees*, 12–15, 22, 356; Miltoun, *Castles and Chateaux*, 258–77; *Dordogne*, 220–23.
37. Labarere, *Laclède*, 23, 84; Costello, *Béarn and Pyrenees*, 29; *Dictionary of Missouri Biography*, s.v. "Laclède"; McDermott, *Libraries*, 13–14; Christian, *Before Lewis and Clark*, 26.
38. Labarere, *Laclède*, 24; Ellis, *Summer and Winter*, 24, 39, 43, 114, 120, 223–25; Costello, *Béarn and Pyrenees*, 362–67. Labarere (p. 25) claimed that Laclède, at a younger age, transacted business on behalf of godfather d'Arret in the Spanish towns of Jaca, Huesca and Saragossa.
39. Ellis, *Summer and Winter*, 24, 43, 37–39.
40. Labarere, *Laclède*, 26; Choquette, *Frenchmen into Peasants*, 31, 78, 85, 195–98; John G. Clark, *La Rochelle and the Atlantic Economy during the Eighteenth Century* (Baltimore, MD: Johns Hopkins University Press, 1981), 30, 41 and passim on the Rasteau family; Shannon Lee Dawdy, *Building the Devil's Empire: French Colonial New Orleans* (Chicago: University of Chicago Press, 2008), 131; John G. Clark, *New Orleans, 1718–1812: An Economic History* (Baton Rouge: Louisiana State University Press, 1970), 83; Bill Marshall, *The French Atlantic: Travels in Culture and History* (Liverpool: Liverpool University Press, 2009), 60–61, 70–73, chap. 2: "Secrets of La Rochelle."
41. Labarere, *Laclède*, 26–27.

The Planners in New Orleans

42. Epigraph from Dawdy, *Devil's Empire*, 226. Sources for the first paragraph are Clark, *New Orleans*, 150–51; Fred Anderson, *Crucible of War: The Seven Years' War and the Fate of Empire in British North America, 1754–1766* (New York: Alfred A. Knopf, 2000), 105, 760; Goubert, *French History*, 169–70.
43. Anderson, *Crucible of War*, 105, 760.
44. James Julian Coleman Jr., *Gilbert Antoine de St. Maxent* (Gretna, LA: Pelican Publishing, 1968), 14–18, 23; *Dictionary of Louisiana Biography*, 2 vols., ed. Glenn R. Conrad (New Orleans: Louisiana Historical Association, 1988): s.v. "Maxent," "Laclède"; Goubert, *French History*, 169.

45. *Dictionary of Missouri Biography*, 75–77, 167–81, 457; Labarere, *Laclède*, 25–27; William E. Foley and C. David Rice, *The First Chouteaus: River Barons of Early St. Louis* (Urbana: University of Illinois Press, 1983), 3; Christian, *Before Lewis and Clark*, 27, 30; William E. Foley, "The Laclede-Chouteau Puzzle," *Gateway Heritage: Quarterly Journal of the Missouri Historical Society* 4, no. 2 (1983): 18–25; John Francis McDermott, "Pierre de Laclede and the Chouteaus," *Missouri Historical Society Bulletin* 31, part 1 (1965): 270–83. The belief that Marie Thérèse was educated by Ursuline nuns cannot be verified because "student records for the years prior to 1797 have vanished," according to a personal communication on June 29, 2008, from Emily Clark, author of the definitive study *Masterless Mistresses: The New Orleans Ursulines and the Development of a New World Society, 1727–1834* (Chapel Hill: University of North Carolina Press, 2007).

Although all recent historians accept the Laclède-Chouteau liaison thanks to the research of McDermott (a descendant), that was not the case in 1928, when the Reverend John Rothensteiner called it a "libel" of "notorious concubinage" that was "too silly to merit attention." He relied on the defensive rebuttal by Alexander N. DeMenil, "Madam Chouteau Vindicated," in the *St. Louis Globe-Democrat* of October 16, 1921, and was convinced that priests in New Orleans and St. Louis would not have administered the sacraments to such sinful people (*History of the Archdiocese of St. Louis* [St. Louis: Blackwell Wielandy, 1928], 1:102, 103n.). The naming of Paul *Liguest* Chouteau (1792–1851) certainly contradicted his opinion. But an even more conclusive rejoinder dates to colonial times. On May 3, 1768, young Marie Pelagie "Chouteau" (1760–1812), the second child of Pierre and Marie Thérèse, revealed the family ruse when she stated her name as "*pelagie laclede*" (my emphasis) in a baptismal ceremony, which the officiating priest, Father Sebastien Meurin, recorded. Personal communication from Professor Sharon E. Person, February 22, 2010, who sent me a photocopy of the original document.

46. Labarere, *Laclède*, 25–27; Coleman, *Maxent*, 23; Stevens, *Fourth City*, xii–xiii; Ellis, *Summer and Winter*, 115, 209–10; Marchand, *Ghost Empire*, 318; Carl A. Brasseaux, ed., *France's Forgotten Legion: Service Records of French Military and Administrative Personnel Stationed in the Mississippi Valley and Gulf Coast Region, 1699–1769*, CD-Rom (Baton Rouge: Louisiana State University Press, 2000), intro., Table 2 (height of soldiers); hereafter cited as Brasseaux Military Bio CD-Rom.

There are at least two painted "Laclede portraits" that are as controversial as they are familiar, and many recent historians of St. Louis have not published one due to doubts about authenticity. I have chosen to use the frontispiece engraving from the 1909 first edition of Stevens, *Fourth City*, because he claimed that it was "a perfect copy" of the 1750s oil portrait that members of the Laclède family in Bedous showed to Theophile Papin Jr. and his mother on a visit from St. Louis in 1905–6. In 1984, Laclède's sole biographer, Lucien Labarère, saw it, too, still in the family home, and was told by descendants that it was an original period portrait of Pierre *or his brother Jean* painted from life by an unknown artist from Bordeaux. But both Stevens and Labarere found that the background scene of a sailing ship approaching an exotic coast tipped the scales in favor of the "American Laclède," since his botanist brother never crossed the ocean. It would have been most appropriate for the family heir to outfit his younger brother in expensive clothing and to commission a portrait of him as he prepared to leave hearth, homeland and any claims to inheritance on a dangerous voyage to Louisiana. That painting, copied for the Missouri Historical Society (now the Missouri History Museum) in 1926, earlier served as the model for George Julian Zolnay's towering statue of Laclède near city hall, commemorating St. Louis's sesquicentennial in 1914 (Labarere, *Laclède*, 88; Stevens, *Fourth City*, xi–xiii; Walter B. Stevens, *Laclede: The Founder of St. Louis* [St. Louis, MO: Merchants-Laclede National Bank of St. Louis, 1910]); Theodore Finkelston, "The Forgotten Founder: The Statue of Pierre de Laclède Liguest," *Gateway-Heritage Magazine* 21, no. 4 (2001): 16–29; "Valuable Gifts to the St. Louis Historical Society" [referring to another Laclède portrait], *St. Louis Republican*, July 15, 1869, and *New York Times*, July 18, 1869; Smithsonian Institution inventories of Laclède portraits and sculptures at http://siris-artinventories.si.edu/ipac20/ipac.jsp. The fact that at least two reputable historians recently published "Pierre Laclede's Portrait" with the permission of both the Missouri History Museum and the State Historical Society of Missouri (assessioned as SHS MO 012594) lend legitimacy to, and imply official authentication of, the image published here.

47. Jacqueline K. Voorhies, comp., *Some Eighteenth-Century Louisianians: Census Records, 1758–1796* (Lafayette: University of Southwestern Louisiana, 1973), 23–29, 145–47, 382–83, 399; Dawdy, *Devil's Empire*, 96, 145–47, 179; Ned Sublette, *The World that Made New Orleans* (Chicago: Lawrence Hill Books, 2008), 98; Coleman, *Maxent*, 50.

48. McDermott, ed., *Libraries*, 14, 21, 26–43, 128–166; [Jean Bernard] Bossu, *Travels Through that Part of North America Formerly Called Louisiana* (made in 1750s), 3rd ed., trans. John Reinhold Forster (London: T. Davies, 1771), 1:174.

49. Marc de Villiers du Terrage, *The Last Years of French Louisiana*, ed. Carl A. Brasseaux and Glenn R. Conrad, trans. Hosea Phillips (Lafayette: University of Southwestern Louisiana, 1982), 35–36; *Dictionary of Louisiana Biography*, s.v. "Kerlérec"; Brasseaux Military Bio CD-Rom, s.v. "Kerlérec."
50. Terrage, *Last Years*, 40–47; Harry Parker, *Naval Battles from the Collection of Prints Owned by Commander Sir Charles Leopold Cust* (London: Parker Galleries, 1911), 51 and passim.
51. Terrage, *Last Years*, 50–53, 65, 89; Gayarré, *History of Louisiana*, 2:68–82.
52. Kenneth J. Banks, *Chasing Empire Across the Sea: Communications and the State in the French Atlantic, 1713–1763* (Montreal, QC: McGill-Queen's University Press, 2003), 113–14, 209–10; Choquette, *Frenchmen into Peasants*, 195–98.
53. *Dictionary of Louisiana Biography*, s.v. "Rochemore."
54. Abraham P. Nasatir and James R. Mills, eds., *Commerce and Contraband in New Orleans during the French and Indian War: A Documentary Study of the Texel and Three Brothers Affairs* (Cincinnati, OH: American Jewish Archives, 1968), 3–11, 163–65, 177, 180–84.
55. Ibid., 116–17, 177; Dawdy, *Devil's Empire*, 219–26. Four of the signers—Denis Braud, Pierre Carresse, Jean Milhet and Jean Charles Le Sassier—did indeed risk their blood nine years later as rebel leaders in the New Orleans Revolt of 1768. Braud, a printer of seditious literature, escaped punishment, but Carresse was executed, Milhet was imprisoned in a Cuban jail and Le Sassier was banished from Louisiana. They protested Louis XV's arbitrary transfer of their persons and property to a foreign power without consent or consultation, but they were probably angrier that a new Spanish regime might actually enforce laws against smuggling. See *The Rebellion of 1768 in Louisiana and the Manifesto of the Inhabitants*, ed. and trans. Wilbur E. Meneray (Harahan, LA: Jefferson Parish Historical Commission, 1997), 1–8 and passim; and *Dictionary of Louisiana Biography* for those named.
56. Dunbar Rowlands and A.G. Sanders, eds. and trans., *Mississippi Provincial Archives*, vol. 5: *French Dominion, 1749–1763*, ed. Patricia K. Galloway (Baton Rouge: Louisiana State University Press, 1984), 24, 116–17, 142, 233 (hereafter cited as *MPA*); Theodore Calvin Pease and Ernestine Jenison, eds. and trans., *Collections of the Illinois State Historical Library*, vol. 29: *Illinois on the Eve of the Seven Years' War, 1747–1755* (Springfield: Illinois State Historical Society, 1940), 253, 277 (hereafter, *Eve of War*).
57. Nasatir and Mills, *Commerce and Contraband*, 163–67, 181; Captain Philip Pittman, *The Present State of the European Settlements on the Mississippi*, intro. Robert R. Rea (Gainesville: University of Florida Press, 1973), 89 [facsimile of the London 1770 edition]; *Eve of War*, xv; J.H. Schlarman, *From Quebec*

to New Orleans: The Story of the French in America (Belleville, IL: Buechler Publishing, 1929), 431; Walter J. Saucier and Katherine Wagner Seineke, "François Saucier, Engineer of Fort de Chartres, Illinois," in *Frenchmen and French Ways in the Mississippi Valley*, ed. John Francis McDermott (Urbana: University of Illinois Press, 1969), 223–27.

58. Kerlérec's *Memoir on Indians* (1758), in *MPA*, 203–09. See Terrage, *Last Years*, 236–38, on the aggressive campaigns launched from Fort de Chartres.

59. Brasseaux Military Bio CD-Rom, s.v. "Neyon de Villiers"; *Eve of War*, xv, 276, 278, 644, 874–75.

60. Pittman, *Present State*, 45–46, 53–55; Nasatir and Mills, *Commerce and Contraband*, 173–79, 182; *MPA*, 124, 245 and passim; *Eve of War*, 267–73; Dawdy, *Devil's Empire*, 136–37, 226–27, chap. 6 passim; Banks, *Chasing Empire*, 210.

61. Nasatir and Mills, *Commerce and Contraband*, 182; Dawdy, *Devil's Empire*, 3–13, 95–96, 125–28; Terrage, *Last Years*, 168–69.

62. Dawdy, *Devil's Empire*, 104–07, 158.

63. Terrage, *Last Years*, 150.

64. *MPA*, 122, 125, 128, 130, 146, 148, 155–58; Banks, *Chasing Empire*, 211. The white feather fans are shown in Patricia Galloway, *Practicing Ethnohistory: Mining Archives, Hearing Testimony, Constructing Narrative* (Lincoln: University of Nebraska Press, 2006), 300–01.

65. Terrage, *Last Years*, 51, 92–94; *MPA*, 129, 144–45, 152; Nasatir and Mills, *Commerce and Contraband*, 172, 181; Khalil Saadani, "Gift Exchange between the French and Native Americans in Louisiana," trans. Joanne Burnett, in *French Colonial Louisiana and the Atlantic World*, ed. Bradley G. Bond (Baton Rouge: Louisiana State University Press, 2005), 51–53.

66. Terrage, *Last Years*, 122–23, 127–29; *MPA*, 242–46.

67. Terrage, *Last Years*, 80, 124; Dawdy, *Devil's Empire*, 125 and passim; Saadani, "Gift Exchange," 53–61.

68. Clark, New Orleans, 61, 123–24; Carl A. Brasseaux, ed. and trans., *A Comparative View of French Louisiana, 1699 and 1762: The Journals of Pierre La Moyne d'Iberville and Jean-Jacques-Blaise d'Abbadie* (Lafayette: University of Southwestern Louisiana, 1981), 139–42.

69. Nicollet quoted in McDermott, *Histories*, 153; Schlarman, *Quebec to New Orleans*, 348–49.

70. Paul Chrisler Phillips (with concluding chapters by J.W. Smurr), *The Fur Trade* (Norman: University of Oklahoma Press, 1961), 1:548; Gayarré, *History of Louisiana*, 2:48.

71. *MPA*, 286; Phillips, *Fur Trade*, 1:546.

72. *MPA*, 278–80; Carl A. Brasseaux and Michael J. Leblanc, "Franco-Indian Diplomacy in the Mississippi Valley, 1754–1763: Prelude to Pontiac's Uprising?" in *The Louisiana Purchase Bicentennial Series in Louisiana History*, vol. 1: *The French Experience in Louisiana*, ed. Glenn R. Conrad (Lafayette: Center for Louisiana Studies at University of Southwestern Louisiana, 1995), 337–38.
73. *MPA*, 280.
74. Terrage, *Last Years*, 168; Clark, *New Orleans*, 123–24.
75. Kerlérec, *Memoir on Indians*, in *MPA*, 225; Phillips, *Fur Trade*, 1: 476–77; Saadani, "Gift Exchange," 56; DuVal, *Native Ground*, 115–18; Willard H. Rollings, *The Osage: An Ethnohistorical Study of Hegemony on the Prairie-Plains* (Columbia: University of Missouri Press, 1992), 84, 136–38.
76. Chouteau, "Narrative" in McDermott, *Histories*, 47; John Francis McDermott, "The Exclusive Trade Privilege of Maxent, Laclede & Company," *Missouri Historical Review* 29 (1935): 272–78; Dawdy, *Devil's Empire*, 11; Coleman, *Maxent*, 20–25; J. Thomas Scharf, *History of Saint Louis City and County* (Philadelphia: Louis H. Everts, 1883): 1:63 n.2; Phillips, *Fur Trade*, 2:174.
77. Chouteau, "Narrative," in McDermott, *Histories*, 47; Labarere, *Laclède*, 32.
78. Coleman, *Maxent*, 24–25; Banks, *Chasing Empire*, 71; d'Abbadie's Journal in Brasseaux, *Comparative View*, 103. The director general's failure to mention the Maxent transaction in his personal diary may indicate how casually he signed off on the deal. Reputable scholars from several generations also have credited Kerlérec for issuing Maxent's original trading license, including N.M. Miller Surrey, *The Commerce of Louisiana during the French Regime, 1699–1763* (New York: Columbia University Press, 1916), 365, and Daniel H. Usner Jr., *Indians, Settlers, and Slaves in a Frontier Exchange Economy: The Lower Mississippi Valley before 1783* (Chapel Hill: University of North Carolina Press, 1992), 118.
79. Louis XV's orders for d'Abbadie's administration, in Terrage, *Last Years*, 179–81; *Dictionary of Louisiana Biography*, s.v. "d'Abbadie"; Brasseaux, *Comparative View*, 84–88.
80. *MPA*, 286. I computed the cost of Indian gifts compared to expenditures for French garrisons based on 1760s documents in Terrage, *Last Years*, 60, 80.
81. Brasseaux Military Bio CD-Rom, s.v. "Aubry," "St. Ange." Note that Saint Ange's father wrote his surname as Grotton, not Groston (Margaret Kimball Brown and Lawrie Cena Dean, eds., *The Village of Chartres in Colonial Illinois, 1720–1765* [Ville Platte, LA: Provincial Press, 2003]: 2:940–43).

82. Brasseaux, *Comparative View*, 139–42; Clarence Walworth Alvord and Clarence Edwin Carter, eds., *Collections of the Illinois State Historical Library*, vol. 11: *The New Regime, 1765–1767* (Springfield: Illinois State Historical Library, 1916), 106.
83. Abraham P. Nasatir, ed., *Before Louis and Clark: Documents Illustrating the History of the Missouri, 1752–1804* (Lincoln: University of Nebraska Press, 1990): 1:61–62 (hereafter cited as *BLC*).
84. Ibid., 62–64; Terrage, *Last Years*, 250–51; *Dictionary of Louisiana Biography*, 807–08; *Eve of War*, 318.
85. *BLC* 1:64–9; Labarere, *Laclède*, 31, 47–55, 116–19 (document transcripts).
86. E. Wilson Lyon, *Louisiana in French Diplomacy, 1759–1804* (Norman: University of Oklahoma Press, 1974), 25, chap. 1 passim; Schlarman, *Quebec to New Orleans*, 349–50; Banks, *Chasing Empire*, 42; Paul Mapp, "French Geographic Conceptions of the Unexplored American West and the Louisiana Cession of 1762," in *French Colonial Louisiana and Atlantic World*, 134–74. Although Louis XV drafted a letter informing Kerlérec of the Spanish cession, it was never sent (*MPA*, 274–75; Terrage, *Last Years*, 178). D'Abbadie heard rumors spread by the British in New Orleans but only received official notice in September 1764 (*MPA*, 291–93; Brasseaux, *Comparative View*, 125, 127–28; Pittman, *Present State*, xviii; Clarence Walworth Alvord and Clarence Edwin Carter, eds. and trans., *Collections of the Illinois State Historical Library*, vol. 10: *The Critical Period, 1763–1765* [Springfield: Illinois Historical Library, 1915], 297–99).

The "St. Louis Project" was one of several proposals by entrepreneurs on both sides of the Atlantic for exploiting the new imperial boundaries in 1762–63 by importing thousands of colonists and slaves and/or to secure a monopoly on the Indian trade. French officials opposed the schemes they knew about to allay Spanish fears about being taken advantage of, which would have jeopardized Louis XV's cession of Louisiana. Given their La Rochelle contacts, Maxent and Laclède may have been involved with a merchant from that city—Daubaret—who "was merely the agent for a larger group of men," probably from there. Between January 1763 and May 1766, Spain permitted thirty-five French ships from La Rochelle and fourteen from Bordeaux to reach New Orleans with food, munitions and merchandise suitable for the Indian trade (Allan Christelow, "Proposals for a French Company for Spanish Louisiana, 1763–1764," *Mississippi Valley Historical Review* 27, no. 4 [1941]: 603–11).
87. Choquette, *Frenchmen into Peasants*, 279; Alvord and Carter, *New Regime*, 134.

88. D'Abbadie journal in Brasseaux, *Comparative View*, 96–98. Gregory Evans Dowd, *War Under Heaven: Pontiac, the Indian Nations, and the British Empire* (Baltimore, MD: Johns Hopkins University Press, 2002), 274–75.
89. Labarere, *Laclède*, 28, 35; McDermott, *Histories*, 31–32, 47; Nina Sturgis, "Traditional Music of the French Pyrenees," *Scribner's Magazine* 13, no. 4 (January 1877), 545; Alvord and Carter, *Critical Period*, 256–58.
90. Brasseaux, *Comparative View*, 118–19; *Eve of War*, 272, 275; Coleman, *Maxent*, 25, 44; Ekberg, *French Roots*, 280; Pittman, *Present State*, 6; Labarere, *Laclède*, 34–36.
91. The only other emigrants from the Pyrenees were Jean Baptiste Ortes, a carpenter from Bedous who arrived in 1765; Laclède's partner and future Chouteau brother-in-law Sylvestre Labbadie Sr. of Tarbes, east of Béarn (1737–1794); John P. Cabanné (1773–1841), born in Pau, who came to St. Louis in 1798, married into the extended Gratiot-Chouteau clan and fathered eleven children; and a baker, Francois Barrere, who was born just north of Béarn and also arrived long after 1764 (Frederic L. Billon, comp., *Annals of St. Louis in its Early Days under the French and Spanish Dominations* [St. Louis: privately printed, 1886], 260–62, 443–44, 473–75).
92. *An Account of Upper Louisiana by Nicolas de Finiels*, ed. Carl J. Ekberg (trans.) and William E. Foley (Columbia: University of Missouri Press, 1989), 29–30; Pittman, *Present State*, 5–7; [Georges Henri] Victor Collot, *Voyage dans l'Amerique Septentrionale/A Journey to North America* (made in 1796), 2 vols. (Paris: Arthus Bertrand, 1826, in both English and French editions), 1: 210–13 (all cites to the English text); *Eve of War*, 274–75; F. Terry Norris, "Where Did the Villages Go?" in *Common Fields: An Environmental History of St. Louis*, ed. Andrew Hurley (St. Louis: Missouri Historical Society, 1997), 82.
93. Rea in Pittman, *Present State*, xxvii–xxviii; Journal of Captain Gordon (1766) in *Travels in the American Colonies*, ed. Newton D. Mereness (New York: Macmillan, 1916), 478–79; Amos Stoddard, *Sketches, Historical and Descriptive, of Louisiana* (Philadelphia: Mathew Carey, 1812), 374 and passim.
94. *Finiels Account*, 30; Brasseaux, *Comparative View*, 109–10, 196; Rea in Pittman, *Present State*, xiv–xvi.
95. Rea in Pittman, *Present State*, xxvii–xxviii; Collot, *Journey*, 1:222–27. In August 1753, eight boatmen were killed in their sleep because they failed to post a lookout (*Eve of War*, 822–23).
96. Collot, *Journey*, 1:223–29; Schlarman, *Quebec to New Orleans*, 430.

THE PEOPLE AND PROSPECTS OF ILLINOIS

97. The epigraph is from Major Robert Rogers, *Ponteach, or the Savages of America: A Tragedy* (London, 1766), 201. Citations for the paragraph are: Bossu, *Travels*, 1:126–27; Collot, *Journey*, 1:242–44, 255–56, 286; Zadok Cramer, *The Navigator*, 8th ed. (Pittsburgh, PA: Robert Ferguson, 1814), 146; Pittman, *Present State*, 51–52; Antoine Simon Le Page du Pratz, *History of Louisiana* (London: Becket, 1744), 162–66 and passim; Thomas Hutchins, *An Historical Narrative and Topographical Description of Louisiana and West-Florida* (Philadelphia, 1774), 26–30; *Eve of War*, 807; M.J. Morgan, *Land of Big Rivers: French & Indian Illinois, 1699–1778* (Carbondale: Southern Illinois University Press, 2010), 1–40.
98. Aron, *American Confluence*, 26–33; Ekberg, *French Roots*, 35–36, 78, 172, 239–40; Winstanley Briggs, "Le Pays des Illinois," *William and Mary Quarterly* 47, no. 1 (1990): 30–56 (hereafter cited as *WMQ*); Robert Michael Morrissey, "'Contrary to Good Order': Political Culture in the Illinois Country Under the French Regime," *Gateway Magazine* 30 (2010): 43–51.
99. Alan G. Shackelford, "On a Crossroads: American Indian Prehistory and History in the Confluence Region" (PhD diss., Indiana University, 2004), 367–400; Theodore Calvin Pease and Raymond C. Werner, eds., *Collections of the Illinois State Historical Library*, vol. 23: *The French Foundations, 1680–1693* (Springfield: Illinois State Historical Library, 1934); Claiborne A. Skinner, *The Upper Country: French Enterprise in the Colonial Great Lakes* (Baltimore, MD: Johns Hopkins University Press, 2008), chaps. 1–3.
100. Emily J. Blasingham, "The Depopulation of the Illinois Indians, Part 1," *Ethnohistory* 3, no. 3 (1956): 195–98; Marchand, *Ghost Empire*, 286–87; Charles J. Balesi, *Time of the French in the Heart of North America, 1673–1818* (Chicago: Alliance Française, 2002), 51–59; Mark Walczynski, "La Salle's Fort Saint Louis of the Illinois: Documentary and Archaeological Evidence for Its Actual Location and Specific Considerations for Why It Was Built Where it Was," *Le Journal of the Center for French Colonial Studies* 26, no. 4 (2010): 1–7.
101. Balesi, *Time of the French*, 128–31; Shackelford, "Crossroads," 400–23; Joseph L. Peyster, ed. and trans., *Letters from New France: The Upper Country, 1686–1783* (Urbana: University of Illinois Press, 1992), 32–85, with king's declaration suspending the fur trade on pp. 61–62. For Illini populations and locations prior to 1700, see Joseph Zitomersky, *French Americans-Native Americans in Eighteenth-Century French Colonial Louisiana: The Population Geography of the Illinois Indians, 1670s–1760s* (Lund, Sweden: Lund University Press, 1994), chap. 3.

102. Zitomersky, *French Americans*, 381; see also 321, 384–85 and passim; Ekberg, *French Roots*, 152; Daniel H. Usner Jr., "The Frontier Exchange Economy of the Lower Mississippi Valley in the Eighteenth Century," *WMQ* 44, no. 2 (1987):165–92.
103. Morgan, *Land of Big Rivers*, 23–68; Ekberg, *French Roots*, 54–61, 152.
104. Natalia Maree Belting, *Kaskaskia Under the French Regime* (Urbana: University of Illinois Press, 1948), 23–40; Ekberg, *French Roots*, 64–73, 152–55; Bossu, *Travels*, 1:141–43; *Eve of War*, 263–64; Carl J. Ekberg with Anton J. Pregaldin, "Marie Rouensa-8cate8a and the Foundations of French Illinois," *Illinois Historical Journal* 84 (1991): 146–60.
105. Aron, *American Confluence*, 40–48; Ekberg, *Colonial Ste. Genevieve*, 42–46, chap. 10; Ekberg, *Vallé and His World*, 48–86; Belting, *Kaskaskia*, 30–31.
106. Chouteau in McDermott, *Histories*, 47; Neyon de Villiers to d'Abbadie, December 1, 1763, in Carter and Alvord, *Critical Period*, 49–57, 435 (loan of king's gunpowder); Brown and Dean, *Village of Chartres*, 2:773.
107. "Official Report Made by Pierre-Joseph Neyon de Villiers on the Visit of Indian Messengers to Fort de Chartres," November 8, 1763, Louisiana Digital Library, http://louisdl.training.louislibraries.org/cdm4/document (accessed March 13, 2008); Brasseaux and Leblanc, "Franco-Indian Diplomacy," 338–39. Kerlérec referred to Wolf, also known as "the Mortar," as "my faithful war chief" because he had kept the Cherokees on the side of the French. Two years before, Kerlérec sent four thousand pounds of gunpowder to Fort de Chartres for the Cherokees, since he wanted them to go there to meet Neyon de Villiers (*MPA*, 277, 278n.).
108. D'Abbadie journal in Brasseaux, *Comparative View*, 97; Neyon de Villiers to d'Abbadie, March 13, 1764, Louisiana Digital Library, http://louisdl.training.louislibraries.org/cdm6/document (accessed March 14, 2008); also noted in McDermott, *Histories*, 33. Neyon de Villiers may have been referring to the "project" he had proposed to d'Abbadie in his December 1, 1763 letter, which he mysteriously stated was "the only one whose execution appears to me fitted not to arouse again our bitter and too powerful neighbors" (Alvord and Carter, *Critical Period*, 49–57). Because d'Abbadie was parleying at Mobile, his first and only response was probably the order of January 30, 1764, requiring Neyon de Villiers to evacuate all troops in Upper Louisiana and bring them to the capital. Since the commandant indicated in March that he was still waiting for a response to his "plan," that had to refer to something else, likely involving St. Louis and his desire to retain a stake in the lucrative fur trade (McDermott, *Histories*, 32).

109. The auction is described in Alvord and Carter, *Critical Period*, 129–31, and Schlarman, *Quebec to New Orleans*, 404–06. A British officer claimed that the Kaskaskia properties sold for over 100,000 livres (Alvord and Carter, *New Regime*, 126). The Jesuits in Illinois were informed about their expulsion on September 23, 1763, giving them two months to prepare for their eventual evacuation. Maxent would have known about the sale of Jesuit properties that occurred in New Orleans on July 18–24, 1763, which resulted in 942,000 livres paid for 136 slaves, 287,350 parcels of land, livestock and personal property (Terrage, *Last Years*, 187–88).

110. Brown and Dean, *Village of Chartres*, 2:788–90; also see the 1762 sale to the soldier by Prunet's wife, Veronique "Panisse" (female Panis, i.e., Pawnee), 2:771.

111. *Eve of War*, 262–63; Morgan, *Land of Big Rivers*, 69–115; Margaret Kimball Brown, *History As They Lived It: A Social History of Prairie du Rocher, Ill.* (Tucson, AZ: Patrice Press, 2005); 1752 census totals in Ekbeg, *French Roots*, 152; Robert Mazrim, "The Ghost House Site: Pierre Laclede's First Residence in the Illinois Country?" *Gateway* 30 (2010): 65–75; Georgina Gustin, "Pottery Called Clue to Pierre Laclede's First Home," *St. Louis Post-Dispatch*, October 3, 2006, D1.

112. Chouteau in McDermott, *Histories*, 48; John B. Marshall, "The St. Louis Mound Group: Historical Accounts and Pictorial Depictions," *The Missouri Archaeologist: Journal of the Missouri Archaeological Society* 53 (1992): 43–79; Carol Diaz-Granados and James R. Duncan, *The Petroglyphs and Pictographs of Missouri* (Tuscaloosa: University of Alabama Press, 2000), 11–15, 73, 162, 249–50; Mark W. Mehrer, *Cahokia's Countryside* (DeKalb: Northern Illinois University Press, 1995), 6 (map).

113. Chouteau "Narrative" in McDermott, *Histories*, 48–49.

114. Collot, *Journey* 1:249–51; Aron, *American Confluence*, intro.; Glen E. Holt, "The Shaping of St. Louis, 1764–1860" (PhD diss., University of Chicago, 1975), 10, 66–67, 124–25, 146–47, 156–57. In addition to having unrivaled river transportation, St. Louis was near salt springs (for curing and preserving pelts) and lead mines (for musket balls)—making it the best location on the continent *specifically* for large-scale fur trading.

115. D'Abbadie ordered the evacuation of French *troops* on both banks of the Illinois Country on January 30, 1764, but he did not know until September 10, 1764, that Spain owned the west bank, so Neyon de Villiers closed Fort Cavagnal—what Chouteau called "Fort des Canses [Kansas]…in Missouri"—solely to honor Maxent's monopoly (McDermott, *Histories*, 32–33, 52).

116. Ekberg, *Stealing Indian Women*, 52. Ekberg constantly refers to St. Louis as a mere "trading outpost" and almost never as a "town" (5, 29, 52, 74). He also makes the dubious claim that "during the late 1760s and early 1770s, Kaskaskia continued to serve as the metropole of the entire region, including both sides of the river, if that designation is determined by population and commercial activity" (p. 124)—by ignoring contrary evidence. In 1770, St. Louis was *not* a "raw frontier fur-trading community" as he claims (p. 63), and if Kaskaskia was so cosmopolitan, how can he state that "Ste. Genevieve of the 1770s was a remote and vulnerable outpost of European colonization" (p. 135), when it was only a short boat ride away?

117. "Lt. Col. James Robertson [of the British army] had previously arranged with Gilbert de St. Maxent, a New Orleans merchant, to construct ten boats for the Illiniois expedition [of Major Loftus]" (Brasseaux, *Comparative View*, 106 n., 134; Robert Rea, "Assault on the Mississippi—the Loftus Expedition," *Alabama Review* 26 [1973]: 175, 179).

118. Morgan, *Land of Big Rivers*, 112–13, 181–87, 195; *Eve of War*, 279, 282, 699.

119. *Eve of War*, xvii, 645, 651; Morgan, *Land of Big Rivers*, 119–31; Bossu, *Travels*, 1:134. Casualty figures for the Mechigamea Massacre vary greatly, and I have used the official ones in Kerlérec's 1758 *Memoir on Indians*, in *MPA*, 204.

120. Bossu, *Travels*, 1:129; Terrage, *Last Years*, 236–38; Balesi, *Time of the French*, 180–85; James R. Atkinson, *Splendid Land, Splendid People: The Chickasaw Indians to Removal* (Tuscaloosa: University of Alabama Press, 2004), 43–48 and chap.1; Peyster, *Letters from New France*, 159–63. Chouteau devoted a large portion of his "Narrative" to that Chickasaw battle (McDermott, *Histories*, 55–59).

121. Dowd, *War Under Heaven*, 168–73, quote on 171; McDermott, *Histories*, 55 (Chouteau's quote); Calloway, *Scratch of a Pen*, 126 ("French Pontiac"). For Indian delegations to New Orleans, see Brasseaux, *Comparative View*, 110–13, 117, 120–23, 136–39. For Indian delegations at Fort de Chartres, see Alvord and Carter, *Critical Period*, 241, 256–58, 289–94, 382, 385.

122. Alvord and Carter, *Critical Period*, 51; Dowd, *War Under Heaven*, 97–104; Peter Silver, *Our Savage Neighbors: How Indian War Transformed Early America* (New York: W.W. Norton, 2008). Two hundred Delawares died from the distribution of smallpox blankets in 1763 (White, *Middle Ground*, 288, n.38). British soldiers regarded Indians as "Vermine" that should be hunted down with dogs rather than being captured alive (Silver, *Our Savage Neighbors*, 132).

123. Helen Hornbeck Tanner, *Atlas of Great Lakes Indian History* (Norman: University of Oklahoma Press, 1987), 42; Zitomersky, *Population Georgraphy*, 339, 341; *Eve of War*, 313, 641, 686, 785–86; Alvord and Carter, *Critical Period*, 224–25. Walter S. Dunn, *Opening New Markets: The British Army and*

the Old Northwest (Westport, CT: Praeger, 2002), 106, 135, found that the Philadelphia firm of Baynton, Wharton and Morgan had less than a 5 percent share of the Illinois fur trade in the late 1760s and only balanced its books by selling merchandise to local habitants and the British Indian Department, until "the French and their influence on the Indians…led to the downfall" of that well-capitalized company.

124. Alvord and Carter, *Critical Period*, 448–54. Pontiac and his allies were furious at Europeans for ceding Native Ground in treaties as if it were theirs, and Indians repeatedly proclaimed that they were *not dead*—meaning they were very visible and should not be overlooked, while also expressing the belief that only death could separate Indians from their lands. Chouteau recalled in 1825 that "the Illinois Indians claimed the land where St. Louis now stands" (quoted in Houck, *History of Missouri*, 2:11 n.).

125. Neyon letter to d'Abbadie, March 13, 1764, Louisiana Digital Library (see note 109 above); *Eve of War*, 914–15; Alvord and Carter, *Critical Period*, 55.

126. Morgan, *Land of Big Rivers*, 104–11, 114–16, 185; *Eve of War*, 680; DuVal, *Native Ground*, 69, 78, 82, 266 n.6.

127. Louis Houck, *The Spanish Regime in Missouri* (Chicago: R.R. Donnelley, 1909), 1:5 (hereafter *SR*); *MPA*, 221 ("pure gift"); Rollings, *Osage*, 157; Louis F. Burns, *A History of the Osage People*, rev. 2nd ed. (Tuscaloosa: University of Alabama Press, 2004), 129–30; *Eve of War*, 300, 313–15, 357. The visit of the Osage and Mechigamea chiefs with Louis XV was described in detail, including their speeches, in the *Mercure de France* of December 1725, trans. Edward A.K. Kilian, typescript at the MHM Library and Research Center. See Frank Norall, *Bourgmont, Explorer of the Missouri, 1698–1725* (Lincoln: University of Nebraska Press, 1988) on Etienne de Véniard, sieur de Bourgmont, who led the trip.

128. Lawrence Kinnaird, ed., *Spain in the Mississippi Valley*, 4 vols. (Washington, D.C.: American Historical Association, 1946): 4:110 (hereafter *SMV*); Rollings, *Osage*, 42–43; DuVal, *Native Ground*, 115, 126–27.

129. D'Abbadie in *MPA*, 296–97; *Eve of War*, 357–59; Morgan, *Land of Big Rivers*, 131.

Most historians emphasize the shortcomings of muskets, without realizing their unique advantage over arrows. While a good bowman might shoot almost a dozen arrows in the time it took to load a flintlock, it could fire multiple projectiles (one or more .58- to .69-caliber lead balls and/or small pellets, nails, glass and even rocks) with each discharge, spraying several enemies in close combat. That shotgun effect of smoothbore muskets gave warriors a definite advantage in battle, but only later rifles, with greater accuracy and range, made firearms good for hunting.

130. Chouteau "Narrative" in McDermott, *Histories*, 48, 54. The short biographical sketches are composites I compiled from the following historical and genealogical sources: Billon, *Annals*, 17–18, 411–31; Scharf, *St. Louis City and County*, 1:141–48, 167–75; *SR*; Houck, *History of Missouri*, 2:7–13; Brown and Dean, *Village of Chartres*; Belting, *Kaskaskia*, 81–120; Frederick A. Hodes, *Beyond the Frontier: A History of St. Louis to 1821* (Tucson, AZ: Patrice Press, 2004), 71–89; Earl Fischer Database and Robert Parkin's "Reconstructed Bicentennial 1776 Census of St. Louis"—both at the St. Louis Genealogical Society website: http://www.stlgs.org/index.shtml.

131. Hodes, *Beyond the Frontier*, 72–76, 85–86, 159, 168, 218, 292, 311–12; Billon, *Annals*, 414–15, 425–26, 431; Brown and Dean, *Village of Chartres*, passim.

132. My computations based on sources in n.130.

133. Briggs, "Le Pays des Illinois, *WMQ*, 49–56; *MPA*, 263–64, 272; Alvord and Carter, *Critical Period*, 57; *Eve of War*, xliii–xlix; Cécile Vidal, "Antoine Bienvenu, Illinois Planter and Mississippi Trader: The Structure of Exchange between Lower and Upper Louisiana," in *French Colonial Louisiana and Atlantic World*, 111–33.

Constructing a Wilderness Civilization

134. Alexis de Tocqueville, *Democracy in America*, trans. Henry Reeve (New York: George Dearborn, 1838), 10. Three decades after the Louisiana Purchase, he did not acknowledge the successful colonization by his fellow Frenchmen, observing that the "Valley of the Mississippi is, upon the whole, the most magnificent dwelling-place prepared by God for man's abode; and yet it may be said that at present it is but a mighty desert" (p. 3).

135. Chapter epigraph is from Cramer, *Navigator*, 121 (full cite in n. 97 above). Information on the Indian diasporas is in Blasingham, "Depopulation of the Illinois Indians," 211–12.

136. McDermott, *Histories*, 32–33, and O'Neil, "Date of St. Louis' Founding Disputed," *St. Louis Post-Dispatch*, February 14, 2010, A1, A6, which shows the visual evidence of Chouteau's numerals and the word *Mars* (March) written by another, later hand in bold ink over his original *Fevrier* (February). Christian fell for that deception; instead of noting the obvious difference in penmanship or consulting Neyon de Villiers's letter of March

13, which verified that work on the new settlement was well underway, she suggested that Chouteau's "memory was off by a month" (*Before Lewis and Clark*, 36). In 1847, the city fathers, including Pierre Chouteau Sr., celebrated the first public anniversary of St. Louis's founding on the appropriate, accurate date—February 15—even though it fell on a less-than-convenient Monday for large parades, banquets and balls (see n.1).

137. The quote is from Wilson Primm's 1832 "History of St. Louis," in McDermott, *Histories*, 106, 111, and the voyageur information is found in Carolyn Podruchny, *Making the Voyageur World: Travelers and Traders in the North American Fur Trade* (Lincoln: University of Nebraska Press, 2006), 212–13.

138. Chouteau "Narrative" in McDermott, *Histories*, 49; Ibrahima Seck, "The Relationships between St. Louis of Senegal, Its Hinterlands, and Colonial Louisiana," trans. Joanne E. Burnett, in *French Colonial Louisiana and Atlantic World*, 266; Cecelia Gaposchkin, *The Making of Saint Louis: Kinship, Sanctity, and Crusade in the Later Middle Ages* (Ithaca, NY: Cornell University Press, 2008), 239–41; http://it'sawonderfulcity.org/frenchstlouis.aspx (accessed March 6, 2009), 9. In his youth, Laclède may have been inspired by Father Pierre Le Moyne's *Saint Louis ou La Sainte Couronne Reconquise: Poeme Heroique* (Paris, 1658), which contained engravings of the crusader king fighting wild beasts and Muslims, as well as conducting diplomacy with "infidels."

139. Chouteau "Narrative" in McDermott, *Histories*, 49; Ekberg, *French Roots*, 96, 99–100; Carolyn Gilman and Emily Troxell Jaycox, "The Chouteau Map Re-Examined: A Quest in Progress," *Gateway* 29 (2009): 25–26.

140. Charles E. Peterson, *Colonial St. Louis: Building a Creole Capital* (Tucson, AZ: Patrice Press, 1993), 6–11, with information on the craftsmen, 38–59, and rare photos of early buildings, 105–39; James Neal Primm, *Lion of the Valley: St. Louis, Missouri, 1764–1980* (St. Louis: Missouri Historical Society Press, 3rd ed., 1998), 13–17; Hodes, *Beyond the Frontier*, 81–83, with individual owners of town lots depicted on 84–87.

141. Peterson, *Colonial St. Louis*, 7–8, 12–23; Reverend Monsignor Elmer H. Behrmann, *The Story of the Old Cathedral* (St. Louis, MO: Church of St. Louis IX, King of France, 1984), viii, 30–32.

142. Wade, *Urban Frontier*, 1; DuVal, *Native Ground*, 103, 121–22; Rollings, *Osage*, 138, 149.

143. Burns, *Osage People*, 29–37, 118–20, 143; DuVal, *Native Ground*, 108–12, 126–27, Rollings, *Osage*, 3–11, 68.

144. Garrick Bailey, "Osage," in *Handbook of North American Indians*, vol. 13: *Plains, Part I*, ed. Raymond J. DeMallie (Washington, D.C.: Smithsonian Institution, 2001), 476–78, 492–94; Burns, *Osage People*, 44–49; Rollings,

Osage, 21, 37–38, 58–60, 69n., 112; Carl H. Chapman, *Osage Indians III: The Origin of the Osage Indian Tribe* (New York: Garland Publishing, 1974).

145. Rollings, *Osage*, 22–53; Burns, *Osage People*, 14–19, 39–43; DuVal, *Native Ground*, 114, 123.

146. Rollings, *Osage*, 18–21; Bailey, "Osage," 479.

147. Rollings, *Osage*, 19–20, 69-80; Bailey, "Osage," 479; *SMV* 4:119.

148. Rollings, *Osage*, 54–55, 84–112; Gilbert C. Din and A.P. Nasatir, *The Imperial Osages: Spanish-Indian Diplomacy in the Mississippi Valley* (Norman: University of Oklahoma Press, 1983), 3–50.

149. Burns, *Osage People*, 19; Rollings, *Osage*, 123, 150–51, chap. 5.

150. George Catlin, *Letters and Notes on the Manners, Customs, and Condition of the North American Indians* (London: privately published, 1841) 2:40–42; *Letters of the Lewis and Clark Expedition, with Related Documents*, ed. Donald Jackson (Urbana: University of Illinois Press, 1978) 1:199 n.; Washington Irving, *A Tour on the Prairies* (Paris: Galignani, 1835), 10–11, 20–21; J. Frederick Fausz, "Becoming 'A Nation of Quakers': The Removal of the Osages Indians from Missouri," *Gateway-Heritage* 21, no. 1 (2000): 28–39 (portrait of Black Dog on the first page).

151. Burns, *Osage People*, 129–30; Marc Lourdes, "Osage Tribe Purchases Historic Mound," *St. Louis Post-Dispatch*, August 1, 2009, A2; Garrick A. Bailey, ed., *The Osage and the Invisible World* (Norman: University of Oklahoma Press, 1995), 284–85, 304 n.24; Robert L. Hall, "The Cahokia Site and Its People," in *Hero, Hawk, and Open Hand: American Indian Art of the Ancient Midwest and South*, ed. Richard F. Townsend and Robert V. Sharp (New Haven: Yale University Press and Art Institute of Chicago, 2004), 102 and passim; DuVal, *Native Ground*, 66–70, 266 n. Supporting that view are William Iseminger, *Cahokia Mounds: America's First City* (Charleston, SC: The History Press, 2010), 156; Timothy R. Pauketat and Thomas E. Emerson, eds., *Cahokia: Domination and Ideology in the Mississippian World* (Lincoln: University of Nebraska Press, 1997), intro., 24–26, and passim. More circumspect are Michael J. O'Brien and W. Raymond Wood, *The Prehistory of Missouri* (Columbia: University of Missouri Press, 1998), 347–49, while a denial of Osage-Cahokia linkages was expressed by Marvin D. Jeter, "Shatter Zone Shock Waves Along the Lower Mississippi," in *Mapping the Mississippian Shatter Zone*, ed. Robbie Ethridge and Sheri M. Shuck-Hall (Lincoln: University of Nebraska Press, 2009), 373–79.

152. Chapman, *Osage Indians III*, 24; Stevens, *Fourth City*, xiii–xiv; Labarere, *Laclède*, 11; Ellen G. Miles, *Saint-Memin and the Neoclassical Profile Portrait in America*, ed. Dru Dowdy (Washington, D.C.: Smithsonian Institution

Press for the National Portrait Gallery, 1994), 154–55, 158, 367; Garrick A. Bailey and Daniel C. Swan, *Art of the Osage* (Seattle: University of Washington Press and Saint Louis Art Museum, 2004), 186–97; illustration of a Missouri war axe on p. 78. *Hero, Hawk, and Open Hand* depicts a Mississippian knapped stone blade in the shape of a raptor talon (p. 199), and the cross-in-circle motif in Indian rock art (p. 43) is identical to the French touchmark on an eighteenth-century axe in my collection. Diaz-Granados and Duncan, *Petroglyphs and Pictographs*, discuss and illustrate bird motifs (pp. 29, 64–65, 77, 92–93, 114, 117, 136, 153, 195, 236) and the cross/quartered circle motifs (pp. 98, 168, 190–91, 194, 223–34). Also see Rollings, *Osage*, 48. The long-bladed spontoon pike axe in the center of the color illustration of furs and weapons in this book dates to the eighteenth century and has a fleur-de-lis stamped into the metal.

153. Bailey, *Osage and Invisible World*, 30–48; Rollings, *Osage*, 47–49; Primm, *Lion of the Valley*, 14; Alice Beck Kehoe, "Osage Texts and Cahokia Data," in *Ancient Objects and Sacred Realms: Interpretations of Mississippian Iconography*, ed. F. Kent Reilly III and James F. Garber (Austin: University of Texas Press, 2007), 246–61, quotes on 261. See Francis La Flesche, "The Osage Tribe: Rite of the Chiefs; Sayings of the Ancient Men," in *Bureau of American Ethnology: Thirty-sixth Annual Report to the Secretary of the Smithsonian Institution for 1914–1915* (Washington, D.C.: Government Printing Office, 1921), 43–597, esp. 69 (illustration of village design with north–south clan divisions), 119 (sun-ray motif) and 104 (young Golden Eagle, with "Hon-ga [as] Sacred Name").

154. Chouteau "Narrative" in McDermott, *Histories*, 51–52; Scharf, *St. Louis City and County*, 139–40; Peterson, *Colonial St. Louis*, 38–39; Primm, *Lion of the Valley*, 15.

155. *SMV*, 2:313 and passim.

156. John Hunter Dunn, *Memoirs of a Captivity among the Indians of North America*, ed. Richard Drinnon (New York: Shocken Books, 1973), 228.

157. *SR* 1:73; DuVal, *Native Ground*, 114; Bailey, "Osage," 482–83; Brasseaux Military Bio CD-Rom, s.v. "St. Ange"; McDermott, *Histories*, 55n., 56n.

158. Alvord and Carter, *Critical Period*, 482; *New Regime*, 196–97. Probably the earliest published account of Pontiac's visit to, and burial at, St. Louis was Richard Edwards and M. Hopewell, *Edward's Great West and Her Commercial Metropolis…and a Complete History of St. Louis* (St. Louis, MO: privately published, 1860), 255–56. Chouteau's "Narrative" did not mention the death or burial of Pontiac. An illustration of the plaque placed in the Southern Hotel is in Stevens, *Fourth City*, 385.

159. Chouteau "Narrative" in McDermott, *Histories*, 49; Alvord and Carter, *Critical Period*, 292; Marjorie M. Schweitzer, "Otoe and Missouria," in *Handbook of North American Indians*, vol. 13: *Plains, Part 1* (Washington, D.C.: Smithsonian Institution, 2001), 447–61; Patricia Cleary, "Contested Terrain: Environmental Agendas and Settlement Choices in Colonial St. Louis," in *Common Fields*, 58–72. Chouteau's original manuscript did not provide a date for the arrival of the Missourias, and McDermott's guess of October (p. 33) was wrong; it had to be in mid-summer, since those Indians dug the cellar for Laclède's house, which was finished by September 1764.

160. Chouteau "Narrative" in McDermott, *Histories*, 50–52. Ignoring Laclède's advice, the Missourias did not return home but crossed the river to Cahokia and then Nouvelle Chartres, where Saint Ange reported they arrived on July 17 (Alvord and Carter, *Critical Period*, 292–93).

161. Kerlérec's 1753 quote in *MPA*, 122; John Francis McDermott, *Old Cahokia: A Narrative and Documents Illustrating the First Century of Its History* (St. Louis, MO: St. Louis Historical Documents Foundation, 1949), 78–79. The one temporary exception that Laclède made was to allow a small group of Peorias, and probably Mechigameas as well, to live for a short time in their own village south of the town (*Prairie de Village Sauvage*), which was probably a concession for their assistance in interceding with the Osages in 1763. Although a British officer claimed in 1766 that Laclède was "readily served by the Indians he has planted within two miles of him," they did not live in the center of St. Louis as the Missourias proposed to do, and there is little evidence of extensive contact with the French population before the Peorias relocated to Ste. Genevieve (*Travels*, 475; Daniel H. Usner Jr., "An American Indian Gateway: Some Thoughts on the Migration and Settlement of Eastern Indians around Early St. Louis," *Gateway Heritage* 11, no. 3 [1990–91]: 45–46).

162. The "transient" quote is from Cramer, *Navigator*, 290. The term "spirit of St. Louis" is borrowed from Burns, *Osage People*, 118. "En dérouine" is a unique vernacular term of the Canadian fur trade with no precise English equivalent, but it means backcountry commerce at Indian villages by individual traders, who often cohabited (Produchny, *Making the Voyageur World*, chap. 7).

163. Jean-Baptiste Colbert to Jean Talon (intendant of Canada, April 5, 1667, quoted in David A. Bell, *The Cult of the Nation in France: Inventing Nationalism, 1680–1800* (Cambridge, MA: Harvard University Press, 2001), 96; Alvord and Carter, *Critical Period*, 157; Guillaume Aubert, "'The Blood of France': Race and Purity of Blood in the French Atlantic World," *WMQ* 61, no. 3 (2004): 439–78; Jacqueline Peterson and Jennifer

S.H. Brown, eds., *The New Peoples: Being and Becoming Métis in North America* (Lincoln: Nebraska University Press, 1985); Watts, *Remote Country*, 160–79; Gitlin, *Bourgeois Frontier*, 5–11 and passim.

164. *Finiels Account*, 120.

165. Scharf, *St. Louis City and County*, 142–44; Chouteau "Narrative" in McDermott, *Histories*, 49, 54; *Eve of War*, 785–86. The advanced planning detailed in this book refutes Cleary's view that "chance and circumstance dictated the 1764 arrival of French colonists at St. Louis" ("Contested Terrain," 58).

166. Brackenridge, *Views of Louisiana*, 12.

167. Houck, *History of Missouri* 2:2, 15–17 (quotes on 15); Gilman and Jaycox, "Chouteau Map Re-Examined," *Gateway* 29 (2009): 26; Philip Skrainka, *St. Louis: Its History and Ideals* (St. Louis, MO: privately printed, 1910), 1–3.

168. McDermott, *Histories*, 33, Alvord and Carter, *Critical Period*, 189–90, 271n.; Alvord and Carter, *New Regime*, 125; Alcèe Fortier, *A History of Louisiana* (New York: Goupil & Co., 1904): 1:151; Brown, *Prairie du Rocher*, 157–62; Pittman, *Present State*, 46–47.

Chouteau's "Narrative" condemned the commandant for "tak[ing] with him a large following" of potential St. Louis settlers, claiming that he promised land near New Orleans to the civilian evacuees and then double-crossed them. They regretted not joining the preferable "exodus" to the true promised land of the Moses-like Laclède, but when the wealthier colonists allegedly returned to Illinois, Laclède assisted them in moving to St. Louis (McDermott, *Histories*, 52–54). Chouteau is the only source on those likely fictitious incidents, and he betrayed the very helpful commandant. Neyon de Villiers was a talented leader, excellent Indian diplomat and an essential component of the Kerlérec cabal. Almost immediately after arriving in New Orleans with the Illinois evacuees, he sailed to France aboard the ship *Missouri*, and in the next decade, he defended Kerlérec's administration in several legal proceedings. He was promoted to brigadier general and appointed governor of a small Caribbean island before dying at sea in 1779 (Brasseaux Military Bio CD-Rom, s.v. "Neyon de Villiers," and Terrage, *Last Years*, 218n.).

169. Aron, *American Confluence*, 116; Collot, *Journey*, 1: 247; Alvord and Carter, *Critical Period*, 292–96.

170. Pittman, *Present State*, 46, 49; Chouteau "Narrative" in McDermott, *Histories*, 54; Alvord and Carter, *New Regime*, 109, 523.

171. D'Abbadie journal, June 12, 1764, in Brasseaux, *Comparative View*, 119; Billon, *Annals*, 20. Only a week after Madame Chouteau and her children departed, d'Abbadie had to make an emergency purchase of flour from Maxent to feed New Orleans.

172. Cession of Fort de Chartres, including final inventory, in Alvord and Carter, *New Regime*, 91–104; Schlarman, *Quebec to New Orleans*, 395–402; Calloway, *Scratch of a Pen*, 83; Pittman, *Present State*, 49; Billon, *Annals*, 69 and passim; Scharf, *St. Louis City and Counry*, 1:71–4; Parkin's Reconstructed Census. In March 1777, Lieutenant de Volsey would succeed Saint Ange as the Spanish-appointed advisor on Indian relations.
173. Skrainka, *St. Louis History and Ideals*, 5; Alvord and Carter, *New Regime*, 108 and 124 (Aubry orders), 140, 146–47 (Aubry letter).
174. *SR* 1:5, 22, 45; Houck, *History of Missouri* 2:17–20; Fortier, *History of Louisiana* 1:236; McDermott, *Libaries*, 24, 33–34.
175. Rea in Pittman, *Present State*, xxix; Alvord and Carter, *Critical Period*, 396; Alvord and Carter, *New Regime*, 108–09, 125, 145.
176. Calloway, *Scratch of a Pen*, 125; July 27, 1766 Militia Roster (PPC Legajo 187A-1), http://www.thecajuns.com; Thomas Hutchins, *A Topographical Description of Virginia, Pennsylvania, Maryland, and North Carolina* (1778), ed. Frederick Charles Hicks (Cleveland, OH: Burrows Brothers, 1904), 109–110; *SR* 1:61; Parkin Census, 1.
177. My computations based on the militia rosters of November 9, 1779, in John Francis McDermott, "The Myth of the 'Imbecile Governor': Captain Fernando de Leyba and the Defense of St. Louis in 1780," in *The Spanish in the Mississippi Valley, 1762–1804*, ed. McDermott (Urbana: University of Illinois Press, 1974), 373–80.
178. Ibid.; Parkin's Census; Clarence Walworth Alvord and Clarence Edwin Carter, eds., *Collections of the Illinois State Historical Library*, vol. 16: *Trade and Politics, 1767–1769* (Springfield: Illinois State Historical Library, 1921), 489, 630.
179. Hodes, *Beyond the Frontier*, 75, 77, 123, 133, 211, 216–18, quote on 219. Regarding racial regulations, see *Code Noir: The Colonial Slave Laws of French Mid-America*, ed. Cark J. Ekberg, Grady Kilman and Pierre Lebeau (Naperville, IL: Center for French Colonial Studies, 2004).
180. Ekberg, *Stealing Indian Women*, 49, 51, 53; Burns, *Osage People*, 34; Person, *Standing Up for Indians: Baptism Registers as an Untapped Source for Multicultural Relations in St. Louis, 1766–1821* (Naperville: The Center for French Colonial Studies, 2010), 7, 37–38, 59, 83, 129–36. See Brett Rushforth, "'A Little Flesh We Offer You': The Origins of Indian Slavery in New France," *WMQ* 60 (2003): 777–808.
181. Computations based on the 1773 census in *SR* 1:61; Parkin's Census.
182. Leslie Choquette, "Center and Periphery in French North America," in *Negotiated Empires: Centers and Peripheries in the Americas, 1500–1820*, ed.

Christine Daniels and Michael V. Kennedy (New York: Routledge, 2002), 198; Marchand, *Ghost Empire*, 283–84.

183. "Of Tyranny, Anarchy, and Free Governments," *London Journal*, January 6, 1733, in Richard Drinnon, *White Savage: The Case of John Dunn Hunter* (New York: Shocken Books, 1972), [231]; Briggs, "Le Pays des Illinois," *WMQ*, 31–32, 55–56; Brackenridge, *Views of Louisiana*, 134, 137; *SR* 1:17; Ekberg, *French Roots*, 240.

184. Brown, *Prairie du Rocher*, 97; Reuben Gold Thwaites, ed., *Early Western Travels* (Cleveland, OH: Arthur H. Clark Co., 1904) 1:170–71; Kinnaird, *SMV* 2:180–81; Brackenridge, *Views of Louisiana*, 134; Alvord and Carter, *New Regime*, 377.

There is broad agreement among historians about the absence of serious physical violence among French residents in the Illinois Country on both sides of the Mississippi—a positive contrast to the notorious lawlessness on Anglo-American frontiers and in New Orleans. See Cécile Vidal, "Greater French Louisiana (1699–1769): A Violent Frontier Colony?" *Le Journal* 23, no. 2 (2007): 1–8; Carl Ekberg's "Reply" (ibid., 11–12); Ekberg, *French Roots*, 250–63; Brown, *Prairie du Rocher*, 48–50; Primm, *Lion of the Valley*, 83–85; Ekberg, *Stealing Indian Women*, 108, 130, 178, 186–87, 221n., chap. 6; Dawdy, *Devil's Empire*, 201–02, 209–17.

185. Belting, *Kaskaskia*, 68, chap. 6; Brown, *Prairie du Rocher*, passim; William E. Foley, "Galleries, Gumbo, and 'La Guignolee," *Gateway Heritage Magazine* 10 (1989): 3–17; Jay Gitlin, "'Avec Bien du Regret': The Americanization of Creole St. Louis," *Gateway Heritage Magazine* 9 (1989): 2–11; Marchand, *Ghost Empire*, 319; Patricia Cleary, "Drinking, Dying, and Lying to Priests: Community Bonds and Conflicts over Authority in Colonial St. Louis," *Missouri Historical Review* 103, no. 1 (2008): 6, 11, 16. See Cleary, annotated documents in "How Did Living in a Frontier Outpost of Empire Influence Perceptions of Women's Sexual, Marital and Public Roles in Eighteenth-Century Colonial St. Louis," *Women and Social Movements in the United States, 1600–2000* 12, no. 1 (2008), ed. Kathryn Kish Sklar and Thomas Dublin at http://www.asp6new.alexanderstreet.com (accessed April 15, 2009).

186. *SR* 1:72–73; Hutchins, *Topographical Description*, 110; McDermott, *Libraries*, 12–13; signatures on 1770 document in *Edwards' Great West*, 258n.; Brackenridge, *Views of Louisiana*, 133.

187. Labarere, *Laclède*, 54; Alvord and Carter, *New Regime*, 120, 144, 146.

188. Alvord and Carter, *New Regime*, 120, 299–301; also see 105; *Trade and Politics*, 633–34.

189. Alvord and Carter, *Critical Period*, 32, 141, 147, 366–69; *Trade and Politics*, 489, 630; *New Regime*, 105, 203–05, 226–31, 379–80, 510.
190. Alvord and Carter, *New Regime*, 510; *SR* 1:37–38; *BLC* 1:66–69; "Gift of Sieur Laclede in favor of the children of Madame Choutaud," May 12, 1768, in Chouteau Papers, MHM Library and Research Center.
191. Foley and Rice, *First Chouteaus*, 16–20; Abraham P. Nasatir, "Ducharme's Invasion of Missouri: An Incident in the Anglo-Spanish Rivalry for the Indian Trade of Upper Louisiana," *Missouri Historical Review* 25, no. 3 (1930): 420–39; DuVal, *Native Ground*, 123.
192. Foley and Rice, *First Chouteaus*, 16–17.
193. Ibid., 23–24; Labarere, *Laclède*, 66–68.
194. Arguing for a May death date are Foley and Rice, *First Chouteaus*, 24, 33 n. 40, and Christian, *Before Lewis and Clark*, 74–75, 446 nn.74–75, among others. Arguing for a June date are Labarere, *Laclède*, 68–69, and McDermott, *Histories*, 6, 36. Coleman, *Maxent*, 92–94, argued against May and also quoted Forstall's letter to Jean Laclède.
195. Labarere, *Laclède*, 68–75.
196. Ibid.
197. Ibid., 76–77, 84; Foley and Rice, *First Chouteaus*, 24–25; Coleman, *Maxent*, 93–95; McDermott, *Libraries*, 21–22, 26–27; Scharf, *St. Louis City and County*, 1:146.
198. *Dictionary of Missouri Biography*, s.v. "Madame Chouteau"; Mary B. Cunningham and Jeanne C. Blythe, *The Founding Family of St. Louis* (St. Louis, MO: Midwest Technical Publications, 1977), intro. by John Francis McDermott, iii, vi; Katherine T. Corbett, "Veuve Chouteau: A 250th Anniversary," *Gateway Heritage Magazine* 2 (1983): 42–48; Gitlin, "House of Chouteau," 7–8 (www.common-place.org). See the pictorial family tree in *Gateway* 29 (2009): 8, and Charles van Ravenswaay, *Saint Louis: An Informal History of the City and Its People, 1764–1865* (St. Louis: Missouri Historical Society Press, 1991), esp. chap. 6, for details and rare anecdotes on many of the principal family members.
199. McDermott in Cunningham and Blythe, *Founding Family*, v–vi.
200. The original manuscript marriage contracts of Auguste Chouteau, September 21, 1786, and Pierre Chouteau, July 26, 1783, Pierre Chouteau Collection, MHM Library and Research Center.
201. Cunningham and Blythe, *Founding Family*, 6; *Dictionary of Missouri Biography*, s.v. "Cerré."
202. Cunningham and Blythe, *Founding Family*, 6–8; Gitlin, "House of Chouteau," 8 (www.common-place.org).

203. Cunningham and Blythe, *Founding Family*, 59–62; *Dictionary of Missouri Biography*, s.v. "Jean Pierre Chouteau Sr."

204. Cunningham and Blythe, *Founding Family*, 62–63; Foley and Rice, *First Chouteaus*, 44–45, 189–90; *Dictionary of Missouri Biography* for Chouteau sons. See Dorothy Brandt Marra, *Cher Oncle, Cher Papa: The Letters of Francois and Berenice Chouteau*, trans. Marie-Laure Dionne Pal, ed. David Boutros (Kansas City, MO: Western Historical Manuscripts Collection, 2001).

205. *Dictionary of Missouri Biography*, s.v. "Cerré," "Gratiot," "Labbadie" and "Papin."

Creating a Congenial Indian Capital

206. Epigraph is from M. Perrin Du Lac, *Travels Through the Two Louisianas and Among the Savage Nations of the Missouri* (London: Richard Phillips, 1807), 99–100. Paragraph sources are: General Amherst letters of June 29 and August 7, 1763, quoted in White, *Middle Ground*, 288–89; Spanish official quoted in *BLC* 1:128. Colin G. Calloway, *The Shawnees and the War for America* (New York: Viking, 2007), xxxiii, compared frontiers to "sponges."

207. Pittman, *Present State*, 53–54; Alvord and Carter, *New Regime*, 229; Kerlérec's praise of Neyon de Villiers in *MPA*, 278; David Hackett Fischer, *Champlain's Dream* (New York: Simon and Schuster, 2008). Galloway, *Practicing Ethnohistory*, 256, wrote that "French and Indian interaction in the Louisiana colony was generally peaceful and nonexploitative by colonial standards" because of "a few enlightened Indian diplomatists"; also see chap. 14. Ekberg revealed his ignorance of fur trade relations when he wrote that "officials in St. Louis were obsessed with Indian diplomacy" and provided "annual tribute" (*Stealing Indian Women*, 147).

208. *Eve of War*, 300–01; *SR* 1:5, 10–12, 22, 26, 39, 44–45, 83; *SMV* 2:59; DuVal, *Native Ground*, 105.

209. *SMV* 3: 367; *SR* 2:301, 306; Schlarman, *Quebec to New Orleans*, 375, 388.

210. *MPA*, 293; *SMV* 4:110; *SR* 1:4; Din and Nasatir, *Imperial Osages*, 134–35. The four governments were Louis XV's France (via New Orleans officials), Spain, Napoleon's France and the United States.

211. *SR* 1:37–38, 69; *BLC* 1:209–11.

212. "Memorial" quoted in Fortier, *History of Louisiana*, 2nd ed., ed. Jo Ann Carrigan (Baton Rouge, LA: Claitor's Book Store, 1966) 1:181.

213. My computations of fur exports from *SR* 1: 86–87, 92–93, 100–01, 139; Rollings, *Osage*, 138; *Finiels Account*, 121, 121n.; *Travels*, 483; *SMV* 2:312–13.
214. *SR* 1:70–71, 77, 209; *SMV* 3:184; *BLC* 1:152; Miro quoted in Din and Nasatir, *Imperial Osages*, 205–06; David J. Weber, *Bárbaros: Spaniards and Their Savages in the Age of Enlightenment* (New Haven, CT: Yale University Press, 2005), 3–8, 47–51, 190–92, 214–18, 250.
215. *SMV* 2:155; 3:102–06, 209; Din and Nasatir, *Imperial Osages*, 121.
216. *SMV* 2: xviii–xix, 298–99; *SR* 1:46–8, 141–48; McDermott, *Spanish in Mississippi Valley*, 354–57.
217. *Travels*, 32; *SR* 1:268–69; *SR* 2:307.
218. Town ordinances in *SR* 1:78, 240–46.
219. *SMV* 2:204–07; *SR* 2:307; Din and Nasatir, *Imperial Osages*, 80–81; DuVal, *Native Ground*, 124.
220. *BLC* 2:128–29; Pittman, *Present State*, 53; *SMV* 2:229, 4:88–89; John C. Ewers, "Symbols of Chiefly Authority in Spanish Louisiana," in McDermott, *Spanish in Mississippi Valley*, 272–76. Although beaded "collars" were not usually given at St. Louis, four were presented to Delaware chiefs in 1792—each six feet long and comprising twelve rows of "porcelain" (glass) beads, which cost 120 pesos at 6 pesos per 1,000 (*SMV* 4:89–90).
221. *SR*, 1:268–69; *SMV*, 2:15–16, 431–34, 117–18; 3: 83–84; *BLC*, 2:768–69.
222. *SR*, 1:210; *SMV*, 2: xxii, 61, 147, 154–55, 296–97, 300; 3:67–68; Coleman, *Maxent*, 36, 41–44; McDermott, *Spanish in Mississippi Valley*, 358–59.
223. *SR* 1:47, 209–10; 2:205; *SMV* 2:214–18; 3: 230, 386–87, 391; Din and Nasatir, *Imperial Osages*, 142.
224. Pekka Hämäläinen, *The Comanche Empire* (New Haven, CT: Yale University Press, 2008), 42, 45, 52, 58–60, 63–73, 82 (quote), 92–98, 102, 108–11, 147–49, 154.
225. *SMV* 3:296; 414–15; *SR* 2: 205; Ekberg, *Stealing Indian Women*, 82–89; *BLC* 1:300; Foley and Rice, *First Chouteaus*, 45, 67n.; Thorne, *Many Hands*, 82, 95, 96, 118, 139, 141, 151; Sophie L. Dahlberg, *Those Illustrious Frenchmen* (Duncan, OK: self-published, 1994), an Osage Chouteau genealogy; Shelby M. Fly, *The Saga of the Chouteaus of Oklahoma* (Oklahoma City, OK: Apache News, 1988); Vinson Lackey, *The Chouteaus and the Founding of Salina: Oklahoma's First White Settlement, 1796* (Tulsa, OK: Tulsa Printing Co., 1961); Gitlin, "House of Chouteau," *Common-Place*, 9, www.common-place.org. On traditional Canadian voyageur sexual relations, see Podruchney, *Making the Voyageur World*, chap. 8 and passim.

226. Burns, *Osage People*, 99; Thorne, *Many Hands*, 114; also see 93–116; Charles J. Kappler, ed., *Indian Affairs: Laws and Treaties* (Washington, D.C.: U.S. Government Printing Office, 1903): 2:218–19 (Article 5 of the "Treaty with the Osage, 1825"); Fausz, "Becoming 'A Nation of Quakers,'" *Gateway-Heritage*, 38–39.
227. Person, *Standing Up for Indians*, 9 (quote), 83, 129–30, 131–38.
228. Foley and Rice, *First Chouteaus*, 25.
229. *Dictionary of Louisiana Biography*, s.v. "Maxent"; Coleman, *Maxent*, 52–59, 105. In 1782, the king of Spain praised Maxent for his "perfect knowledge of the [trade] relations the colony can have with the mother country and the neighboring [native] nations" and, based on his recommendations, granted a ten-year exemption of the 6 percent duty on Louisiana furs exported to Spanish ports (*SMV* 3:2–5).
230. New Orleans birth data from St. Louis Militia Roster of 1779, in McDermott, *Spanish in Mississippi Valley*, 375; Gratiot letter of March 22, 1778, in McDermott, *Old Cahokia*, 197; also see 194 and mentions of Chouteau activities between St. Louis and New Orleans (207, 212).
231. Coleman, *Maxent*, 76–82 and chap. 8 passim; Foley and Rice, *First Chouteaus*, 26–27; McDermott, *Spanish in Mississippi Valley*, 328–36, Kathrine Wagner Seineke, *The George Rogers Clark Adventure in the Illinois and Selected Documents of the American Revolution at the Frontier Posts* (New Orleans, LA: Polyanthos, 1981).
232. *SMV* 3:217, 391; 4:48.
233. Sinclair quoted in McDermott, *Spanish in Mississippi Valley*, 339–40; *SR* 1:167–78; Carolyn Gilman, "L'Année du Coup: The Battle of St. Louis, 1780—Part 1," *Missouri Historical Review* 103, no. 3 (April 2009): 142–45; Gilman, "Battle Part 2," *MHR* 103, no. 4 (July 2009): 199, 204; John F. McDermott, "The Battle of St. Louis, 25 May 1780," *Missouri Historical Society Bulletin* 36 (1980): 131–50.
234. McDermott, *Spanish in Mississippi Valley*, 340–44, 358–59; James B. Musick, *St. Louis as a Fortified Town* (St. Louis, MO: Press of R.F. Miller, 1941), 33–34.
235. St. Louis Militia Rosters for 1780, in *SR* 1:182–96; McDermott, *Spanish in Mississippi Valley*, 361–62.
236. Musick, *Fortified Town*, 36–39; McDermott, *Spanish in Mississippi Valley*, 344–47, 361–72, 386–87; Gilman, "Battle, Part 2," 197–99, 201–05.
237. *SR* 1:175–77; McDermott, *Spanish in Mississippi Valley*, 367; Gilman, "Battle, Part 2," 205.
238. *SR* 1:177, 183–84, 202–03, 262; Foley and Rice, *First Chouteaus*, 29–30; Gilman and Jaycox, "Chouteau Map Re-Examined," 26–27.

239. *SR* 1:235, *BLC* 1:372; *Outpost on the Wabash, 1787–1791: Letters of Brigadier General Josiah Harmar and Major John Francis Hamtramck*, ed. Gayel Thornbrough (Indianapolis: Indiana Historical Society, 1957), 49; "The Western Journals of Dr. George Hunter, 1796–1805," ed. John Francis McDermott, in *Transactions of the American Philosophical Society* 53, part 4 (1963): 31, 31n.; Ekberg, *French Roots*, 156; Sublette, *World that Made New Orleans*, 127–28, 168; Ekberg, *Stealing Indian Women*, 107 ("new towns"), 138 (map showing old and new Ste. Genevieves).
240. John F. Darby, *Personal Recollections of Many Prominent People Whom I Have Known* (St. Louis, MO: G.I. Jones, 1880), 10–11; John Francis McDermott, "Auguste Chouteau: First Citizen of Upper Louisiana," in McDermott, *Frenchmen and French Ways*, 8–10; Foley and Rice, *First Chouteaus*, 45–46, 172; Christian, *Before Lewis and Clark*, 89, 248.
241. Coleman, *Maxent*, 47–49 (illustration of Marigny House opposite p. 48).
242. Ibid., 49–52, 114–15, chaps. 10–11, passim; *Dictionary of Louisiana Biography*, s.v. "Maxent."
243. Houck, *Missouri* 1:180; Burns, *Osage People*, 212; "virtues" quote adapted from the toast in Foley and Rice, *First Chouteaus*, 132, 140 n.67; Irving, *Tour on the Prairies*, 22; *SR* 2:204–05; DuVal, *Native Ground*, 194. In 1830, some three hundred Osage warriors slaughtered eighty or ninety Pawnees using mainly tomahawks and spears (Rollings, *Osage*, 274).
244. When President Jefferson first met the Osages in 1804, he called them "the finest men we have ever seen. They have not yet learnt the use of spirituous liquors" (Jackson, *Letters of Lewis and Clark*, 1:199n.). In 1767–8, the Philadelphia firm of Baynton, Wharton and Morgan in British Illinois listed the liquor sold to area Indians: 216 gallons of rum to the Kaskaskias, 192 gallons to the Peorias, 136 gallons to the Missourias and 96 gallons to the generic "Illinois"—but a *mere 32 gallons to Osages*, the lowest total of any nearby tribe (Peter C. Mancall, *Deadly Medicine: Indians and Alcohol in Early America* [Ithaca, NY: Cornell University Press, 1995], Appendix I, 181–82; and see 53–55, 163). A high-ranking British officer at Fort de Chartres wrote in 1766 that "Indians are…in general great Drunkards. *I must except the Ozages*," who are *not* "so passionately fond of drink as other Nations are" (my italics; Alvord and Carter, *New Regime*, 231). "[B]y no means was [alcohol] central to the pre-American trade" (William E. Unrau, *White Man's Wicked Water: The Alcohol Trade and Prohibition in Indian Country, 1802–1892* [Lawrence: University Press of Kansas, 1996], 121). Auguste Chouteau built St. Louis's first distillery in 1799, but just a decade later, there were eleven more (Unrau, *White Man's*

Wicked Water, 30). Ann M. Carlos and Frank D. Lewis, *Commerce by a Frozen Sea: Native Americans and the European Fur Trade* (Philadelphia: University of Pennsylvania Press, 2010), 89–95, dispute broad generalizations about all Indians being addicted to alcohol.

245. Burns, *Osage People*, 18–19; Din and Nasatir, *Imperial Osages*, 23; DuVal, *Native Ground*, 115; Bailey, "Osage," 481; *SR* 2:105.

246. *SMV* 3:170–74, 187, 244–47, 253, 256, 295–97, 316, 332–33.

247. Alvord and Carter, *New Regime*, 494.

248. *SMV* 3:170–74, 187, 247, 256, 295–97, 316, 332–33; trail map in Burns, *Osage People*, 73.

249. Din and Nasatir, *Imperial Osages*, 190–91, 208, 266. The commandant of Arkansas Post in 1790 wrote that *bohemes* (unruly white vagabonds) "suffer less from the Osages than they claim," intruding on Osage lands by "call[ing] themselves hunters without being so" (*SMV*, 3:333).

250. Din and Nasatir, *Imperial Osages*, 189; Burns, *Osage People*, 19, 115; Bailey, "Osage," 482–83.

251. *SMV* 3: 246–47, 253, 312, 316, 369; *SR* 2:103; Din and Nasatir, *Imperial Osages*, 387; *Seeking a Newer World: The Fort Osage Journals and Letters of George Sibley, 1808–1811*, ed. Jeffrey E. Smith (St. Charles, MO: Lindenwood University Press, 2003), 170–71.

252. *SR* 2: 96, 303; *BLC* 1:172; *SMV* 1:206–07; 3:296, 406; Din and Nasatir, *Imperial Osages*, 81, 150–51, 267.

253. *SMV* 3:312; 4:119; *BLC* 1:145–50 (quotes on 149); Perrin du Lac, *Travels*, 95–96; Din and Nasatir, *Imperial Osages*, 178–83, 211; Foley and Rice, *First Chouteaus*, 50–52, 57.

254. *SMV* 3:145, 196–97, 295, 414–17; *Dictionary of Louisiana Biography*, s.v. "Carondelet."

255. *SMV* 3:414–15, 417; *BLC*, 1:199; Primm, *Lion of the Valley*, 56.

256. *BLC* 1:152, 2: 527; Din and Nasatir, *Imperial Osages*, 320. Perez had earlier suggested such a trading fort to Governor Miró in October 1791 (*BLC* 1:150, 150n.; *SMV* 3:416).

257. *SMV* 4:299; *SR* 2: 93; Din and Nasatir, *Imperial Osages*, 258–61; Foley and Rice, *First Chouteaus*, 47, 52–53; Rollings, *Osage*, 173–212. Most sources agree that the Chouteaus' manipulations were a key factor in the political factionalism and major diaspora of the Osages. But there is disagreement about whether the Chouteaus induced other relocations to Arkansas in 1802 to thwart Lisa. Some Osages who moved south earlier or later did trade with two generations of Chouteaus; however, they were not pawns who did the bidding of whites.

258. *BLC* 2:534–39 (quotes on 538), 584; *SR* 2:100–10; Carl H. Chapman, "The Indomitable Osage in Spanish Illinois (Upper Louisiana), 1763–1804," in McDermott, *Spanish in Mississippi Valley*, 300–08; Foley and Rice, *First Chouteaus*, 54–58; Din and Nasatir, *Imperial Osages*, 291, chaps. 8–9 and passim.
259. *BLC* 2:526–27, 677–80; Din and Nasatir, *Imperial Osages*, 336, 347; Rollings, *Osage*, 191–92. The Chouteaus controlled sixteen of the twenty-nine shares/licenses of all St. Louis traders and 96,000 of 175,000 livres in trade goods (*BLC* 1: 209–10). On anti-Chouteau free trade advocates, see *BLC* 2:622–51 and *SR* 2:194–208; on the Company of Discoverers, see *BLC* 1:217–311 and *SR* 2:148–93.
260. Phillips, *Fur Trade*, 2:3–13, 129, 235, 241–43, 250 and chap. 41 passim; Jacques A. Barbier and Allan J. Kuethe, eds., *The North American Role in the Spanish Imperial Economy, 1760–1819* (Manchester, UK: Manchester University Press, 1984), 75, 100–01, Table 34. The Chouteaus traded with Cavelier et Fils in New Orleans from 1800 to 1816 (Phillips, *Fur Trade* 2:250, 250n.).
261. Perric du Lac, *Travels*, 56–57; Ekberg and Foley, *Finiels Account*, 84–85, 113; Reuben Gold Thwaites, ed., *Collections of the State Historical Society of Wisconsin* (Madison, WI, 1912), 20:97; Phillips, *Fur Trade* 2:34–35; Walter Havighurst, *Three Flags at the Straits: The Forts of Mackinac* (Englewood Cliffs, NJ: Prentice-Hall, 1966), 150.
262. Phillips, *Fur Trade*, 2:241, 250.
263. Schneider Invoice, March 27, 1794, Chouteau Collections, MHM Library and Research Center; Todd, McGill and Co. letter to A. and P. Chouteau, July 31, 1794, announcing arrival of Schneider shipment, Chouteau Collections; Schneider Letter re: Chouteau account, May 7, 1795, Pierre Chouteau Collection; Charles Gratiot list of merchandise from Schneider via Todd, McGill and Co., April 23, 1795, Henry Chouteau Dyer Collection, all from that same repository.
264. Accounts of Auguste and Pierre Chouteau with Andrew Todd & Co. of Mackinac, dated July 14–July 29, 1794, July 30, 1794–November 16, 1795, and September 24, 1796, all in Henry Chouteau Dyer Collection, MHM Library and Research Center; Chouteau to William Grant, May 8, 1797, Auguste Chouteau Papers, MHM.
265. That summary is based on my analysis of two dozen documents of the Chouteau-Canada trade from 1794 to 1804 in MHM Library and Research Center. Astor's letter proposing a partnership, January 28, 1800, is in the Pierre Chouteau Collection at that repository.

266. Brackenridge, *Views of Louisiana*, 122; *SR* 2: 141–43, 198–99, 247–50; Ekberg and Foley, *Finiels Account*, 69, 70–79, 107, 122; Stoddard, *Sketches of Louisiana*, 209–26; *BLC* 2:648; Chouteau "Narrative" in McDermott, *Histories*, 48; Gilbert J. Garraghan, S.J., *Saint Ferdinand de Florissant* (Chicago: Loyola University Press, 1923). Population estimates are from Paul Lachance, "The Louisiana Purchase in the Demographic Perspective of Its Time," in *Empires of the Imagination: The Transatlantic Histories of the Louisiana Purchase*, ed. Peter J. Kastor and François Weil (Charlottesville: University of Virginia Press, 2009), 149, 151. He noted that the annual growth rate of Upper Louisiana was 4.9 percent between 1766 and 1788 but increased to 7.4 percent in the period from 1789 to 1803—surpassing that of Lower Louisiana and attaining 15 percent of the population in all of Spanish Louisiana. Under the Americans, population growth in Upper Louisiana "continued to outpace that of the state of Louisiana in the last forty years of the antebellum period" (174n.).

267. Brackenridge, *Views of Louisiana*, 124; McDermott, *Libraries*, 8, 9–10 (quotes), 21–22, 65, 77, 87, 89, 90, 112, 128–30 and passim.

268. Ekberg and Foley, *Finiels Account*, 121–22; *SR* 2:656; Stoddard, *Sketches of Louisiana*, 297–98; *SMV* 2:xxiv; William E. Foley, *The Genesis of Missouri: From Wilderness Outpost to Statehood* (Columbia: University of Missouri Press, 1989), 96, 314 n.61. In 1800, even the St. Louis merchants who were opposed to monopolies estimated the annual volume of furs at 221,000 pounds (*SR* 2:195). See Table A for the distribution of $180,000 in trade goods. In 1789, Spain decreed that "no white person shall be admitted to reside in this territory [of Upper Louisiana] who shall…be a hunter by profession….This regulation is intended for the preservation of those animals [deer and buffalo], and for the benefit of neighboring Indians, whose dependence is on hunting" (*SR* 1:305).

269. Billon, *Annals*, 298.

270. *Dictionary of Missouri Biography*, s.v. "Delassus"; *SR* 2:301–12. Din and Nasatir, *Imperial Osages*, 318–19, asserted that the culprits were rogue warriors from the separatist Arkansas Osages, leaving the Fort Carondelet Osages blameless (p. 310).

271. Newspaper accounts from eastern cities on the Osages' 1804 visit, in Luke Vincent Lockwood, *The St. Memin Indian Portraits* (New York, 1928), 12 and passim; Washington quoted in J. Frederick Fausz, "'Engaged in Enterprises Pregnant with Terror': George Washington's Formative Years among Indians," in Warren R. Hofstra, ed., *George Washington in the Backcountry* (Madison, WI: Madison House, 1998), 140, 142, 153–54.

272. McDermott, *Libraries*, 174–75. Napoleon quoted in François Barbé-Marbois, *The History of Louisiana, Particularly of the Cession of that Colony to the United States of America* (Philadelphia: Carey & Lea, 1830), 293. The best source on the international intrigues that led to the Spanish retrocession of Louisiana to France on October 1, 1800 (not "delivered" until October 15, 1802), and Napoleon's agreement to sell that huge territory to the United States on April 30, 1803 (ratified by the Senate on Oct. 19, 1803), is Jon Kukla, *A Wilderness So Immense: The Louisiana Purchase and the Destiny of America* (New York: Alfred A. Knopf, 2003).

273. *BCL* 2: 592.

274. Perrin du Lac, *Travels*, 47–48; James Pitot, *Observations on the Colony of Louisiana from 1796 to 1802*, trans. Henry C. Pitot (Baton Rouge: Louisiana State Press, 1979), 36; Vilemont letter of 1802, in *BCL* 2: 683, 687; Ekberg and Foley, *Finiels Account*, 110–11.

EPILOGUE. FINDING AND "FIXING" ST. LOUIS

275. Epigraph from William Fisher, *New Travels Among the Indians of North America* [based on] *the Communications Already Published of Captains Lewis and Clark* (Philadelphia: James Sharan, 1812), vii. Paragraph citations: Ekberg and Foley, *Finiels Account*, 112. "Trauma" is not usually associated with the Louisiana Purchase, especially in St. Louis, but there is ample evidence for French discontent with that jarring and unexpected territorial transfer in both Upper and Lower Louisiana. See Barbé-Marbois, *History of Louisiana*, 333–35, 357; *A Whole Country in Commotion: The Louisiana Purchase and the American Southwest*, ed. Patrick G. Williams, S. Charles Bolton and Jennie M. Whayne (Fayetteville: University of Arkansas Press, 2005); Moore, "Déterminé L'Effacement," 18–29; *The Louisiana Purchase: Emergence of an American Nation*, ed. Peter J. Kastor (Washington, D.C.: CQ Press, 2002); "The Louisiana Purchase and The West," *Journal of the West* 43, no. 3 (2004).

276. Stoddard, *Sketches of Louisiana*, 108 (star quote), 219–20 (town description). Also see Foley and Rice, *First Chouteaus*, 93, 102 nn.14–15; McDermott, "Captain Stoddard," *MHS Bulletin* (1954): 328–35; Thomas C. Danisi and W. Raymond Wood, "Lewis and Clark's Route Map: James MacKay's Map of the Missouri River," *Western Historical Quarterly* 35 (2004): 53–72. Regarding "tears," see Darby, *Personal Recollections*, 459; Elizabeth Gentry Sayad, "Louisiana Purchase: Celebrations and Legacies," *Gateway Heritage*

21, no. 2 (2000), 32–45. Lewis knew so little about Upper Louisiana that he was shocked to find the Spanish still governing St. Louis, since Jefferson had given him official credentials for French officials.

277. Stoddard, *Sketches of Louisiana*, 211 (precarious subsistence), 218 (emporium of trade); *The Life and Papers of Frederick Bates*, ed. Thomas Maitland Marshall (St. Louis: Missouri Historical Society, 1926), 1:267.

278. *SMV*, 4:106; *SR* 2:12; *Dictionary of Missouri Biography*, s.v. "Clark," "Lewis," "Harrison"; J. Frederick Fausz, *The Day Kikotan Became Hampton: England's First Indian War, 1609–1614* (Hampton, VA: Port Hampton Press, 2010); Fausz, "Washington's Formative Years," in Hofstra, *Virginia Backcountry*, 118–19, 136–37; Daniel M. Friedenberg, *Life, Liberty, and the Pursuit of Land: The Plunder of Early America* (Buffalo, NY: Prometheus Books, 1992), 276–77, 303–05, and passim; James H. O'Donnell, "The Native American Crisis in the Ohio Country, 1774–1783," in *The Old Northwest in the American Revolution*, ed. David Curtis Skaggs (Madison: State Historical Society of Wisconsin, 1977), 156; Walter Nugent, *Habits of Empire: A History of American Expansion* (New York: Alfred A. Knopf, 2008); Barbara Alice Mann, *George Washington's War on Native America* (Lincoln: University of Nebraska Press, 2008); J. Hector St. John de Crevecoeur, *Letters from an American Farmer* (London, 1782). See two recent biographies of leading Virginia "land-stealers": Robert H. Owens, *Mr. Jefferson's Hammer: William Henry Harrison and the Origins of American Indian Policy* (Norman: University of Oklahoma Press, 2007) and Jay H. Buckley, *William Clark, Indian Diplomat* (Norman: University of Oklahoma Press, 2008).

279. Kukla, *Wilderness So Immense*, 292–93; Friedenberg, *Pursuit of Land*, 163 (Walker quote) and chaps, 15, 18; Donald Jackson, *Thomas Jefferson & the Stony Mountains: Exploring the West from Monticello* (Urbana: University of Illinois Press, 1981), 4–12; Le Page du Pratz, *History of Louisiana*, title page ("western Virginia").

280. Peter S. Onuf, "'Empire for Liberty': Center and Peripheries in Postcolonial America," in Daniels and Kennedy, *Negotiated Empires*, 308; *SR* 2:12; *SMV* 3:117; prospectus for the history of the Lewis and Clark Expedition (1810) in Jackson, *Letters of Lewis and Clark*, 2:547; speech to the Hanover Country militia, 1758, quoted in Charles Campbell, *Introduction to the History of the Colony and Ancient Dominion of Virginia* (Richmond: William McFarlane, 1847), 126. Jumonville's death became a cause celebre in France, "proving" that the British were ruthless "barbarians" (Bell, *Cult of the Nation*, 13, 78–85 and passim).

281. George Croghan in Thwaites, *Early Western Travels*, 1:141, 152; Merrill D. Peterson, ed., *Thomas Jefferson: Writings* (New York: Library of America,

1984), 818 (TJ to John Jay, August 1785), 1081 (to Dr. Benjamin Rush, September 1800), 1311 (to Alexander Humboldt, December 1813); Carroll, *Eulogy on George Washington, February 22, 1800*, quoted in Fausz, "Washington's Formative Years," Hofstra, *Virginia Backcountry*, 115–16. An English pamphlet in 1720 warned Virginians about the growing threat of French and Indians in Louisiana—a dangerous frontier force enlarged by "intermarrying" and Jesuit conversion efforts (*Some Considerations on the Consequences of the French Settling Colonies on the Mississippi*). Jefferson's complex and often contradictory opinions about Indians and his policies regarding them are best summarized in Anthony F.C. Wallace, *Jefferson and the Indians: The Tragic Fate of the First Americans* (Cambridge, MA: Harvard University Press, 1999).

282. Jackson, *Letters of Lewis and Clark*, 1:199–202; Jefferson to Harrison in Peterson, *Jefferson Writings*, 1118; Stoddard, *Sketches of Louisiana*, 410; see also 291–306; 411–18.

283. DuVal, *Native Ground*, 184–87, 200–01; Rollings, *Osage*, 183–84; Din and Nasatir, *Imperial Osages*, 295, 304, 311–14, 349–51; *The Expeditions of Zebulon Montgomery Pike*, ed. Elliott Coues (Minneapolis, MN: Ross & Haines, 1965) 2:530–31.

284. Onuf, "'Empire for Liberty,'" in Daniels and Kennedy, *Negotiated Empires*, 302; Jefferson to Jay, 1785, in Peterson, *Jefferson Writings*, 819; Jefferson to the Osages, January 4, 1806, in Jackson, *Letters of Lewis and Clark*, 1:281–82. Note Jefferson's message to the Indians near Detroit in November 1807: "If ever we…lift the hatchet against any tribe, we will never lay it down till that tribe is exterminated or driven beyond the Mississippi" (*American State Papers: Documents Legislative and Executive of the Congress of the United States, Class 2: Indian Affairs* [Washington, D.C.: Gales & Seaton 1832], 1:745; hereafter cited as *ASP: Indians*).

285. Meriwether Lewis, "A Statistical View of the Indian nations inhabiting the territory of Lousiana…April 1805," in *ASP: Indians*, 2:707–08; and Lewis to President Jefferson "relative to the treaty with the Osage Indians," December 15, 1808, 766–67. Lewis confirmed that the Grand Osages still had twelve hundred warriors and a total population of five thousand, while the Petit Osages accounted for another three hundred warriors and thirteen hundred total people. Together, their fur trade was valued at $28,000 worth of merchandise, which Rollings, *Osage*, 219–20, claimed would yield $63,000 worth of furs.

286. Account of Governor Meriwether Lewis, May 26, 1808, published in *Massachusetts Spy, or Worcester Gazette*, Wednesday, August 3, 1808, 3,

columns 1–2; Jefferson to Harrison, 1803, Peterson, *Jefferson Writings*, 1120; Din and Nasatir, *Imperial Osages*, 372–83; Jackson, *Letters of Lewis and Clark*, 2:704, and see 696–719; Burns, *Osage People*, 168; Clark to Secretary of War James Barbour, June 11, 1825, in *ASP: Indians*, 2: 592; Treaty of 1808 with Lewis commentary, *ASP: Indians*, 1:763–67.

287. Clark's "damned" quote in *Fifty Years in Camp and Field: Diary of Major-General Ethan Allen Hitchcock, U.S.A.*, ed. W.A. Croffut (New York: G.P. Putnam, 1909), 140; Clark's admission to Jefferson, October 10, 1816, in Jackson, *Letters of Lewis and Clark*, 2:625; Second Treaty of St. Louis, June 11, 1825, in *ASP: Indians* 2:592; Clark's report to Congress, March 1, 1826, in *ASP: Indians*, 2:653; Fausz, "Nation of Quakers," 37–39; John Mack Farragher, "'More Motley than Mackinaw': From Ethnic Mixing to Ethnic Cleansing on the Frontier of the Lower Missouri, 1783–1833," in *Contact Points: American Frontiers from the Mohawk Valley to the Mississippi, 1750–1830*, eds. R.L. Cayton and Fredrika J. Teute (Chapel Hill: University of North Carolina Press, 1998), 304–26.

288. Quote on fur traders in Thwaites, *Collections of Wisconsin* 20:258. See similar prejudices in Stoddard, *Sketches of Louisiana*; 302–03 and passim.

289. Albert Gallatin quote in Jackson, *Letters of Lewis and Clark*, 1:209. He said that Pierre Chouteau sought "power and money" as agent to the Grand Osages. Stoddard described that initial probationary period of mutual probing as "cordial acquiescence" (quoted in Aron, *American Confluence*, 114).

290. Aron, *American Confluence*, 111 and passim; Gitlin, *Bourgeois Frontier*, 61 (Chouteau acreage); Primm, *Lion of the Valley*, chap. 3; Kukla, *Wilderness So Immense*, 351 and chaps. 15–16 on controversies involving Louisiana residents; Robert Moore Jr., "The French Connection of Lewis and Clark," *Le Journal* 25, no. 1 (2009): 1–7; Jay Gitlin, "A Place Beyond Words: Using the Creole Corridor to Rediscover the Terms of Early American History," *Gateway* 30 (2010): 9–17. Auguste Chouteau was one of the leaders in preparing petitions to Congress that were critical of U.S. policies (*ASP: Miscellaneous*, 1:400–04, and Foley and Rice, *First Chouteaus*, 90–101).

291. Brackenridge, *Views of Louisiana*, 143–45.

292. Foley and Rice, *First Chouteaus*, 92–95, 101, 160–61. Removing the Osages from Missouri was equivalent to burying the outlines of French St. Louis, as United States policies amounted to "out of sight, out of mind and ultimately out of memory" (Fausz, "Nation of Quakers," *Gateway*, 39).

293. Foley and Rice, *First Chouteaus*, 142–48; Articles of Association and Partnership for the St. Louis Missouri Fur Company, March 7, 1809, in Pierre Chouteau Collection, MHM Library and Research Center; J. Frederick Fausz, "'Pacific Intentions': Lewis and Clark and the Western Fur Trade," in *Lewis & Clark: Journey to Amother America*, ed. Alan Taylor (St. Louis: Missouri Historical Society Press for the Oasis Institute, 2003), 120–43; Gitlin, "'Avec Bien du Regret,'" 9.

If the Chouteaus wished to remain involved in fur trading, they had to adapt to new American policies and personnel as that industry became more bureaucratized under government control. While outsiders condemned Spanish "despotism" in its governance of Upper Louisiana, merchant insiders like the Chouteaus enjoyed lax enforcement and large official subsidies, as Spain bore the brunt of perennial deficits (see *SR* 2:194 and Barbier and Kuethe, *Spanish Imperial Economy*, 182 and passim). Merchants in the new American capital of the West profited from outfitting expeditions, opening stores, having Indian debts paid for by treaty provisions and selling to tribes receiving government annuities (see Gitlin, *Bourgeois Frontier*, chaps. 3–5, and Aron, *American Confluence*, chap. 6 and epilogue).

294. Foley and Rice, *First Chouteaus*, 176 (quote), 194–98, and passim on offices and philanthropies; Barbier and Kuethe, *Spanish Imperial Economy*, 101, Table 34; Collot, *Voyage*, 1:153–55.

295. Edwards to Secretary of War William H. Crawford, November 15, in *ASP: Indians*, 2:65–66; and Chouteau's "Report on the Fur Trade," 1815, 66–67; "Notes on Indian Boundaries," 1816, *Glimpses of the Past* 7 (October–December 1940).

296. *Messages and Letters of William Henry Harrison*, ed. Logan Esarey (Indianapolis: Indiana Historical Commission, 1922), 1:110, 744; Darby, *Personal Recollections*, 31–32; Foley and Rice, *First Chouteaus*, 175, 196.

297. Holt, "Shaping of St. Louis," 222, 238, 508–10.

298. Susan Dunn, *Dominion of Memories: Jefferson, Madison, and the Decline of Virginia* (New York: Basic Books, 2007), 1–29 and passim; Foley and Rice, *First Chouteaus*, 172, 180–81, 201; Christian, *Before Lewis and Clark*, 248–49; Chouteau obituary, *Missouri Republican*, February 24, 1829.

299. Stoddard, *Sketches of Louisiana*, 460; Alvord and Carter, *Critical Period*, 257; Hunter, *Memoirs*, 225.

300. Chouteau's "Report on the Indian Trade," in *ASP: Indians* 2:66.

About the Author

Fred Fausz is a history professor and former dean of the Pierre Laclede Honors College at the University of Missouri–St. Louis, specializing in the ethnohistory of Indian-European relations in colonial America. He received an AB degree in European history from Thomas More College in his native Kentucky; earned his PhD in early American history from the College of William and Mary, with Phi Beta Kappa honors; and was a fellow of the D'Arcy McNickle Center for the History of the American Indian at the Newberry Library, Chicago. Three of his many publications have won "best of the year" awards from historical societies in Missouri, Virginia and Maryland, and in May 2007, *Time* magazine cited his research on early Jamestown. Committed to sharing historical knowledge with the general public, he was a consultant on Kevin Costner's eight-hour Indian documentary, *500 Nations*, and has exhibited his extensive collection of fur trade artifacts in major museums and at other sites in seven midwestern states. In 2006, he was the lead organizer and program chair for the Ninth North American Fur Trade Conference in St. Louis and received the 2007 Missouri Governor's Award in the Humanities for Enhancing Community Heritage.

Visit us at
www.historypress.net

This title is also available as an e-book

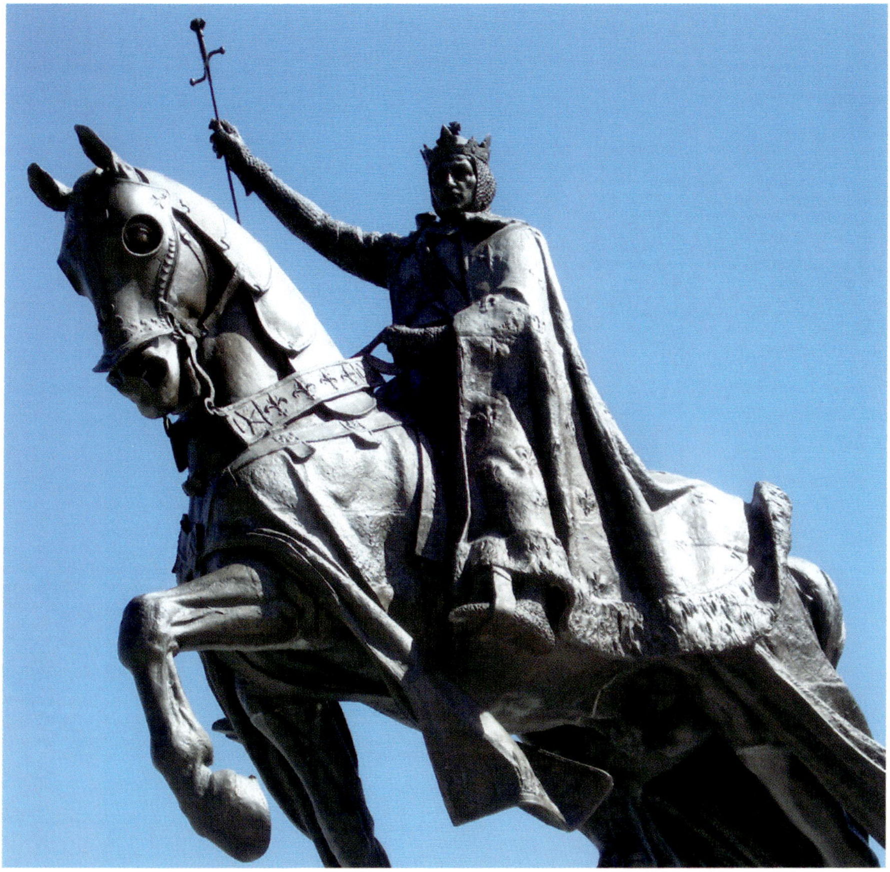

Apotheosis of Saint Louis, King Louis IX of France. Designed by Charles H. Niehaus, 1903; erected in 1906. *Photograph by Jeanette Fox Fausz.*

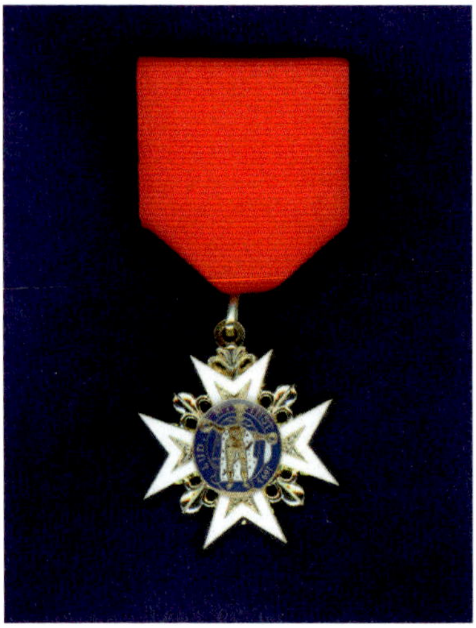

Left: Cross of the Royal and Military Order of Saint Louis—medal awarded to Kerlérec, Neyon de Villiers and Aubry. *Replica owned and photographed by author.*

Below: Church of St. Michel in Bedous, where Laclède was baptized. *Photographed in 2009 by Ian Stokes of Stroud, Gloucestershire, United Kingdom; used with permission.*

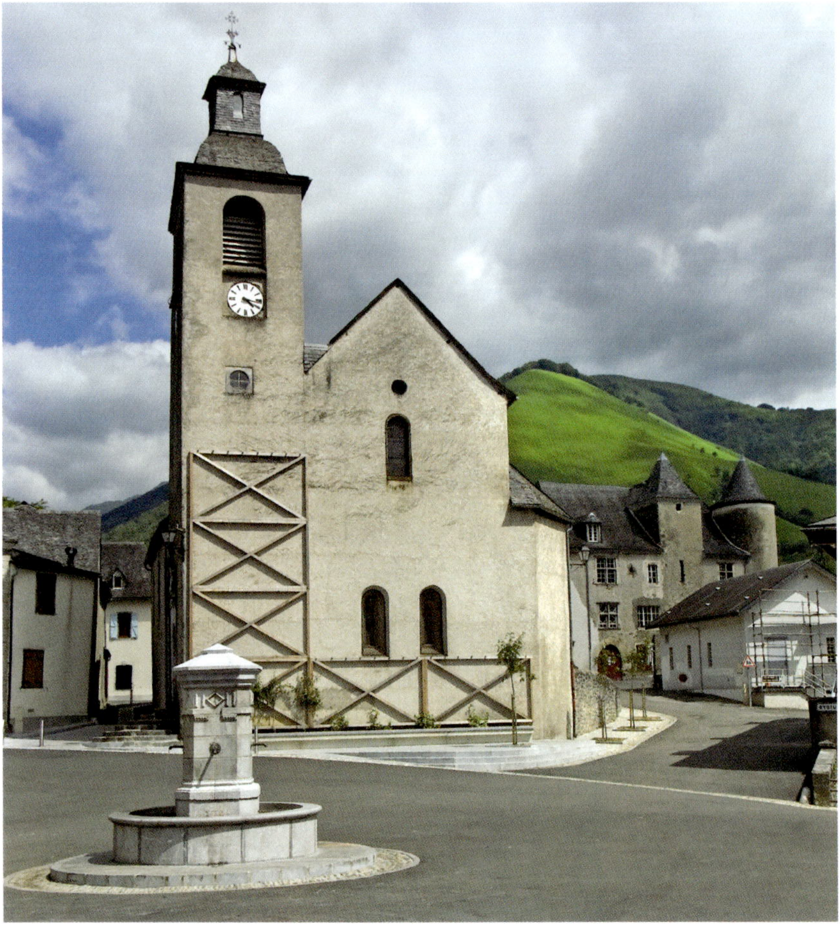

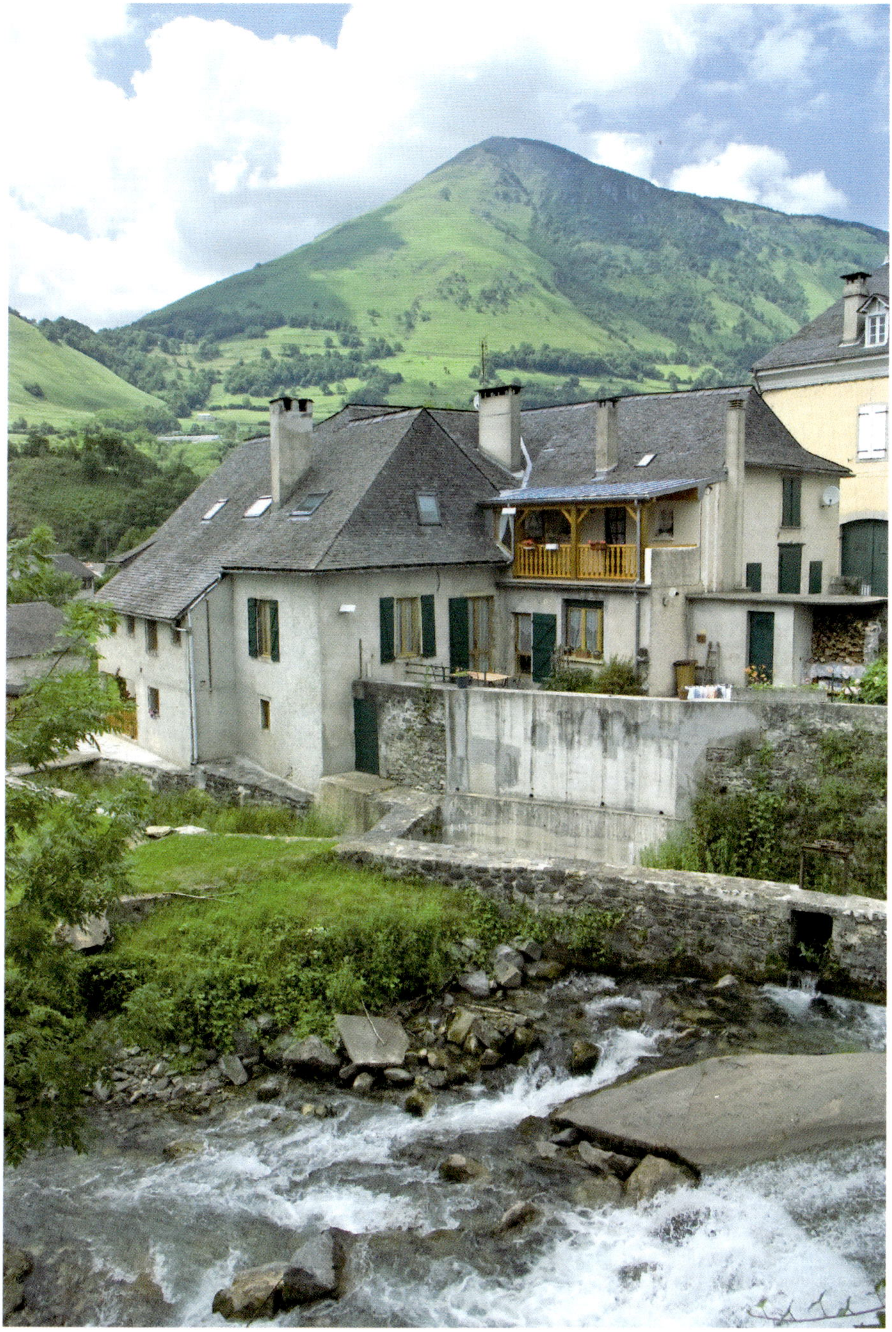

The Gabarret River at Bedous, near Laclède's home. *Courtesy photographer Ian Stokes of Stroud, Gloucestershire, United Kingdom; used with permission.*

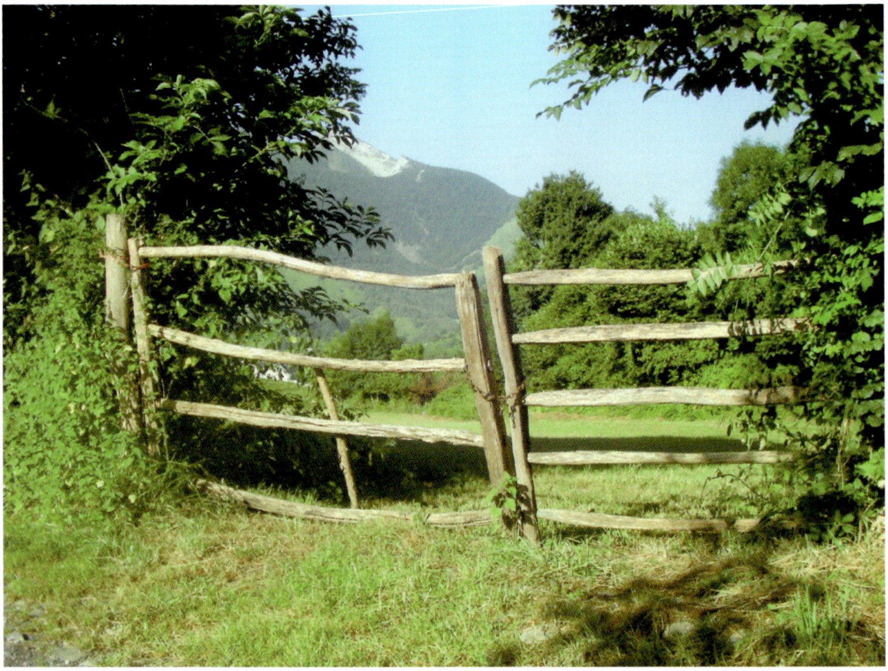

A Béarnais *clede* ("gate"), origin of Laclède's surname, photographed near his willow grove.
Courtesy Jean Caillabet of Christchurch, New Zealand; used with permission.

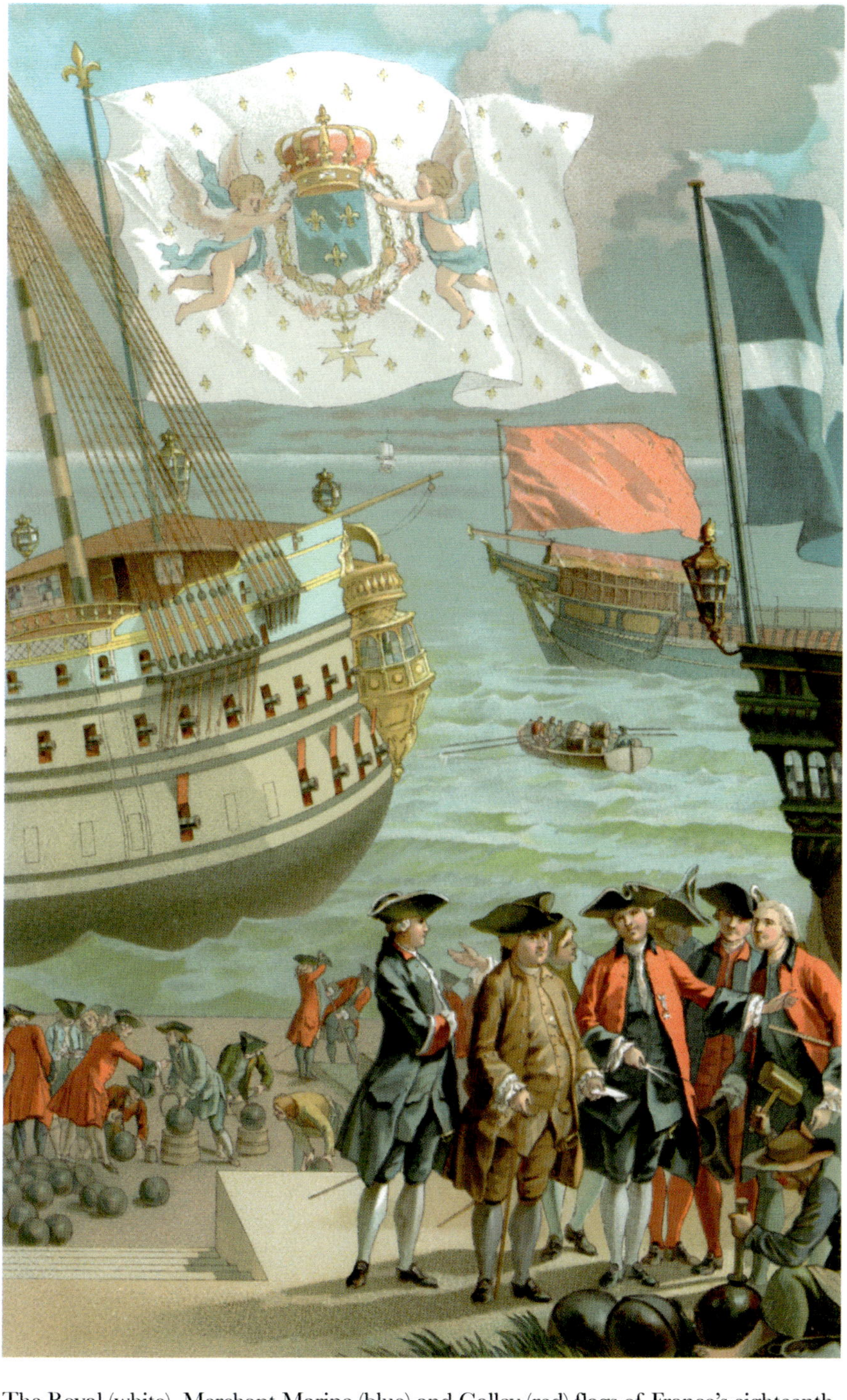

The Royal (white), Merchant Marine (blue) and Galley (red) flags of France's eighteenth-century ships, as painted by Joseph Vernet. *1864 lithograph owned by author.*

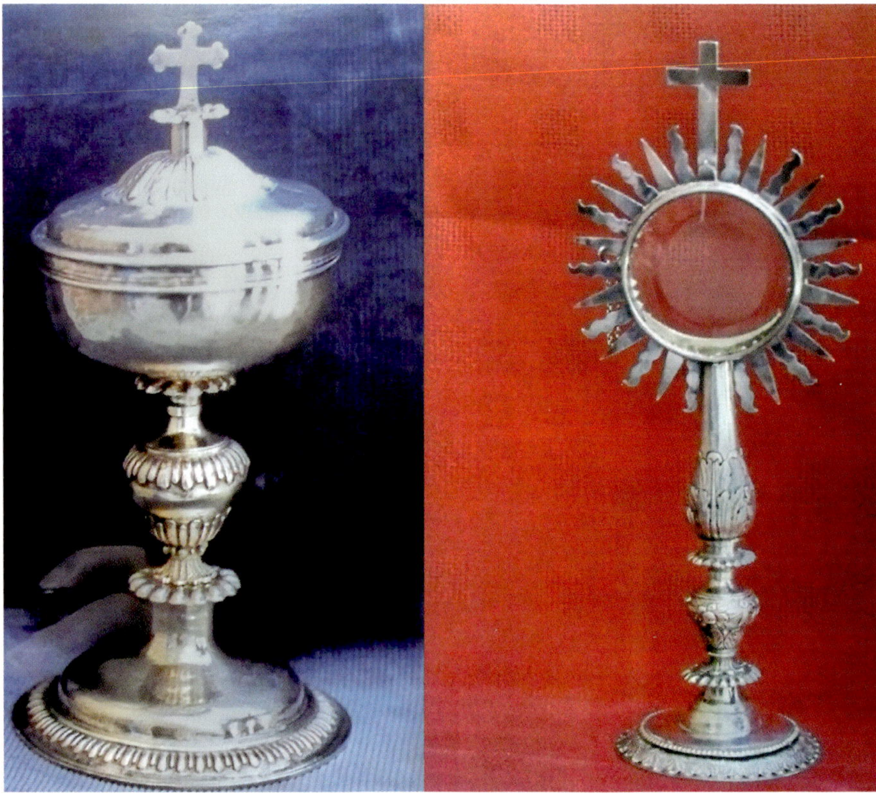

Seventeenth-century French silver vessels from Ste. Anne Church, where Laclède worshipped in Nouvelle Chartres. *Courtesy Fort de Chartres State Historic Site, Illinois.*

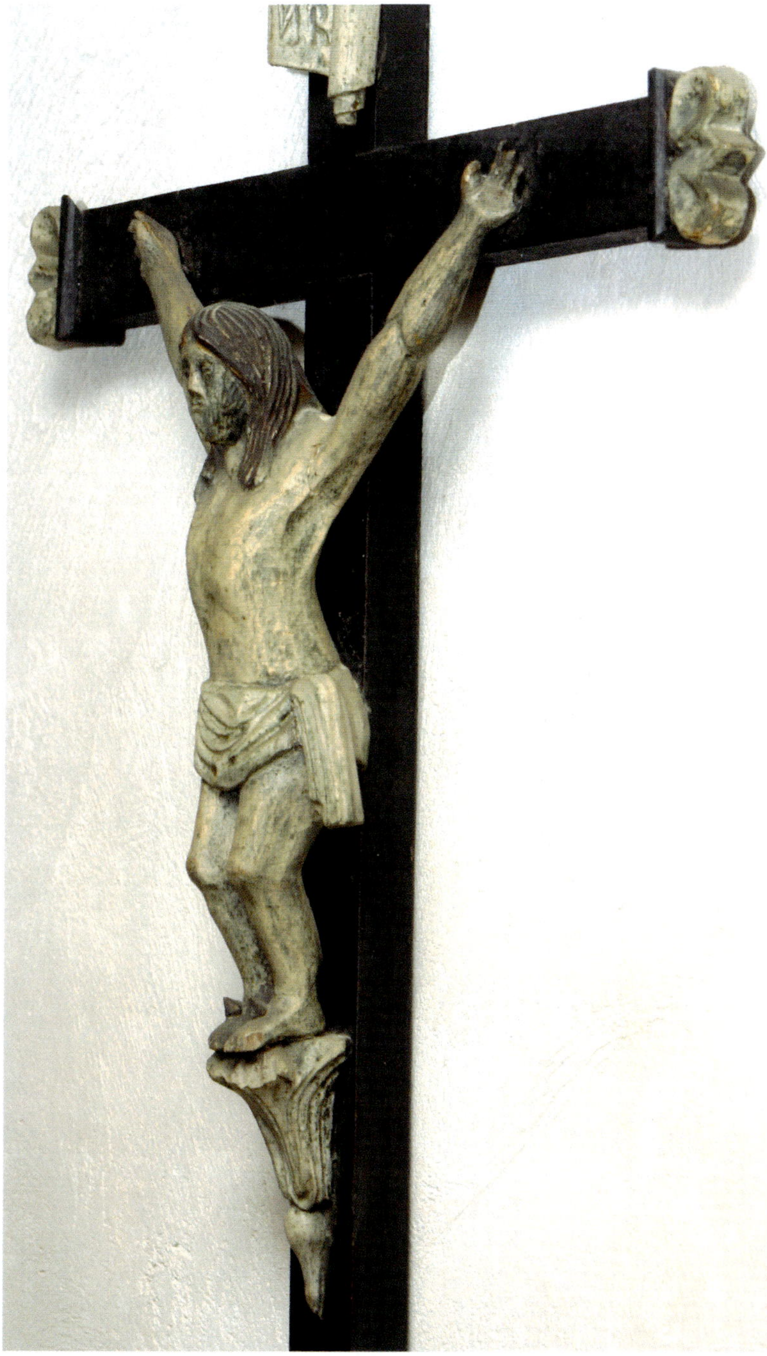

A so-called "voyageur crucifix" (long arms, barrel chest and short "canoe legs"). *Photograph by Bill Naeger; used by permission of Bolduc House Museum, Ste. Genevieve, Missouri.*

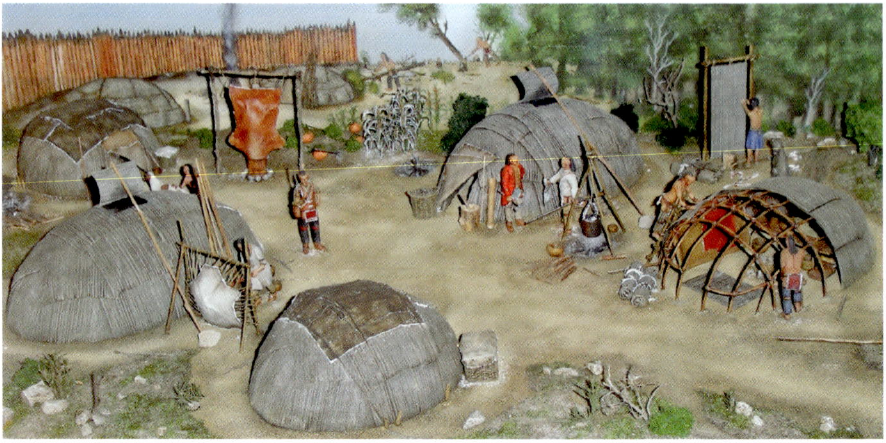

Museum model of eighteenth-century Mechigamea village in Illinois, when that tribe was allied with the Osages. *Courtesy, Fort de Chartres State Historic Site, Illinois.*

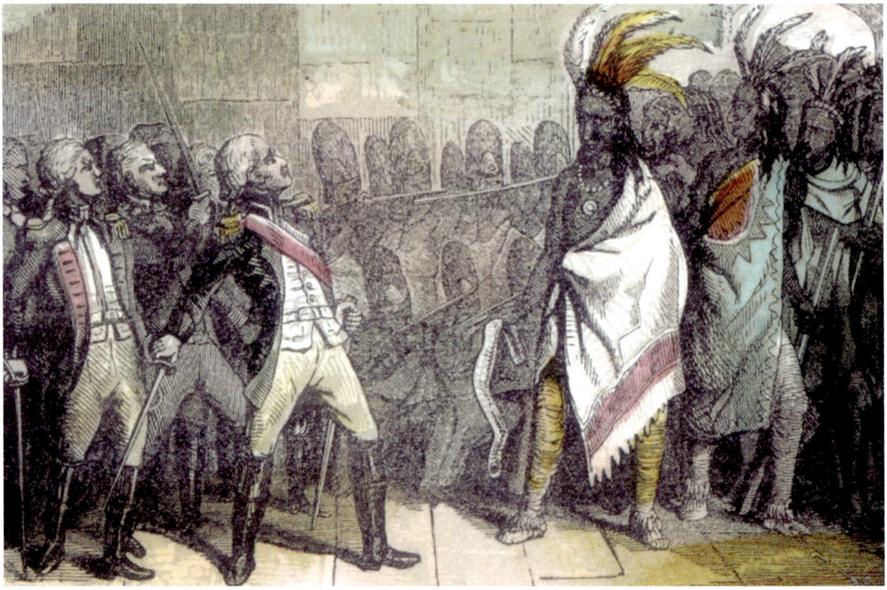

Pontiac was truly larger than life in influencing events when St. Louis was founded. *From author's Henry Howe,* Historical Collections of the Great West *(1856).*

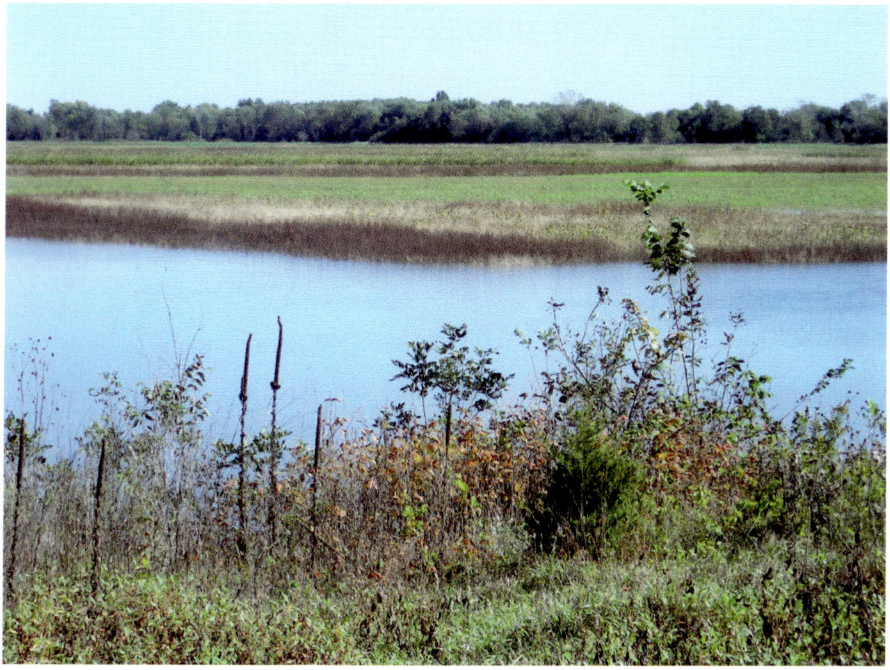

The Grand Osages' famous *Marais des Cygnes* ("Marsh of Swans"), which nourished their towns in southwestern Missouri and eastern Kansas. *Author photograph, 2007.*

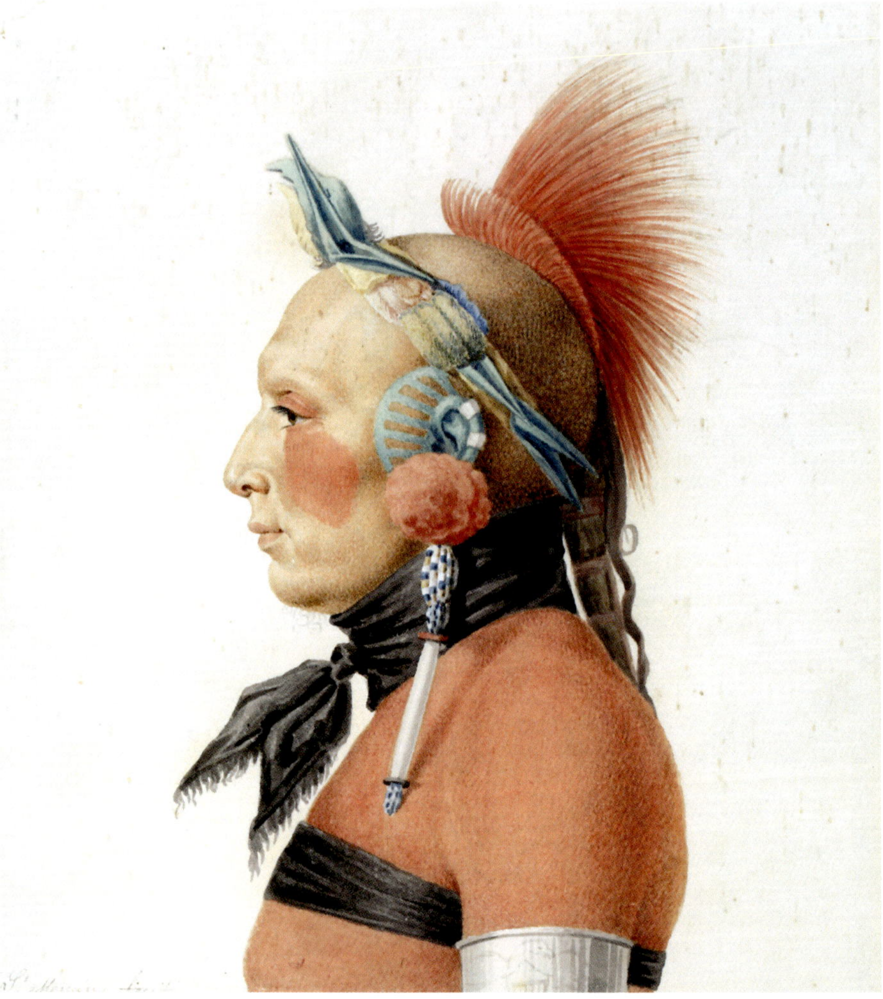

"Osage Warrior" who visited Jefferson in 1806, wearing a vulture beak "crown." Painted from life by Charles Balthazar Julien Févret de Saint-Mémin. *Courtesy Winterthur Museum.*

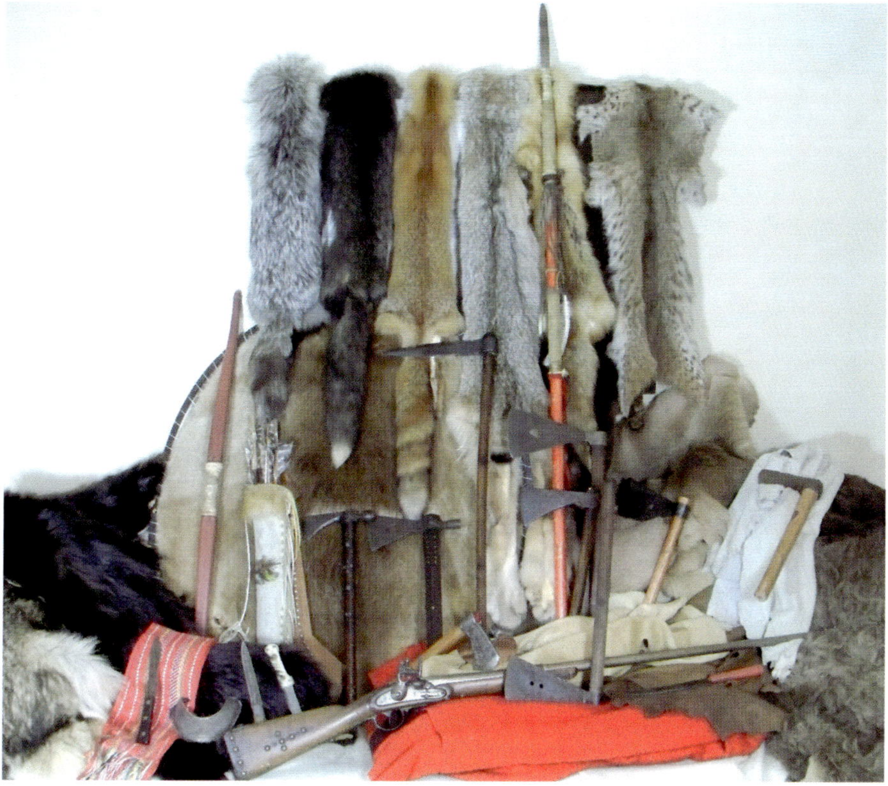

Objects representing the eighteenth-century St. Louis fur trade: pelts, hides, deer leather, Missouri war axes and a 1790 musket. *Owned and photographed by author.*

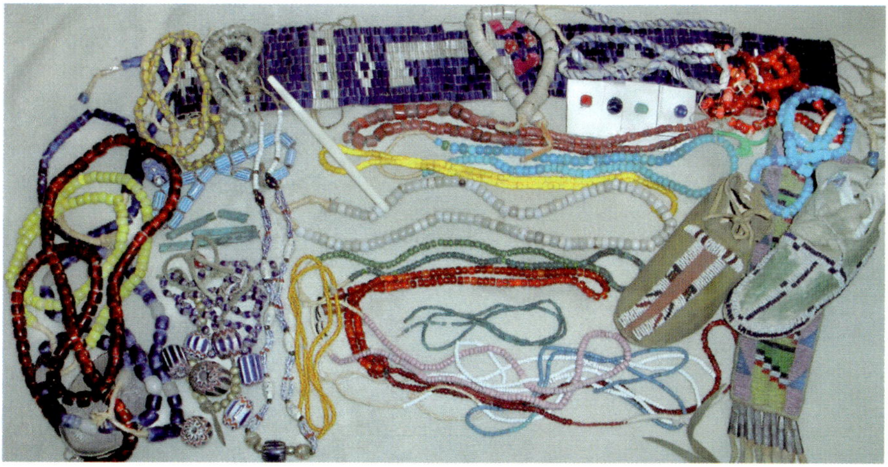

Glass trade beads from several European countries were desirable gifts received at the Indian capital of St. Louis. *Owned and photographed by the author.*

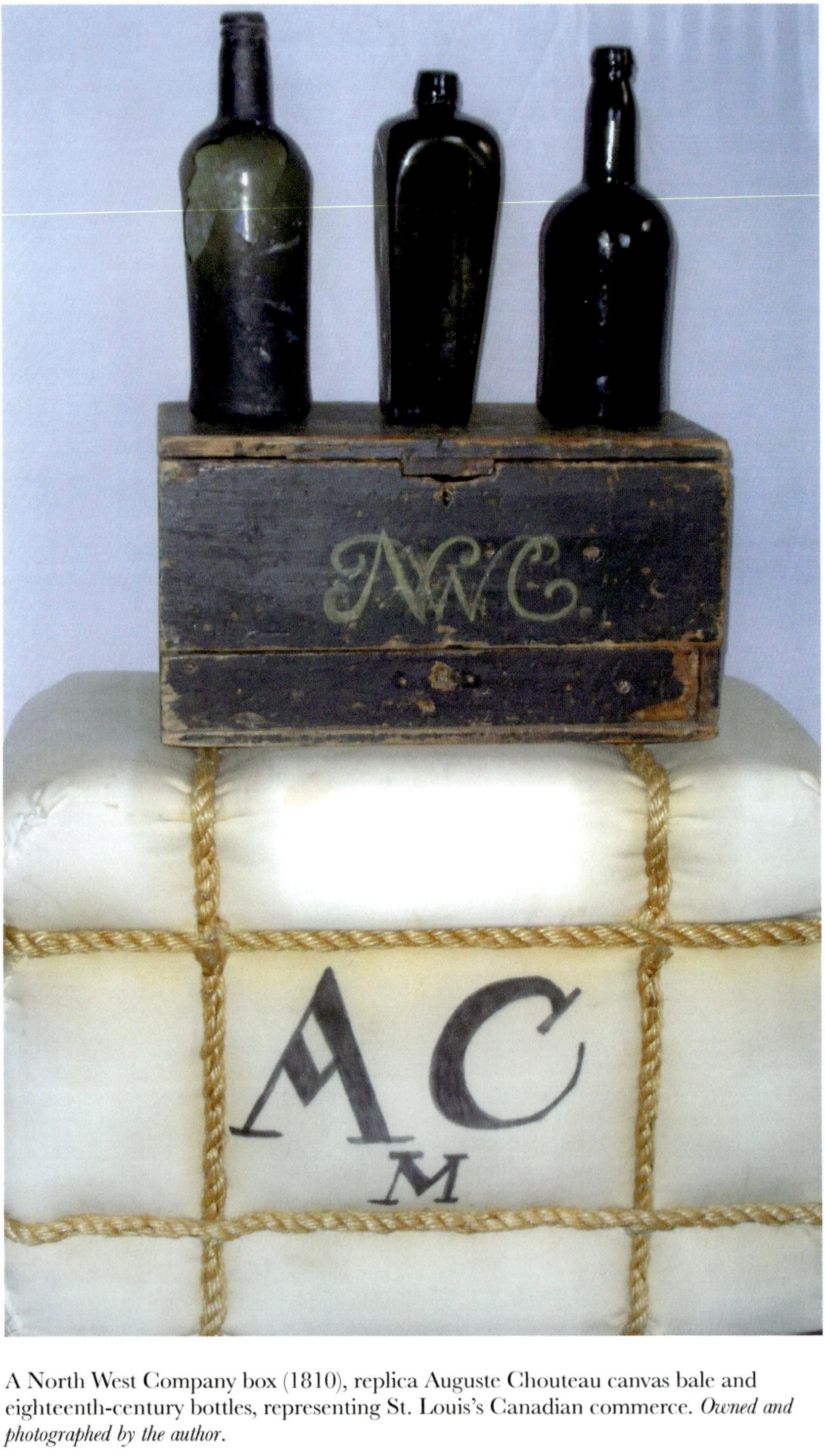

A North West Company box (1810), replica Auguste Chouteau canvas bale and eighteenth-century bottles, representing St. Louis's Canadian commerce. *Owned and photographed by the author.*

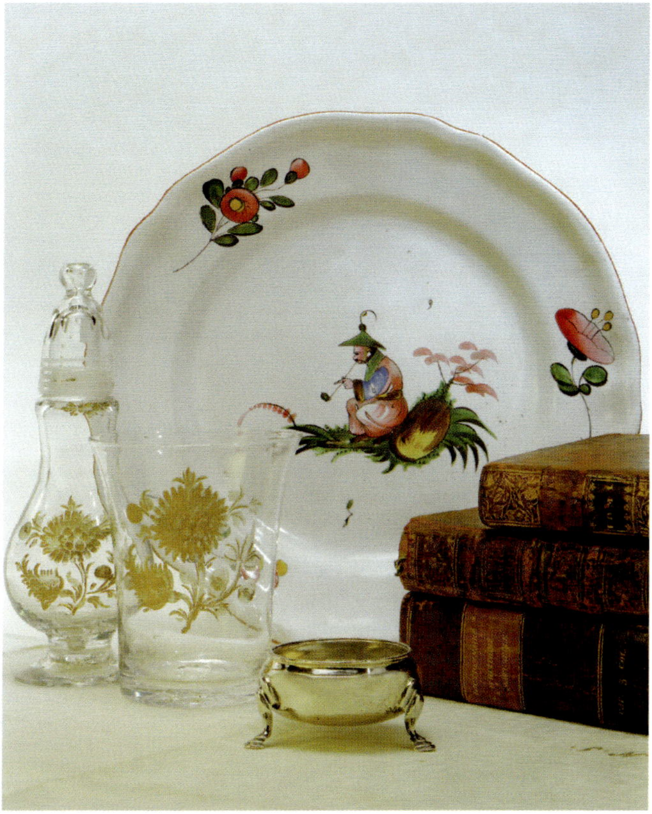

Right: Wealth from the Osage "wilderness" provided the Laclède-Chouteau family with Spanish glassware, French china and libraries that complemented Indian knowledge. *Courtesy Missouri History Museum, St. Louis.*

Below: First published "portraits" of Meriwether Lewis (right) and William Clark, from William Fisher's *New Travels among the Indians of North America* (Philadelphia, 1812). *Author's collection.*

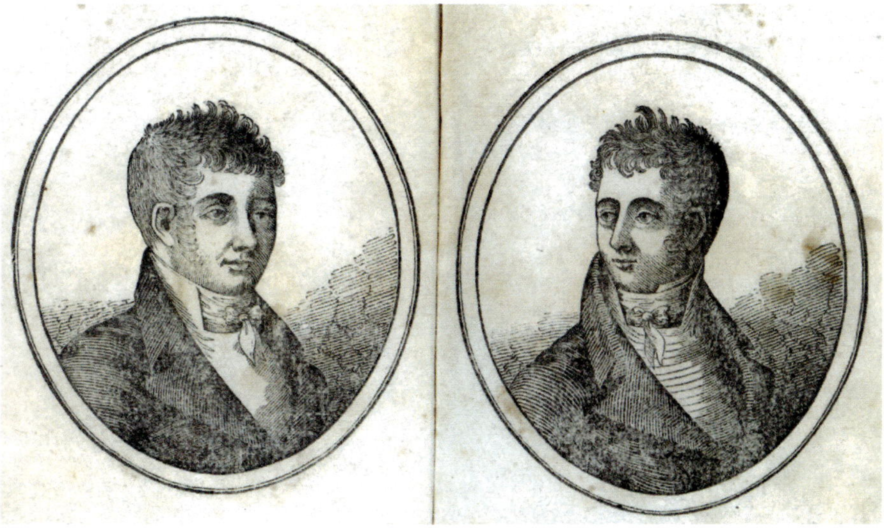

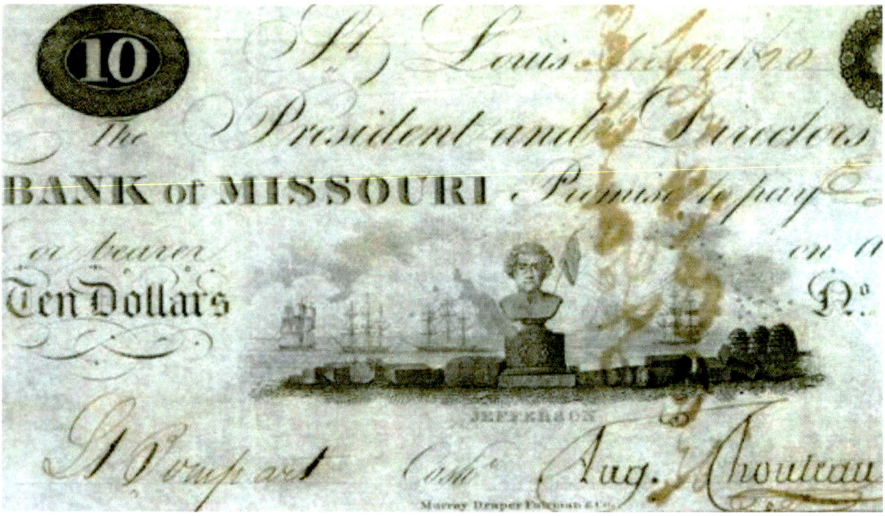

1820 Bank of Missouri bill, signed by president Auguste Chouteau, portraying an imperious Jefferson surrounded by symbols of commerce, not agriculture. *Author's collection.*

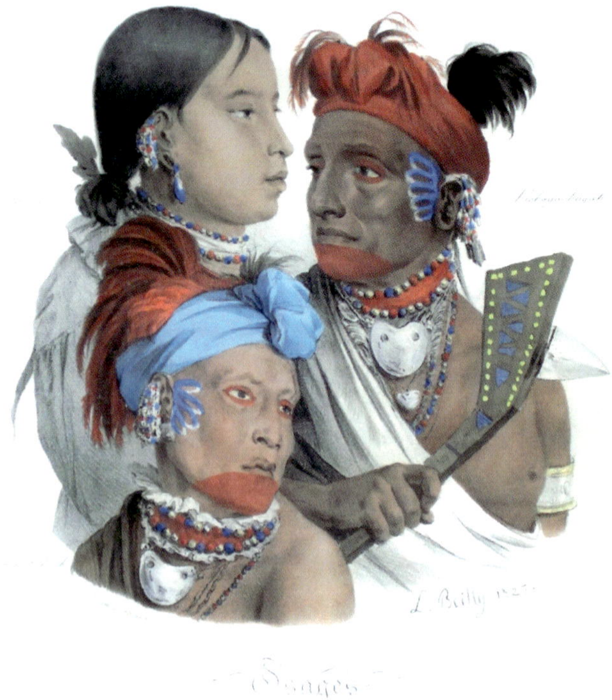

Three of the six Osages who toured Paris after losing their homeland. *Signed and numbered 1827 Louis-Leopold Boilly lithograph in author's collection.*

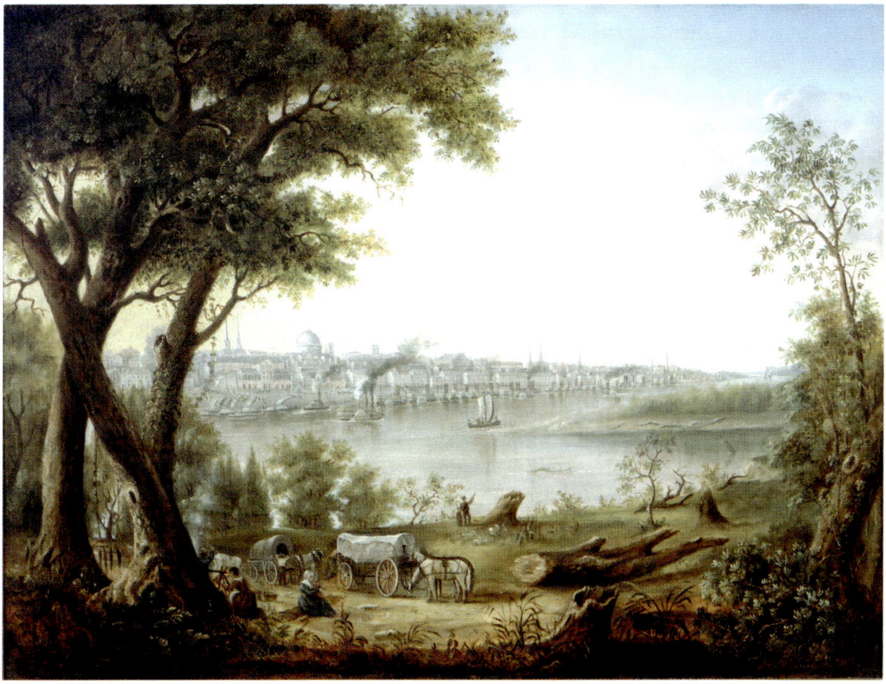

St. Louis in 1846 by Henry Lewis, 1846, symbolizing the historic connection between rural Illinois and St. Louis. *Courtesy Saint Louis Art Museum. Eliza McMillan Trust.*

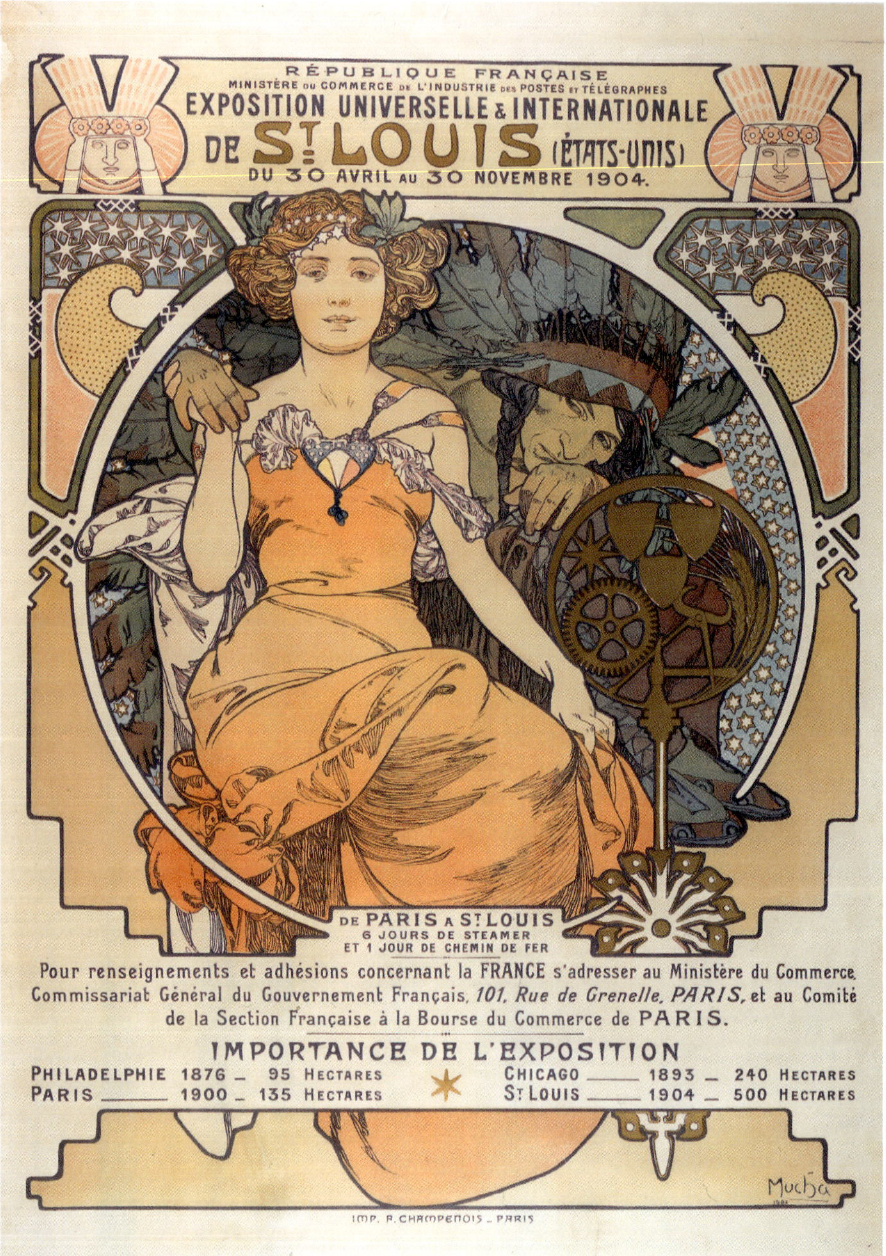

1904 World's Fair advertisement by Alphonse Mucha, symbolizing French St. Louis's historic association with Indians. *Courtesy Saint Louis Art Museum. Gift of Alice P. Francis.*